I, KOCH

I, KOCH

A Decidedly Unauthorized Biography of the Mayor of New York City, Edward I. Koch

⟫⟫ ⟪⟪

ARTHUR BROWNE,

DAN COLLINS, &

MICHAEL GOODWIN

DODD, MEAD & COMPANY
New York

To
Gretchen, Christian,
Brendan, Courtenay,
Patrick, Gail,
and Scott

No part of this book may be reproduced in any form
without permission in writing from the publisher.
Published by Dodd, Mead & Company, Inc.
79 Madison Avenue, New York, N.Y. 10016
Distributed in Canada by
McClelland and Stewart Limited, Toronto
Manufactured in the United States of America
Designed by Claire Counihan

First Edition

Library of Congress Cataloging in Publication Data

Browne, Arthur.
  I, Koch.

  Includes index.
    1. Koch, Ed, 1924–   . 2. New York (N.Y.)—Mayors
—Biography. 3. New York (N.Y.)—Politics and govern-
ment—1951–   . I. Collins, Dan. II. Goodwin,
Michael, 1949–   . III. Title.
F128.54.K63B76 1985   974.7'1043'0924 [B] 85-6893
ISBN 0-396-08647-0

CONTENTS

INTRODUCTION

Being a reporter covering a major public figure is both the best and worst assignment that journalism can offer. On the plus side is the chance to be close to the center of the action, to report the ongoing and important stories that the public wants and often needs to know. Many of those stories require the reporter to come to grips with complicated issues and to present them in language comprehensible to the general public. Doing this well, on deadline, of course, is perhaps the highest reward our profession can offer.

On the other hand, reporters covering a major newsmaker often feel a sense of frustration that they are failing to tell the whole story about their subject. They are so busy with the day-to-day responsibilities of coverage that they rarely have time to lift the veil that shields the less-than-obvious issues as well as the motives and personalities. Sometimes this feeling can be relieved temporarily by writing a story that, by analyzing some of the causes and effects, puts the news events and the newsmaker in perspective.

And sometimes, only a book will do.

Our decision to do a book about Ed Koch came about both slowly and quickly. During our years at City Hall, we were constantly amazed by the hunger the public had for more information about Koch. When people, some of them strangers encountered at dinner parties, learned that we covered the Mayor, they inevitably asked two questions: What's he really like, and is he gay? Our responses, replete with behind-the-scenes mayoral anecdotes, usually seemed to surprise them. We were, in turn, struck by how little the public seemed to know of him.

Moreover, our own knowledge was constantly expanding,

thanks in part to some after-hours sharing of ideas over a drink. Arriving at Suerken's or Pier 6—one a high-class saloon, the other a gin mill—we would often be greeted by mayoral aides who were engaged in some retrospection of their own about Koch. Why did he say this? What did he hope to achieve by doing that? Was he being honest about his reasons? This cross-pollination of perspectives further convinced us that the public knew only a sliver of who and what Koch was. It was only natural that we would frequently talk about "someday" putting together, in one place, everything that we knew and suspected about one of the most successful and unorthodox politicians of our time.

The "quickly" part of our decision came not long after Koch published his autobiography, *Mayor*, in February 1984. The book was a catalyst because much of what we knew and believed about Koch was absent from it. The powerful ego guiding the book was familiar, but the heroic dimensions of his self-portrait burst the bounds of even our expectations. The Goliath that emerged from the pages of the book won every argument and caused opponents to weep, sweat, twitch, and turn gray. Major players in the Mayor's rise to success—including friends and colleagues— were reduced in size and importance to bit players. Granted, an author is allowed a certain license with his own book, but there is simply no human, especially one involved in New York politics, as pure and perfect as the Ed Koch of *Mayor*.

The book distorted reality by omitting facts that did not fit Koch's view of himself (to use his own words) as "reasonable and responsible" and all of his opponents as "vile and vicious." Koch's view of history also virtually ignored his premayoral existence. It was almost as if he were born in 1977, the year he was elected mayor. The first thirty-two years of his life were written off in four short sentences. His early political development and a long stint in Congress were reduced to a summary that spanned fourteen pages and stray paragraphs that focused on his virtues and victories. Even his stunning victory in 1977 was portrayed as a one-man performance. Only in 1982, when he suffered an embarrassing loss to Mario Cuomo in the race for governor, did those around him take life in the pages of *Mayor*, but only as blunderers who had contributed to his defeat.

Yet knowing of Koch's errors and omissions amounted to what reporters call nickel—useless—knowledge. Or would have been were it not for the brilliantly simple suggestion put forth by a friend named Jane Moni. Upon hearing one of us gripe about the distortions in Koch's book, she said, "Why don't you write a book on Koch?" Bingo. An idea was born. Two days and a little recruiting later, the three of us met to chew it over. We decided immediately—it really was that spontaneous—to do a book that would respond to *Mayor*. Our book would offer the opinions and experiences of others who dealt with Koch on many of the events described in his book, especially those that offered a more balanced view of reality.

It seemed like such an easy thing to do, because none of us had ever attempted a book. Before we knew it, however, we had spent the better part of two months researching enough material and doing enough interviews just to put together an outline. Writing it seemed to take forever, with one of us writing and the other two looking over his shoulder, sometimes making good suggestions, sometimes just second and third guessing.

Slowly but surely, concepts took shape, chapter ideas came together and then we had a ten-page outline to give to our agent, Betty Marks. We called it *Equal Time: Talking Back to Mayor Koch*, and Betty promptly got it out to the usual suspects on her list of publishers. Dodd, Mead liked it and made an offer that we accepted, and we got to work.

At the same time, it was becoming increasingly clear that our response to Koch's book was growing into something more substantial, though just exactly what we weren't certain. For one thing, it certainly wasn't quick—two more months passed with nary a chapter written. Secondly, interviews with more than 200 people meant that there would be nothing small about the product. Then, one day, while talking with Jerry Gross, our fine and patient editor at Dodd, Mead, one of us used a word that hadn't crossed our lips before—*biography*. That, of course, was not what we had set out to write, but there was little doubt that was what we had got ourselves into. How else to describe our efforts to unearth the nuggets of Koch's boyhood, what kind of high school student he was and what he did and experienced in the army? The idea of simply responding to Koch's book fell by the wayside. On the other hand we didn't try to emulate the encyclopedic works of biographers such as Robert Caro, whose recent tome on Lyndon Johnson included rainfall statistics for the Texas Hill Country covering the years *before* Johnson was born. In that sense, we do not think the weather had anything to do with shaping Ed Koch's personality. Moreover, we are journalists, not historians, and we wanted to have a little fun writing a book that would entertain and inform.

Our task was complicated by Koch's shifting attitude toward us. In April of 1984, for example, soon after we had started our research, he asked with a smile, "How's the counter-book coming?" When we told him fine, he said he hoped that we would adhere to high journalistic standards. We assured him we would, but his concern was pretty funny, considering the standards he had employed.

"I'll write a chapter for you," he offered cheerily.

We thanked him, but declined, saying he'd had his chance. That same day, while in Boston for a lecture at Harvard, he confided to two people that he was pleased about our book because he thought that it would help the sales of the paperback version of *Mayor.*

In September, when it was clear that our book was moving closer to reality, we got a different kind of message from Koch. Using his favorite newspaper as his messenger, the Mayor made it clear that he was unhappy with what we were doing. An item on "Page Six," the gossip column of the *New York Post,* attacked our motives and suggested that our collaboration was unethical. Koch told the *Post:* "I'm not going to pass judgment. I assume they're in it for the money." The next day we sent our own message to the Mayor correcting his misperception: We were doing it for love.

After being told by a *Post* reporter that Koch aides had planted the item—a fairly routine occurrence—we requested an interview with Koch to find out just what was on his mind. We spent about ten minutes with him and Bill Rauch, his press secretary and coauthor, on September 11 in Koch's City Hall office.

We asked how much cooperation we could expect from him.

"None," Koch said.

We said we supposed he was only joking when he had offered to write a chapter that April day in Boston.

He said that he didn't remember saying that, but yes, if he had, he was only joking.

"What should we do if we get allegations about you?" we asked. "Do you want us to come to you so you can respond?"

"I will not aid or assist you in any way," he said.

We made it clear that responding to allegations was not help-ing us, it was helping him.

"I will not aid or assist you in any way," he repeated.

We asked whether he would discourage friends and city offi-cials from talking to us. He said he would tell them that he was not cooperating—which was his way of saying yes.

As time would show, his attitude was not open to challenge. Reports reached us that at least one of his aides had received a tongue-lashing for talking to us, while others were apologetic as they declined to be interviewed. They said that Koch was so de-termined to freeze us out that they risked banishment by coop-erating. Nonetheless, the degree of help we received from many people close to Koch was extraordinary. Some have done so "on the record," while others talked about him on the condition that they not be identified. We are grateful to all those who risked his wrath, and sometimes their jobs, by sharing their experiences with us. One personal friend of his, Al Nahas, a Brooklyn restaura-teur, not only agreed to talk to us, but also told us of how Koch pleaded with him not to.

We asked Koch about his family.

"My family will not talk to you," he said.

On that, he was at least half right. His sister Pat followed his orders, but his brother Harold, who is very fond of Ed, was helpful in telling some stories and offering some important in-sights into Koch's childhood and family life.

Finally, we asked the Mayor with the reputation for openness about retrieving information from the vast newspaper and video library city employees keep of his statements, speeches, and in-terviews. Such material is readily made available to reporters covering City Hall.

Koch said that, in our regular jobs, we would be accorded the same treatment as all other reporters. But when it came to the book, forget it, the library was off limits. Asked on what basis he could make such an arbitrary distinction with city property, Koch said, in effect, "I'm the Mayor."

So getting information for the book was at times difficult, but that only made our successes that much sweeter. Such was the case with Bunny Grossinger, née Persky, Koch's date for his high school prom in 1941. Her description of Koch's sexual advances provided enough laughs and inspiration to keep us going for weeks. We first learned of Bunny's existence in a casual conversation with Bronx Democratic boss Stanley Friedman in the waiting room of Governor Mario Cuomo's office in New York. We tracked her down, interviewed her four times, and through a mayoral aide confirmed that Koch knew her. Koch told the aide he had a "vague recollection of taking her to a dance once." We don't blame him for having a memory lapse about the evening.

Then there were Koch's army days, a secret to his closest friends and family. Even Dan Wolf, the Mayor's best friend, once said that Koch never told him about his army experience. Howard Blum, another friend who was kept in the dark on the subject, once speculated that Koch must have been involved in some nasty combat that he would just as soon not relive with anyone. Virtually every large profile written on Koch says exactly the same thing about his military experience: Drafted out of City College in 1943, served in the combat infantry in Europe, was discharged as a sergeant in 1946. Nothing more.

Koch's silence on the subject is unusual for two reasons—most politicians are quick to exploit their military service, and modesty is not one of Koch's dominant qualities. We were able to piece together a solid picture of Koch's combat experience by finding and interviewing GIs scattered across the country. They patiently shared with us their memories of the horrors of Europe's battlefields. Just listening to some of their stories, such as Mike Berrigan's account of how a land mine turned his foot into a ball of bloody flesh, was difficult. We thank the survivors of the Timberwolf division.

Obtaining information about Koch's postwar life was somewhat easier, if only because many of the people he crossed paths with in his early political days are still around and active in the business. Perhaps the most interesting aspect of those days was how singlemindedly Koch devoted himself to politics. For nearly thirty years, he has thought of little else. The pictures of him working late into the night at a Greenwich Village political club, of carrying a notepad and pencil in his breast pocket at the beach, and of being unable to sit still in a canoe on an upstate lake because he wanted to know what political news was in the papers—these are striking images of a man possessed. In that sense, there is a certain justice in Koch having reached such great heights of success and popularity—he got there the old-fashioned way. We came to admire his willingness to pay his dues in exchange for reaching the one goal he had set for himself—becoming Mayor.

As our research focused on the more mature Koch, including his days in Congress, the problem for us became not one of obtaining information. We were, in fact, inundated with anecdotes, documents and newspaper clippings of Koch and the issues he tackled. Instead, our challenge became one of going beyond the obvious to reach some conclusions about the Mayor-in-the-making. What was most striking was Koch's pragmatic approach to politics, his chameleonlike willingness to suddenly assume positions that offered the prospect of gain. He had no patience with losing, regardless of the price for winning.

Perhaps our most valuable source of information and perspective for Ed Koch as Mayor was David Garth, a media whiz long before he helped make Koch Mayor. While Garth initially distrusted our motives, because Koch did, many hours of interviews gave us the opportunity to persuade him that our approach was valid, even if he usually didn't agree with our conclusions. Thereafter, he shared with us some of the tricks of his trade as well as giving us some insight into the operation that propelled Koch from obscurity to City Hall. We are grateful to David Garth and his entire staff for their help.

Assessing Koch the Mayor was in some ways both the easiest and most difficult part of the book. It was easy because at least one of us has covered City Hall virtually the entire time Koch has been Mayor. Our first-hand knowledge led us to respect many of the things he's done, as well as sharply disagree with him on others. We saw him almost every day, and many days had two or three separate encounters with him. While most of these were in press conferences, many of the settings were less formal. We rode in cars with him. We had lunch with him. We went to Gracie Mansion for dinner. He met our wives and children. He even sent us autographed pictures of himself.

The difficult part was that, while a front-row seat is invaluable to a daily journalist, it offers too narrow a view from which to write a biography. The city, its government, and Koch's life are too big and too complex to be understood without some perspective. And so we often stepped back a bit to see the entire picture.

At the same time, some of the issues we had to deal with are probably better left to historians because they have not yet played themselves out. For example, Koch's relationship with blacks is a very distinct one, set in the larger context of the relationship of whites to blacks and, especially, Jews to blacks. What his problems with blacks will ultimately mean for Koch's career, for blacks, and for race relations in the city have not yet been resolved. Therefore, we sought to focus on Koch, his attitude and actions, leaving the cosmic judgments to others.

Finally, we come to conclusions about Koch as he readies to run for a third term in office. He is not the same man today as when he entered Greenwich Village politics or even when he took over City Hall, politically or personally. Once viewed as an ultra-liberal, he is now a neoconservative on many issues. Many of his former supporters now revile him. Many of those he attacked are now counted among his staunchest backers. Once poor, he is now rich. Once an outsider, he is now New York's ultimate insider. The energetic reformer determined to return New York City to its days of glory is now the loudest defender of the status quo.

When he came into office in 1978, he said he hoped to be the best Mayor the city ever had. Now he says only that he wants to be Mayor forever.

In that sense our book tells a tragic story. As time has passed, Ed Koch has frittered away a potentially brilliant career in pursuit of fame, fortune, and press clippings.

What a pity.

A WORD ABOUT
THE TITLE

Room 9, the high-ceilinged room that serves as the den for the City Hall press corps, was ajangle with ringing phones and the clatter of computer keyboards as late afternoon deadlines approached for the arbiters of all good and evil in New York City politics. Into the din was thrown a fresh-faced reporter. As he sat down to compose his story, he looked at the top of a press release he'd been handed by the Mayor's press office. It had the standard opening phrase: "Mayor Edward I. Koch today . . . "

The reporter had never covered Koch, but still knew a lot about him. You found out more than you wanted to know just reading the papers. But now he began to wonder about something.

He called across to one of the older reporters, a veteran of many wars with Koch.

"What's the *I.* stand for?" he asked.

"His favorite personal pronoun," the veteran answered without looking up.

True story.

"And I know that nothing happens here on this earth that wasn't ordained by God. And while I know that it was the people who elected me, it was God who selected me."

—Mayor Edward I. Koch at the Mount Nebo Baptist Church in Harlem, Easter Sunday, 1985.

HAPPY BIRTHDAY, ED

The several hundred demonstrators who had gathered outside the Sheraton Centre Hotel in midtown Manhattan were angry. They pushed against the wooden police barricades, trying to get a closer look at the parade of limousines and taxis that pulled up to discharge passengers. They slumped slightly with disappointment each time the person who emerged was not the one they were waiting for. Then, at a few minutes after 7 P.M., a tall, bald man with a face made familiar by television and newspaper photos stepped from a car and hurried for the entrance. Like electricity, word spread through the crowd, "There he is. It's him. It's Koch." The fury the demonstrators had been holding back came tumbling out in a torrent. "Dump Koch, the landlords' man," "Hey, you mobster, choke on your lobster," they shouted, placards waving wildly. It went on like that for nearly a minute before the rage suddenly turned to a murmur, then silence, and, finally, sheepish laughter. The crowd had gone after the wrong man, a case of mistaken identity. The man they were jeering was a ringer for Ed Koch, and was probably just as famous. He was the King of Chicken, Frank Perdue.

After a few laughs, the demonstrators regrouped to wait again for the real thing. But they were not to get their chance this night, for Edward I. Koch, the 105th Mayor of the City of New York, had entered the hotel through the garage.

Although he was accompanied by his usual retinue of aides and heavily armed bodyguards, Koch had avoided the main entrance because he did not want to be bothered by the mob outside. December 12, 1984 was a special day—his sixtieth birthday—and he did not want it ruined, nor was he in a mood to placate his enemies. He rarely is. He had come to celebrate at a lavish party he was throwing for himself in the Imperial Ballroom with a few "friends"—1,500 of the richest, most powerful people in New York. And why shouldn't he?

Poor and Polish from the Bronx, the son of immigrant Jews, he had climbed and clawed his way to the top of New York's political establishment. For seven years, he'd ruled municipal government, with its 200,000 employees and its budget of more than $18 billion, with a flair unmatched in modern times. Even the image of Fiorello La Guardia, the battling Little Flower, seemed to wither next to Koch's flamboyance and chutzpah. For Koch was more than a mayor. He was a best-selling author, a movie and TV personality who had appeared in everything from soap operas to feature films. He was rich. He was a celebrity. All over the country, indeed, the world, people recognized his face. King of the hill, top of the heap—that's what they said about Ed Koch.

Deep in the bowels of the hotel, he emerged from his chauffeured Lincoln Town Car in black tie. With his bodyguards leading the way, and a bomb-sniffing Labrador from the Police Department nearby, Koch and Diane Coffey, his daytime chief of staff and "date" for the evening, were ushered into an elevator and whisked to a cocktail reception on the third floor. Koch and Coffey were excited. Rockefellers and Astors were expected, along with scores of Wall Street financiers, real estate tycoons, sports and culture barons, and captains of commerce and industry. It was the sort of gathering that could happen only in New York, and Koch was looking forward to being the center of attention in such a glittering assembly.

But Ed Koch is a pragmatic man, and so he wanted more from his birthday than a party and cake. After all, he could have had that anywhere. What he wanted was to do a little business. The business was money. He would need lots of it—at least $3 million—to finance his upcoming reelection effort, and what better place to get it than from "friends." So the word had been put out through the mail and through the political grapevine that anybody who wished to help Edward I. Koch celebrate his birthday would have to buy a ticket. The price would be either $1,000 or $2,500. Those 280 people who paid the top price would get to meet him at a private cocktail reception and sit closer to him during dinner in the Imperial Ballroom.

Not so many years ago Koch was repelled by people who went

in for that sort of thing. "Richies and snobs" he had called people who seemed to believe that their contributions could buy influence, or at least protection, at City Hall. If he ever got to be
Mayor, things would be different, government would not be for
sale. He boasted of his simple tastes—he lived in a cramped, rent-
controlled apartment, liked wine that sold for three dollars a bottle, and rode a public bus to his first inauguration in 1978. But
times had changed, and so had Ed Koch.

He lived in a mansion now, with a chef and butlers. He had
a big car and police officers to drive it. The officers had a siren
so the Mayor never had to sit in traffic jams. A city helicopter
awaited his command. His net worth was growing daily, thanks
to sales of his autobiography. And it was remarkable how everything he said was considered news. Why, just that day, the front
page of the *New York Post* was given over to his suggestion that
the United States bomb Iran. That New York City could be such
a wonderful place to live was not something everyone appreciated equally. He knew the guests at his party did, and that's why
they were invited.

The crowd at the $2,500 cocktail event parted as Koch walked
in. Every head seemed to turn his way. He shook hands, mur-
mured pleasantries, and kissed a few women dressed in furs and
diamonds. They were all so happy to see him. The ever-present
bodyguards hung back discreetly, as did Diane Coffey. Careful
not to upstage him or appear to be giving directions, she occasionally reminded him that he should keep moving so he could
greet everybody personally because they had all paid so much to
be with him. The visit over, he moved downstairs to a more
crowded reception, where his $1,000-a-ticket friends waited.

He was intercepted in a hallway by reporters who asked
whether he was concerned that the dinner would mark him as
the candidate of the fat cats. Koch said he regretted that he had
to raise so much money, but that the villain was not him or his
guests. The problem was that the television stations charged too
much for political advertising. Further, he said it was outrageous
for the reporters to even ask such questions because their sala-
ries were paid out of the stations' income from the ads. They were
the hypocrites, not he.

What about the demonstrators outside, he was asked. They
seemed so angry, especially those who feared that his plan to
rehabilitate Times Square would force them out of their nearby

homes. Koch seemed exasperated that he had to deal with such a question on a night such as this. Rolling his eyes heavenward, he said: "You didn't recognize them? They're from Central Casting."

He turned on his heel and, led by a phalanx of aides, began moving through the $1,000 crowd. They, too, were happy to see him. Shouts of "Happy birthday" and "Keep up the good job" rang out as Koch shook hands, slapped backs, and kissed cheeks. Preston Moore, a tall man who builds and renovates housing, brushed close to Koch to say something and shake the Mayor's hand. As Moore was elbowed away by the surging crowd, he stretched his hand over the heads of those nearby and slipped his business card into the breast pocket of Koch's tuxedo jacket. "I do business here in New York so I just wanted to meet the Mayor," he said. Others had met the Mayor at similar functions in the past, men and women whose business had prospered under Koch. They were there to wish him well and let him know they were still with him.

Koch beamed when he entered the Imperial Ballroom, where the huge chandeliers were turned low to add a romantic touch. Potted flowers adorned each of the 143 tables, as did a floral-like arrangement of helium-filled balloons. Burgundy balloons, pink balloons, white balloons. The tablecloths were burgundy, the walls were burgundy. As Koch entered, waiters were adding the final touch to each place setting—a four-inch wheel of chocolate bearing a snapshot of Ed Koch as a toddler. Many people remarked what a cute baby he had been.

The turnout was impressive.

Executives from such leading financial institutions as American Express, Citibank, Manufacturers Hanover Trust, and Republic National Bank were there. The big Wall Street investment houses—Bear Stearns, Merrill Lynch, Smith Barney, and Kidder Peabody—all sent delegations. The politically active law firms, many of which earn big money helping wealthy clients get tax breaks from the city, turned out in large numbers. A contingent from Finley, Kumble, Wagner, Heine and Underberg was there, led by its two stars, Hugh Carey, a former governor, and Robert F. Wagner, a former mayor. Hawkins, Delafield and Wood. Rogers and Wells. Shea and Gould. Tufo and Zuccotti. They were all there.

Donald Trump, the millionaire wunderkind who built the obscenely opulent Trump Tower and owns the Generals of the United States Football League, shelled out $25,000 for a table of ten tickets at the top price. He said he did it because he thought Koch was a good mayor, but that he didn't expect anything in return. George Steinbrenner, owner of the Yankees, and Fred Wilpon, president of the Mets, bought tickets for themselves and guests. The beer distributors association was there, as were the cigarette people from Philip Morris and Reynolds Tobacco. The North Star Contracting Corporation was at table 41. Since 1980, the firm has held more than $38 million in contracts with the Transit Authority and other agencies. Benjamin Holloway, a major real estate financier and executive vice president of Equitable Life Assurance, was at one of the $2,500-a-plate tables. He sat with Jerry Speyer, of the Tishman-Speyer real estate empire. Lawrence Wien, a real estate investor who recently gave Columbia University enough money to build a football stadium, was there. Harold Fisher, the rotund, gravel-voiced Brooklyn power broker–lawyer, sat at one of the $2,500 tables with his son, Kenneth. Martin Segal, chairman of Lincoln Center, and Nathan Leventhal, the president of Lincoln Center and a former deputy mayor, each bought a ticket. The theater owners association was there. And so was Frank Perdue.

Many others in the room were not as wealthy, but they had something the wealthy need—political connections. Party leaders, city councilmen, deputy mayors, commissioners, deputy commissioners and their staffs. In short, everybody was there whom an outsider looking to do business with the city would have to know and cultivate. What were Trump and Tony Gliedman, the housing commissioner, talking about? What was Bob Linn, Koch's labor expert, talking about with Jack Bigel, the brains behind the municipal unions? Whatever it was, they could thank Ed Koch. He had brought them all together. Howard Rubenstein, the leading public relations man in the city, thanked the Mayor personally. He led two of his clients—an international financier and a major developer—over to Koch's table for introductions. Would they be satisfied with a handshake for $2,500?

Koch was pleased. He scanned the crowd of those who had come to pay their respects, and remembered it had not always been this way. His eye roved from table to table, where rich and famous men in black tie sat with their wives and mistresses in diamonds and furs. The take would be close to $2 million. He allowed himself a smile and said to a reporter, "Not bad, huh?"

Dinner started with cold poached salmon, followed by rack of lamb, one of Koch's favorite dishes. Imported French wine was delivered to each table. Entertainment was provided by Judy Collins, one of Koch's favorite singers, who serenaded him from a large stage. A band was behind her. Speakers lauded Koch the Man and Koch the Mayor. A congratulatory telegram from Governor Mario Cuomo was read. Finally, the Mayor went to the stage to speak. He talked of how honest his administration had been, how it had guided the city away from bankruptcy, and how much he cared for the people, all the people. He said the large turnout of such important people proved how good a mayor he was. They applauded. Then the signal was given and the crowd began singing "Happy Birthday" as white-jacketed waiters carried, sedan-chair–style, a huge, four-tiered cake to him. Behind them trailed a long line of waiters delivering small cakes to each table.

But the finale was not grand. As Koch was speaking, some people got up to leave. By the time the cakes were brought out and "Happy Birthday" was being sung, nearly half the seats were vacant. So the Mayor ate his birthday cake in an emptying ballroom in a hotel as the waiters began clearing away the dirty dishes and linen around him. The people had paid to be with him, but they did not want to stay longer than necessary. Even power has its limits.

ED KOCH'S NEW YORK

Ed Koch rules a city of more than 7 million people, and like its Mayor, New York is not subtle. As visitors learn, it tends to shout at anyone whose stance or step betrays the least indecision. But it is not a place that can be comprehended in a glance. A municipality that suspends its parking regulations for both Simhath Torah and the Feast of the Assumption requires some careful observation. So does a city where you can find the Gutenberg Bible and Cupid's Retreat within a few blocks of each other along 42nd Street.

Servants of the Lord and servants of the king may have founded most of the New World, but New York was first settled by traders in search of a deal. People come to New York from someplace else, planning to be something other than what they are. It is the most optimistic and most nervous city in the world.

It is a city heterogeneous beyond imagining. Restaurant critics can fill an entire column reviewing New York's Afghani dining spots. Astoria, Queens, claims more Greeks than Athens. The Albanians tend to live in the Bronx, the Rastafarians mainly in Brooklyn. The Satmar and Lubavitcher Hasidic Jews have been known to carry their theological differences into the streets of Borough Park or Williamsburgh. Ethnic identities are most often celebrated by parades, with the city averaging one parade every three days. There are parades to honor the Irish, Italians, Puerto Ricans, Afro-Americans, Poles, West Indians, Chinese, Germans, Turks, and Ukrainians. When the police themselves are marching, they do it as members of the department's Columbian Association (Italian), the Emerald Society (Irish), the Guardians (black), the Pulaski Association (Eastern European), or the Shorim Society (Jewish).

People are everywhere. White people, black people, Hispanics from a dozen countries, Asians, and Indians. The subways are crowded. The parks are crowded. The sidewalks are shoulder-to-shoulder. It has more residents than forty-one of the fifty states—more people than Massachusetts, Indiana, or Virginia. It has more people than Bolivia, Denmark, Ireland, Israel, Norway, Switzerland, or Zambia. There are more than 100,000 births and about 75,000 deaths each year.

The tolerance of New Yorkers is a tolerance bred of lives spent cheek-to-jowl with wildly divergent throngs of strangers. Although the city averages only 2.5 people per household, and more than 900,000 New Yorkers live alone, the most important factor in the city's life is not isolation, but enforced proximity. The vast majority of its residents live in buildings of five or more apartments. They commute to work on subways, not in cars. A trip to the store may be simply a matter of walking to the corner, but along the way, one might be asked to sign a petition, register to vote, donate money to feed the poor, buy cookies to support a day-care center, and do something about American troops in El Salvador.

The city is crowded and uncomfortable but never boring. All over Manhattan, musicians play for pay, their hats or guitar boxes strategically placed to collect the cash. There is a percussionist in the company of an energetic tap dancer, and a saxaphonist whose entire repertoire consists of "Over the Rainbow." There is a man who recites poetry and a man who writes poetry on demand. There are breakdancers, mimes, and a beggar who will show you the scar from his stomach surgery. Young people pass out leaflets promoting a new hairdresser, hamburger stands, health clubs, Jews for Jesus, and massage parlors. A smiling, well-dressed matron distributes typewritten messages from God announcing that He has designated His special messenger Monica to save mankind from its sins.

Off the streets, New York offers more diversions than any other city in the world. It has 150,000 restaurants, which means that everybody could go out to dinner at the same time and find a table. There are more than a hundred movie houses, serving an audience so movie-mad that a French film about a peasant in the Middle Ages could run for six months and sell out on the Fourth of July. New York has 434 museums and galleries—more than four times as many as any other American city—and there are an estimated 90,000 local artists who plan to see their work shown someday. There are scores of live theaters, not counting the dozens of lofts, churches, and schools where actors perform in "showcase" productions for free hoping to land something bigger and more lucrative. There are 15,000 stage actors who have qualified to join Actors Equity, but only about 15 percent have theater jobs on any given week. There is nowhere on earth that you are as likely to have your hamburger served and your purchases rung up by a person with an intimate knowledge of Shakespeare and Stanislavsky.

Walk through midtown Manhattan and you will see people hustling. The first sign of a storm cloud produces street peddlers offering umbrellas. Five thousand two hundred licensed vendors sell hot dogs, souvlaki, knishes, empañadas, Tofutti, Italian ice cream, and shish-kebab from their carts, along with hordes of unauthorized competitors. Small-time drug dealers murmuring "smokesmokesmokesmoke" stake out the parks, the side streets, or stand beneath the marquees of seedy movie houses. In Harlem and the Lower East Side, youngsters hawk brand-name heroin.

The hustle generally comes attached to a dream. The man selling hot dogs on the corner of Tenth Avenue says he is really a television producer looking for a break. The clerk behind the information desk at the Port Authority is really a computer programmer, and the cabbie outside on the street is writing a novel. New Yorkers are inclined toward secret careers, or at least lead an extremely active fantasy life. The security guard at the old McGraw-Hill building on 42nd Street has worked his way into his fifth job before age twenty: "In a factory, a fast food place, a pharmacy, unloading furniture." His real identity, of course, is something else: "I'm going to school to be a commercial artist."

The city almost went bankrupt in the 1970s, but a decade later it had recovered and become the world's greatest center of financial services, the city Business Week called "the capital of capital." The strong dollar, high interest rates, and relaxation of regulations on international financial transactions have turned the old mercantile city into the hub of the mysterious money manipulations of the 1980s. More than 300 foreign banks had offices in New York in 1984. Financial services accounted for the creation of 200,000 new jobs, but almost all of the new jobs were in Manhattan, and two-thirds went to commuters who live outside the city.

The number of financial jobs in New York now surpasses manufacturing employment for the first time. Office construction chugs ahead, and rents for prime buildings hover at forty to fifty dollars a square foot, despite the continually expanding number of new fifty-story glass boxes at desirable addresses. Manhattan, which has been growing in size since Peter Minuet bought it from the Indians for twenty-four dollars in trinkets in 1626, continues to expand as still more landfill is poured along the shoreline to build new facilities for the banks and brokerage houses. Money spills out of Wall Street, supporting fifty-dollar theater tickets and hundred-dollar-per-person restaurant tabs, and pressuring rents up even higher.

The new wealth flows down to the humbler citizenry in the smallest of trickles. Banks and brokerages do not welcome high-school dropouts with reading problems or new arrivals from Central America with a shaky command of English. There are jobs at the bottom at minimum wage. But missing are those middle rungs that have always enabled people to climb up from the bottom.

While Wall Street thrives, New York is creating its own permanent underclass, made up of families headed by women, families with no experience with anything but welfare and unhappy endings. One out of three children born in the city in 1983 was born to an unmarried woman. More than 14 percent of the city's residents are receiving public assistance, and 25 percent are below the poverty line. The city has 635,000 drug abusers.

The South Bronx has become a nationwide symbol of urban misery. The area was convulsed by blight, poverty and rage in the late sixties and early seventies. The Bronx was on fire, with arson bred of landlord greed, despair, and the neglect of the junkies and winos who camped out in what had been the fine, high-ceilinged apartments of the borough.

Then, suddenly, it was over. The Bronx had worn itself out, burned itself out. The 43rd Precinct, nicknamed "Fort Apache" when it was the last bastion of civil order in a borough under siege, was renamed "The Little House on the Prairie." The buildings around it had all been burned away, and there were not enough people left in the neighborhood to create a crime wave. By 1980, there were 1.1 million people in the Bronx—a 37 percent decline from the decade before.

The Bronx shrinks, Staten Island swells. Nothing stays the way it was very long in New York. Neighborhoods rise and fall, ethnic group replaces ethnic group. "The whole of New York is rebuilt once every 10 years," wrote diarist Philip Hone in 1839. "Everything in New York is at an exorbitant price. Rents have risen 50 percent for the next year."

One hundred and fifty years later, Manhattan's shrinking Italian community watches unhappily as Chinatown gobbles up Little Italy. In Brooklyn's Crown Heights, the growth of the Hasidic community is evident on sunny Sundays, when bearded, black-hatted men and their wives push their children's strollers through the streets, creating veritable baby-carriage gridlock at the corners. In Bedford-Stuyvesant, once a prosperous Jewish neighborhood, then an impoverished ghetto, middle-class black families restore the elegant old brownstones and plant flowers in their tiny, reclaimed front yards. In Queens, the unlovely commercial streets of Flushing sport Chinese and Indian signs, marks of the latest influx from Korea, Hong Kong, and Gujerat.

The outside world tends to see New York in terms of Manhattan—and why wouldn't it, when the mayor and almost all his chief deputies are Manhattanites, when the borough has been the magnet for the city's real estate developers, the beneficiary of most of its tax breaks, and the center of its job boom? But the city, as the politicians know well, lies beyond the boundaries of Peter Minuet's land grab.

Queens, where 1.9 million people live in middle- and working-class respectability, gives the lie to every generalization about the city that Manhattan calls forth. If New York is supposed to have tall buildings, there are sections of Queens where single-story commercial structures and modest homes mix together in a sprawl crisscrossed by highways. If Manhattan's housing is impossible to afford, a one-bedroom apartment in Astoria is still renting for $500 a month. If a native New Yorker is a rarity in Manhattan, there are neighborhoods in Bayside in Queens where children can walk to their grandmothers' houses down the street.

Those simple virtues are not much appreciated in Manhattan. Woody Allen, the hero of the cosmopolitan camp, described a nightmare in which he was captured by a roving gang of secretaries who "brandished knives and forced me to say favorable things about the borough of Queens."

Queens tends to return the sentiment. Consider the community group formed to oppose extension of the subway system into the southeast corner of the borough. "We don't want access to the city," explained the group's co-chairman. "If we want to get to Manhattan, we find a way. But we don't want Manhattan coming here."

Consider Staten Island, which regularly threatens to secede from New York. More than 85 percent white, more than 58 percent homeowning, conservative Staten Island is a suburb in everything but name. The only source of vast desirable stretches of undeveloped land within the city's borders, Staten Island has become a mecca for real estate developers, sprouting dozens of subdivisions with names like Wishing Well Acres. While the city's population began to decline after 1950, Staten Island's doubled.

Brooklyn, if it were still an independent city, would be the fourth largest in the nation, after New York, Los Angeles, and Chicago. Before its amalgamation into the city at the turn of the century, it was pure nineteenth-century suburbia—known as the "city of churches," one would-be booster said bitterly, "because we have nothing but churches."

Now it is the city of neighborhoods, where if you are from Bay Ridge, you are probably Italian; Borough Park means Jewish and Brooklyn Heights yuppie; Brighton means Russian immigrants and Greenpoint Polish. Beset by more poverty and crime than most places, Brooklyn still has a sense of identity and neighborhood, where it is possible to live where everybody knows your name and shares your nationality and religion. In Bay Ridge, housewives rest from their shopping at a genuine old soda fountain. Even the "pioneers" of Park Slope who hang ferns in their windows and scour antique stores for the perfect knobs for their stripped-down refurbished doors, hold block suppers and take turns tending the communal tulips.

Walk through any neighborhood in New York and you will see flowers in the springtime—well-funded spreads of begonias on Park Avenue; humbler and more diverse community gardens in abandoned lots; single tulips attached to the trees attended by Brooklyn's block tree committees; barrels filled with impatiens in front of Village brownstones; sunflowers, showy and defiant, in the yards of Bedford-Stuyvesant's reclaimed row houses. People in New York will do almost anything they are not supposed to do, but in general they will not molest a public flower.

Walk through any neighborhood and you will also see the pigeons, sometimes sunbathing on the sidewalk, their wings spread out defiantly. They will move only grudgingly when a human foot comes near. New York pigeons are tougher than members of their species who live in less challenging environs. Like their human neighbors, they have to be.

Enduring the subways is one reason New Yorkers are so tough. The Straphangers Campaign, an organization of beleaguered subway riders, estimated in 1984 that riders had a one-in-four chance of getting on a subway car with a door that would not open, encouraging shoving and bad tempers among commuters fearful of being caught on the wrong side when the train pulled out. Chances were one-in-three the cars would be badly lit, and one-in-six there would be no readable subway map, and one-in-seven the car itself would be mislabeled. In February of 1984, the Transit Authority acknowledged the doors on cars on moving subway trains had flown open at least thirty-two times in the preceding twenty-one months. No one was injured—a miracle considering how frequently crowding forces riders to lean against the doors for support.

If the door of your subway car did not fly open, the car itself could always catch fire. Sixteen underground blazes lit up the subways on Koch's birthday, trapping thousands of riders in smoky tunnels and delaying many thousands more whose trains came to a sudden halt all under town. An ancient subway car showering sparks onto tracks littered with trash touched off the day-long bonfire—one of more than 5,000 fires that year.

If your door did not open and the train did not ignite, you could always be killed by a crazy person. In February 1984, a man wielding a two-foot-long sharpened metal pipe told passengers on the AA train in Manhattan: "This is my car and I'm taking over." Despite the best efforts of the conductor, he pursued the passengers through two cars, swinging his pipe, until he was shot and killed by transit officers. Days later Ly Yung Chung, a 19-year-old Chinese newlywed who had been in the country four months, was pushed in front of a train at Canal Street and decapitated. Witnesses said a third-grade teacher with a history of mental problems had begun shouting obscenities about the Board of Education and muttering "push push push" before shoving the young woman, whom he did not know. One midtown Manhattan station entertained passengers for a time by playing a recorded message warning them to stand behind the yellow line to avoid being shoved in front of a train. It also requested help in locating a man armed with a hatchet who was wanted for hacking away at riders.

The violence and the fires and the doors were irregular atrocities. Day-to-day life was trains that did not come, trains that developed problems and discharged their passengers halfway through their routes, trains that were much too hot or much too cold, trains that were much too crowded to provide any hope of a seat, or even a strap to hang upon. Trains that were always dirty and incredibly noisy. Trains that would stop, their public address systems spewing forth inaudible announcements that sent confused riders darting off, then back on again, unsure whether the express had become a local, gone out of service, or was simply departing for the next station. All this for just a ninety-cent token.

Rider frustration spawned revolt. Angry straphangers sometimes simply refused to leave trains that were "taken out of service." Riders who refused to leave one Manhattan train that was going out of service were taken on a thirty-minute "mystery ride" to nowhere by an angry conductor who shouted obscenities at them on the public address system. What was most shocking was that the PA system worked.

People could try to rise above the subways, but they could not really avoid using them. Buses do not run from borough to borough. Cars do, at a rate of less than six miles an hour in midtown, on streets where potholes six inches deep appear out of nowhere, cracking axles and crunching suspensions. The city's 12,000 medallion taxi cabs are no solution either. If you are lucky enough to find one, it will no doubt be dirty and dangerous. And if the driver speaks English, he may be able to get you to your destination without first taking you on an expensive sightseeing tour.

The trauma of crime cuts across an even wider swath than transit. In New York, a safe neighborhood is one with the luxury of worrying about car theft and burglaries. A dangerous neighborhood is one where mothers sleep during the day, the better to guard their children against the junkies and arsonists at night.

The late Anthony Williams lived in such a neighborhood in Brooklyn. Williams was killed—shot twice in the back—about the same time Ed Koch arrived at the Sheraton for his birthday bash. More than 1,300 New Yorkers met the same fate in 1984.

For the average New Yorker, crime means the daily necessity of taking petty thieves and the occasional lunatic into consideration, a wearying need to keep an eye out for trouble. If chances are only one out of 5,000 you will be murdered in New York (and in fact much lower if you live in a "safe" neighborhood and have the luck not to be a young male), the chances are one in 20 that your house will be burglarized, and nearly one in 14 that your life will be touched by some felony. Everybody in New York knows somebody who has been mugged, robbed, lost a car to theft, or been otherwise undone by serious crime.

Major crime appeared to peak in New York in 1981, before dropping by 5 percent in '82 and 9 percent the following year. Still, there were 550,339 reported felonies in 1983, only 16.1 percent of which were "cleared" by the arrest of a suspect or some other final resolution.

If crime and transportation are the day-to-day burdens New Yorkers must bear, housing is the single obsession. The blessings and woes of a two-percent vacancy rate fall unequally on the rich and the poor, but also on the lucky and the cursed, the newcomer and the long-term resident. Thanks to the city's rent control and rent stabilization laws, which cover about 1.2 million apartments, there is a bizarre sense of democracy to the housing scene. Elderly women on Social Security live next door to East Side yuppies, who shell out $1,000 a month for studios next to the old ladies' $200-a-month, four-room apartments. Middle-class families who happen to live in buildings slated for co-oping receive windfalls thanks to state laws that encourage landlords to sell at a discount to existing tenants. One appraiser pointed to an East 86th Street building where residents bought their two-bedroom apartments for $36,000 and could sell them two years later for more than $200,000.

The housing crunch brings out the worst in everybody. Rent-controlled tenants sublet their bargain-rate apartments for two or three times what they pay the landlord, or charge thousands of dollars up front for "furniture rental." Landlords hire goons to harass the poor and elderly out of their apartments, so the space can be renovated and rented at ten times present rates. Donald

Trump, the boy wonder of Manhattan's luxury housing market, offered to put up the city's homeless in a building he was unsuccessfully trying to empty of its present tenants. When Trump was asked to lend the vacant apartments to middle-class Polish refugees instead, his office quickly backtracked, announcing the offer was good only for "people who live in America now."

New York's housing situation causes unhappily married couples to think twice about divorce. A young artist or stockbroker or secretary looking for an apartment in a "safe" section of Manhattan could expect to pay $800 for the humblest of studios, and give the rental agency up to $1,600 for disclosing the location. Real estate developers brag about "affordable" co-ops in fifth-floor walk-ups at $70,000 for 400 square feet of space. Landlords demand $5,000 a month for small commercial spaces in unglamorous locations like Broadway above 100th Street.

The nightmare is worse for the poor. About 175,000 poor families are on a waiting list for apartments in the city's dreary public housing projects. The projects already have a population of about 500,000.

The search for living space sends the more adventurous, particularly the artists, into territories as yet untouched by the city's real estate developers. But the developers, who buy low and sell high, are never too far behind. Working-class families who had once feared "tipping" that would bring in "a bad element" and ruin property values now have a greater fear of "gentrification" that would triple their rents and replace the corner grocery with a David's Cookies Shop.

"Ethnic businesses and services will gradually be forced out. Anyone else can be paid to leave," a thirty-three-year-old real estate investor told *New York* magazine. "If you can get rid of the rent-controlled tenants, renovate the place and charge $700 a month, it's worth paying them $10,000 or so just to get them out and raise the rent. They'll all be forced out. They'll be pushed east to the river and given life preservers. It's so clear. I wouldn't have come here if it wasn't."

Some people do not even get life preservers. Near Times Square, there is a hotel called the Holland House, a place whose lobby evinces all the native charm of a pawnshop. The Holland House is a welfare hotel. Children live there, playing on the sidewalks they share with the pushers and prostitutes, sitting outside watching the nighttime action. To wind up in a welfare hotel is to fall about as far as you can fall in New York. The hookers at Times Square turn up their collective noses at places like the Holland House. "What do I look like?" demanded one prostitute indignantly when a sympathetic cop suggested she take refuge for the night in one.

The 3,000 homeless families who live in filthy places like the Holland House at city expense are mostly single women with two or three or four children, have been evicted or burned out of their old apartments, have no friends or relatives willing to take them in, and will remain an average of six months in rooms that are often small, usually filthy, and frequently dangerous. The cops at the local precinct house that covers the Midtown welfare hotels keep a supply of Pampers on hand, so often are they called upon to tend small children who have been abandoned or temporarily forgotten by their mothers.

On the coldest days of the year, more than 7,000 single men and women seek refuge in the city's shelters—often armories where people sleep in military cots lined up row after row, while food and showers are a bus ride away. Thousands of others sleep in the streets, subways, parks, and abandoned buildings. They include many ex-mental patients, now "deinstitutionalized"—released from hospitals and left to wander the city helplessly. About 200,000 New Yorkers are destitute enough to get their daily ration of bread from soup kitchens operated by churches and other private groups. Not since the Great Depression have so many New Yorkers been down and out.

And never, it seems, have so many been so opulently rich. The ex-wife of a Texas oilman reportedly bought a 37-room spread in the Trump Tower condominiums for $9.7 million. At the River House cooperatives, so exclusive that Gloria Vanderbilt was rejected as a potential tenant, the wife of a Wall Street financier spent $3,000 hoisting a 22-foot Christmas tree into her penthouse, where it was decorated with hundreds of orchids and mimosa. New York's number-one landlord, Harry Helmsley, once announced his premier hotel, the Palace, was overpricing its triplex penthouses at $1,800 a night: "I'm reducing it to $1,250. That's a good buy for $1,250. You get three bedrooms."

Many worry that New York is splitting into two cities: a citadel of wealth in Manhattan and encampments of the dispossessed in the fringes of the outer boroughs. Everyone turns to City Hall for support, the rich sniffing after access and clout, the poor beseeching aid, and the middle class demanding protection from encroachment on either end.

The largest city in the nation also has the country's largest municipal government—a sprawling bureaucracy that includes offices as small as the Commission on Distinguished Guests and agencies as large as the $4-billion-a-year Welfare Department, which serves more than one million New Yorkers. The police department, with 24,000 cops, makes more than 400,000 arrests a year. The fire department's 12,000 firefighters battle more than 90,000 blazes and responded to 136,000 false alarms. The sanitation department picks up more than 3.4 million tons of garbage. The transportation department fills nearly a million potholes and issues more than six million parking tickets. The parks department oversees 227 parks, 850 playgrounds, 45 swimming pools, 526 tennis courts, seven ice skating rinks, 14.3 miles of beach, four stadiums, and 2.6 million trees.

The man at the top is Edward I. Koch. The 104 mayors who preceded him have included rogues and reformers—characters ranging from Jimmy Walker, the nightclubbing Jazz Age mayor, to Abe Beame, described by one writer as the little guy who would have advised Peter Minuet to hold out for $19.95. Becoming the Mayor of New York City is all that Ed Koch ever really wanted in life, and he made the most of it when the dream came true in 1978.

He lives in a mansion that has been newly refurbished at a cost of $6 million. He is surrounded by bodyguards twenty-four hours a day. He is chauffeured wherever he goes. A retinue of aides stands ready to attend his every whim. For him, New York is a safe, secure, comfortable, and wonderful place to live.

But being mayor also offers Koch something more important than creature comforts. It gives him power, and he wields it mightily. He is a man who cherishes vindictiveness—getting even—as his chief political currency; who verbally brutalizes friends and enemies alike; who boasts that he has made people cry, sweat, twitch, and turn gray; who demands absolute loyalty from those around him, but thinks nothing of publicly humiliating the few dedicated souls who have supported him longest and most unwaveringly; who believes it is more blessed to give ulcers than to get them.

THE OUTSIDER

Bunny Persky knew him when he was a shy and frightened loner.

She was an adolescent, naively innocent, and terrified that her mother would find out that she had snuck off to Weequahic Park with her ice skates. For high school kids in Newark in the winter of 1941, the park's frozen pond was the place to be. That's where they did the whip. In frolicking bunches, Bunny and her friends would line up single file, each one would grab the waist of the person in front of him, then the line would skate in loops until the speed was fast enough to send those on the end hurtling outward at glorious peril.

In the beginning, Bunny had watched the fun from afar. She was a loner, a shy girl, inhibited by her buck teeth, a pair of gleaming silver braces that covered them, and an overprotective mother who had forbidden her to go to the pond and join in. She did nonetheless—for her an act of great daring—and this time wound up on the end of the chain, moving far faster than she wanted to. Unable to hold on anymore, she whipped across the ice and skittered away precariously, certain that she was going to crash and die. But Bunny was not injured. At the last second, a hand reached out and grabbed her. She was being rescued—by a boy.

He was not, as she might have hoped, a knight on a white charger. He was gawky, skinny, and tall, with a head topped by a bush of curly dark hair. He smiled at her nicely and set her upright. He certainly wasn't handsome, but he still looked wonderful. His name was Eddie Koch, and Bunny Persky was about to become his girlfriend.

Bunny and Eddie, they were to discover, had a lot in common. Both were sixteen, studious, shy and, for the most part, without friends. Bunny, dark-haired, five-feet-five-inches tall, and scrubbed-faced, had only recently moved to Newark, after her father's jewelry business in Connecticut went bankrupt. Although she was a drum majorette and a sorority member, Bunny still felt like an outsider, in part because her parents would not let her participate in many of the teenage pastimes of the era. Bunny wasn't even allowed to hang out in the local sweet shop where her classmates at Weequahic High gathered to giggle in their Pringle sweaters and saddle shoes.

Eddie was even further from the center of the in crowd. He'd lived in Newark for nine years, since his father's fur business had gone broke in the Great Depression, but still seemed to lack close friends. Classmates, using the parlance of the time, thought of him as an egghead. In part that's because he preferred cooking class to playing football, and writing dreamy poetry to engaging in horseplay. His body didn't have much meat on its long bones, nor was it strong or coordinated. His large, angular nose dominated the better part of his face, except for his mouth, which always seemed to be moving. Painfully shy in some ways, Eddie sought to make up for his adolescent shortcomings by talking. And talking. And talking. His penchant for nonstop patter drove away some would-be chums. To some, the talking was boring. To others, it was a form of aggression.

Frances Shantz was another Newark schoolgirl who remembers Eddie. She lived around the corner from his family's apartment on Milford Avenue and would pass the time chatting with her girlfriends on the sidewalk, at times about the "gatherings" or dance parties they would organize. "We had cliques. I'd say, 'Alice, see if you can get Joan and Nancy, and ask John and Jim and Mack. We'll have a gathering.' We'd put on records in the living room and dance." Sometimes their planning would be interrupted by Koch, who, walking alone, would stop and volunteer his opinions on "everything."

"He'd come by jabbering," Mrs. Shantz says. "We'd say, 'Eddie, get lost.' "

But Bunny enjoyed his patter.

"I think our friendship was based on loneliness," she says. "Maybe the fact that I felt isolated, he found in me a kindred person." One thing she learned was that he wasn't too fond of being on the end of the skating whip either. She could relate to that sort of thing.

After the ice-skating incident, Eddie called Bunny and asked her out. Through the spring and into the summer of 1941, they dated. He came over to her house and met her parents. They liked Eddie and felt his intentions were honorable. The young couple went skating in the winter and took long walks in the woods, or near the pond in Weequahic Park in warmer weather. He often brought a picnic basket full of food from his uncle's catering hall on Belmont Avenue, a spread that she recalls as "scrumptious." They would sit and eat and talk about Newark, about being teenagers, about the world. Religion was also a topic. Both were Jewish, though it was of little consequence at the time, especially to Bunny. Only recently, her father had resumed using the name Persky after calling himself Perkins in Connecticut to hide his Jewish identity. Koch's family observed some, but not all, Jewish religious practices.

The young couple also found a common ground in the business failures that had brought both families to Newark. The fall wasn't as far for the Perskys, who were able to live in the predominately white, middle-class section of town and send their daughter to Weequahic. The Koches, on the other hand, had come to town as squatters in a relative's apartment and were still struggling. They lived in the South Ward, a tougher part of town, and Koch attended South Side High along with the children of other not-so-well-off families. Bunny was conscious that she and Eddie came from different economic classes, and that she was breaking an unwritten rule in dating him.

"You weren't really supposed to go with boys from Southside," Bunny remembers. "That was a lower-class thing. But I liked him."

Once or twice in the park, Eddie kissed Bunny. Not with great passion, but in a tentative, exploring way. It was something new for both of them, and they were frightened because they didn't even know much about that sort of thing. Necking and petting, let alone sex, simply were not even discussed in most nice families in Newark in 1941.

"We were both awkward, young teenagers," Bunny says of that time forty-four years ago. "It was scary stuff."

As the school year drew to a close, Eddie asked Bunny to be

his date for his senior prom. Even though it was to be held in the school gymnasium and not at an elegant hotel, it was the high point of their limited social calendar. On the appointed night, Bunny primped and readied herself expectantly and wore a pretty white dress with red polka dots. Eddie was all dressed up, too, and he presented her with a wrist corsage before they rushed off. An indication of how special the night was to be was that one of the kids had a car. Eddie and Bunny piled into it with what seemed a dozen classmates, and Bunny wound up sitting on his lap in the back seat. Such intimacy was not part of their routine, and the temptation was apparently more than Eddie could bear. He reached up and grabbed Bunny's breasts.

She was shocked, horrified beyond belief. Instantly, she bolted off his lap, slid down between his legs and onto the floor. She sat there, mortified, for the ride to the prom. The night was ruined—and so was their relationship.

"I do distinctly remember his hands on my bosom and me sitting on the floor, feeling violated and crushed that a good person could do this," Bunny now says with a laugh. "I sat right there on the floor and refused to talk to him all night because I thought this was a terrible thing to do to a friend. I really thought he was a rogue, a cad."

Bunny never again dated Eddie Koch. She didn't call him and he didn't call her. "I guess neither one of us knew how to handle it from that point on," she says. "I didn't know how to, and because he was a shy boy, I guess he didn't know how to handle it either. It's not your most thrilling moment to take out a girl and touch her and then she sits on the floor and doesn't talk to you."

Bunny only saw Koch again years later when he was a congressman. By coincidence, she bumped into him at a political affair. By then, she was an independent businesswoman and the wife of Paul Grossinger, president of the famous Catskill Mountain resort that bears his family's name. Stunned that her old boyfriend had made such a success of himself, Bunny approached Koch and asked his age—just to make sure he was the same "cad" who had touched her girlish bosom without permission. She was about to identify herself, but thought better of it, and he did not recognize her.

"He was more sensitive than people may have realized," she says. "He was not easy in that, if you did something, you couldn't talk to him afterwards. I think that's probably true of him today. Maybe some of the bluster one sees in the Mayor today is to make damn sure that the frightened young boy is well protected and taken care of." She allowed herself a chuckle, before adding, "And to think I could have been in Gracie Mansion."

Louis Koch and Joyce Silpe arrived in New York as teenage Polish immigrants about 1910. Like most of those who formed the human wave that was America-bound early in this century— the Irish, the Italians, and those from other countries—they entered the New World through the teeming portal of Ellis Island and plunged into New York City's ever-churning ethnic cauldron. They brought with them the immigrant's dream of a better life and enough energy, resourcefulness, and patience to make the dream come true. If not they, at least maybe their children could prosper.

Sophie Kottler, then a twelve-year-old girl from a small village on the Russian-Polish border, came to America in the same wave as Louis and Joyce Koch. Seven decades later, she vividly recalls the two-week ocean voyage and the excitement on the boat as the immigrants reached their destination:

"The night before, everybody on the ship said we're going to reach America in the morning. So we all washed our hair and dressed up. We all took the shoes, polished the shoes, even washed the sole of the shoes because they say this is golden land. There's no mud. There's cleanliness here and here we come from a dirty little town. So we all polished our shoes at night and made them shiny and washed the soles of the shoes and went out in the morning and we seen the Statue of Liberty. We were all dancing. What a beautiful day. We were laughing and crying for joy. We came to America at last."

But New York in the early twentieth century was a tough town by any measure. Though most immigrants came expecting to find the streets paved with gold, the life they found here was anything but easy. Whole families worked long hours as laborers for subsistence wages and at night went home to cramped, cold, damp railroad flats that were little more than multi-story shacks. Children had little time for education, and tuberculosis kept the infant mortality rate high. The streets were clogged with horse-drawn carts, causing a primitive form of gridlock that was made more odious by the manure. The Irish-dominated police force was notoriously corrupt, with officers as likely to accept a bribe as make an arrest.

The government in the teeming metropolis of have-nots from around the world was headed by William J. Gaynor, the city's ninety-fourth chief executive. A crusty, peevish reformer, Gaynor was in many ways a precursor of the kind of mayor Louis and Joyce's son was to become. Gaynor took great delight in publicly excoriating and browbeating his aides, the citizenry, reporters, and anybody else he chose. A flamboyant showman and the consummate politician, Gaynor's antics brought him great popularity. His bullyboy ways were described in a 1910 profile by William B. Hale in a publication called *World's Work*:

"You see he is far from possessing or cultivating the grace of a popular idol. No man was ever so apparently indifferent to the good opinion of the public. He is much sought after as a speaker for public occasions; if anybody is tardy or undignified he is likely to snub the committee which asks him to speak, lecture the gentlemen who come to escort him, admonish the chairman of the meeting and scold the audience—but before he sits down he has everybody cheering."

In such a world, Louis Koch and Joyce Silpe found each other, and eventually, the Bronx. Driven by a desire to get ahead, they worked long hours in what was known as the "needle trades." Because Jews had been denied the right to own land in many countries, such as Poland and Russia, most of those who came here had worked as tailors in their native towns and villages. Arriving as they did in such great numbers—more than 1 million immigrants came through Ellis Island annually during the early part of this century—the new Americans found themselves competing with one another in New York's fledgling garment industry. At times, it seemed that every immigrant was a tailor setting up shop on the Lower East Side of Manhattan.

Joyce Silpe brought with her some training and talent, and she worked hard as a designer of women's blouses. Louis Koch was a pantsmaker. By 1920, they had married and moved to the Bronx. That was the year Harold, the first of their three children, was born. Four years later—in 1924—was born a second son, Edward Irving. Honest John Hylan was the mayor then, presiding over an administration that, in return for $1 million in bribes, approved the sale of vast quantities of tainted, watered-down milk that was blamed for spreading typhoid and causing brain damage in infants. Later, the Koches had a daughter, Paula, who would change her name to Pat.

Before the Roaring Twenties ended and the Great Depression came crashing down on their lives, the Koches had begun to make progress toward their dream. Louis, at his wife's urging, had moved up from pants to furs and was a partner in a small company. "He was a pantsmaker, which was considered the lower end," said Harold Koch. "She persuaded him to raise his sights because at that time with her job as a ladies' blouse designer she was a high-end lady and pantsmakers weren't really in."

Joyce was so determined to make it in America that she hired a tutor to teach herself to read and write English and insisted that it, and not Yiddish, be the primary language spoken at home.

The family was securely tucked into an apartment in the Morrisania section of the Bronx, at 1660 Crotona Park East. The newly constructed building faced Crotona Park and had spacious apartments and an elevator—a major status symbol of the time. Residents of the area regarded the park as the Bronx's answer to Central Park and their street as its answer to fashionable Central Park West. Much of the Bronx, as was much of the city, had just undergone a gigantic residential building boom. Immigrant families such as the Koches were flocking to the "suburbs" of the Bronx, Brooklyn, and Upper Manhattan in an effort to escape the ghetto of the Lower East Side. The journey was made easier, as was the commute to work everyday, by the expanding subway system. Over succeeding generations, new waves of immigrants from other parts of the world would move into those same buildings and ride those same subway lines.

For Jews, however, the choices in the 1920s were not always as wide as for the other groups. Old guard landlords hung out signs that said NO JEWS, and the courts upheld their right to maintain segregated buildings. So Jewish developers constructed their own buildings, outposts of middle-class respectability. These apartment buildings with elevators substituted for the single-family home as the symbol of a better life.

The Koches were among the many working-class Jewish families, most of them from Eastern Europe, who found a home in the Bronx. Commercial streets in their neighborhood teemed with pushcarts, delicatessens, kosher restaurants, and specialty stores. The neighborhood also had a reputation for radicalism. Socialist and union groups attracted greater interest than the temples. The aristocratic German Jews who had arrived earlier, and now owned many of the sweatshops on the Lower East Side, were Republicans. Those from Eastern Europe, those who worked in the sweatshops, organized unions to fight back. They became Democrats, an affiliation their children would cling to generations later despite entering the ranks of the professions.

The world was small for those who lived near Crotona Park in part by choice, in part not. After the pogroms of Europe and the trauma of immigration, there was a natural suspicion of the outside world and so children were schooled to maintain their heritage. At the same time, although anti-Semitism was not a pressing reality for many, as it had been in Europe, there were barriers for those who wished to leave the home base and seek their fortunes elsewhere. Ivy League schools such as Harvard, Yale, and Columbia established quotas limiting the number of Jewish students they would admit. As a result, New York Jews built Yeshiva University for their own children, while many other families sent their children to City College, where Jews were welcomed. For Ed Koch's generation, which came of age between the wars, "quota" is still a word that smacks of discrimination against Jews rather than equal opportunity for blacks and other racial minorities.

The Koch family was closely knit, with both parents working hard to give their children comfort and a fighting chance to make it in the world. The parents fulfilled the traditional roles, with Louis spending long hours hunched over his sewing machines, while Joyce ruled the home with a forceful, even dominant hand. Speaking of his father, Koch has described him as an energetic man, who always seemed to have two jobs and never needed more than five hours of sleep a night. In height, facial appearance, and the absence of hair, Koch strongly resembles his father.

Yet, as perhaps befits a matriarchal household, Koch was apparently closer to his mother. Later friends would recall how much he revered her, and the memories he has shared of his mother have been mostly humorous. Her cooking, he has said, got better the minute he stopped having to eat it—after-dinner heartburn was apparently a family malady, even if chicken soup was the main course. By all accounts, Mrs. Koch was a tall, handsome, feisty woman who did not shrink from a good fight, and sometimes went out of her way to find one. Indeed, Koch has on several occasions used the word "torture" to describe his mother's methods of fighting with his father. Once he told an interviewer that his mother sent him as a child to take Hebrew lessons rather than allow him to stay home and take the harmonica lessons he preferred "so she could torture my father while I was gone." Another time, Koch told of his mother's ultimate weapon against his father. Louis was more zealous about observing kosher dietary laws than his wife, and when she was very upset at him, she would cook bacon and wave the pan under his nose. The Mayor laughed heartily when he told the story recently. And he laughed when he said his government bumps along "like a very large and quarrelsome Jewish family," a clear indication of what home must have been like.

By 1931, the rising tide of the Depression had swamped the Koches. Furs were a luxury item that few people could afford, and sales plummeted overnight. Three-quarters of the fur companies went bust. Suddenly Louis's skills and products were no longer in demand, and without his steady income, the family could not meet its rent payments. Destitute, they turned for help to Bernard Koch, Louis's brother in Newark. Though the brother, his wife, and two children had little room to spare in their two-bedroom, $45-a-month flat at 90 Spruce Street, they opened their doors to their impoverished relatives. Their pride crushed, their dream derailed, Louis and Joyce packed their bags and brood and moved across the Hudson River. Life in the land of opportunity had come down to nine people in two bedrooms in Newark.

The apartment was located in Newark's South Ward, a tough, working-class part of town. The neighborhood was a traditional entry point for poor people moving into Newark, and contained a sizable number of blacks from the South as well as immigrants. Though they lived in the same neighborhood, and the children attended the same schools, the two groups were virtually segregated into separate enclaves. Some blocks were white, others black. The two most powerful local figures were white—Abner "Longie" Zwillman, leader of the city's Jewish mafia, and Meyer Ellenstein, a flamboyant populist and Newark's first Jewish mayor.

Although most of the whites viewed relations between blacks and whites as cordial, the blacks were in fact less equal. They were forced to sit in the balcony of downtown movie theaters, were refused service in many restaurants, and were barred from

driving a bus or operating a trolley. Calvin Smith, a black Newark physician who went to high school with Eddie, remembers
the segregation of the 1930s. "That was devastating to us," he
says. "It made us feel we were somehow inferior despite the fact
that we were competing academically and athletically." Judith
Mischel also went to high school with Koch and she, too, remembers the racial caste system. Angered at the treatment of
blacks, Mischel, who is white, joined the local branch of the
NAACP at thirteen only to discover that it made her an outcast.
She came to be regarded as a "nigger lover" by the parents of
some of her white friends who forbade their children to play with
her.

Eddie's mother also had a brother in Newark, Louis Silpe, to
whom she turned for help. The oldest and most successful of the
Silpes, Louis was the family patriarch. He leased and operated a
prosperous catering hall in Krueger's Auditorium on Belmont
Avenue. The huge building had an auditorium, several dining
rooms, and two full kitchens where Louis Silpe's wife Mary
oversaw the preparation of kosher food for bar mitzvahs, weddings, and other celebrations. Family members describe Mary's
cooking as delicious. It was the same food that Bunny Persky
called scrumptious. In the auditorium, the Jewish Theater, with
stars like Molly Picon, staged performances, and the big bands
of the era appeared. "We had all the big bands play there from
Benny Goodman to Tommy Dorsey, one night stands in the
1930s," said Louis Silpe's son, Abraham.

The hall also had a hat-check concession, which Eddie's uncle,
Louis Silpe, sold to the Koch family. Louis and Joyce plunged
into working the concession with the help of Harold and later
Eddie. Patrons were charged 25 cents to check their coats and
hats, and when the evening was over they stampeded the
concession, demanding that the Koches produce their garments
in a hurry. "When they left, everybody wanted their coat at one
time," said Seymour Bodner, Koch's first cousin. "It used to be
quite a hassle. That's when someone like me would help out."

In addition to returning the coats, the Koches were busy hustling for tips. Baskets were placed on the counter, and signs were
posted reminding the patrons not to forget to tip the hat-check
people. A dime was a common tip. On weekend nights, the
Koches closed up the stand at about 2:00 A.M. and went home
to enjoy cake before going to bed. "In the morning," Koch has

remembered, "we would roll the dimes in paper, my parents and myself."

Looking back, Koch has bittersweet memories of the time. The experience of being poor clearly left a deep, formative impression on him. He remembers fondly his father's ingenuity at feeding his wife and three children. Later a family legend for his hamburgers and carrot cake, Louis in those days soon figured out that he could stretch his meager budget by waiting until fruit turned overripe so he could get it at a discount. Taking them home, Louis would peel, then stew the mushy peaches and plums and serve them cold with week-old bread. Koch remembers the cold fruit soup as "delicious," but his eyes positively twinkle with delight when he talks of the not-so-fresh chocolate cake his father used to bring home from Dugan's bakery. "Really good," he says.

But it is not with fondness that he recalls his uncle, Louis Silpe, and hustling for tips. He has described his uncle as "not such a nice person," and has said that he sold the family the hat-check concession on "onerous" terms. The rolls of coins from the concession weren't enough to support the family. Louis Koch, exhausted from working the hat-check concession at night, rose early to leave the house at seven to seek work in New York's garment center. Harold, a powerfully built man, bitterly remembers his father's struggle and shares his brother's anger at the Silpe patriarch. Indeed, at Koch's sixtieth birthday party, Harold began to tell a story of how he once became "physical" with Silpe, but broke off the story in midsentence. Money, or the lack of it in the Koch family, was the problem.

"I suspect Eddie's father wanted to go back into business, since being a furrier was the only thing he knew," says Seymour Bodner. "Since Krueger's Auditorium was a profitable business, I would assume he may have asked Louis Silpe for money."

For Eddie, however, the worst part—the part that left a lasting scar—was watching his father struggle so hard to put food on the table while the whole family had to beg for tips from those more economically fortunate. "It was very demeaning," Koch told journalist Ken Auletta in 1979. "It was demeaning to ask people as we did, 'Don't forget the hat-check boys.' That left a trauma, I must say. To live on the largesse of people is something I consider demeaning."

After a year or so, Louis Koch was able to move his family out of his brother's crowded flat and into an apartment of his own and about one-half mile away, at 61 Milford Avenue. Eddie attended the neighborhood elementary school with his mother's demand that he do well so he could get ahead. He obeyed, as did many of his peers for whom an education was viewed as the ticket to a better life. With Louis's fur business picking up some momentum again, the family was able to put much of the trauma of the Depression behind it, and life on Milford Avenue took on a more routine flavor. There were family gatherings involving aunts and uncles and cousins, with the extended Silpe clan going to each other's homes for socializing and eating.

"I remember that very fondly," says Seymour Bodner. "The whole family used to come. They'd come on a Sunday and we'd have a family get-together." The men, in addition to talking business, would sometimes talk politics—Democratic politics. Franklin Delano Roosevelt was the President, a hero attempting to lead the nation out of the Depression, and the Silpe clan was behind him.

For Eddie, the growing stability in his family's finances meant that his days consisted mostly of schoolwork and play. There were hot dogs and custard pie to be had at Sabin's, movies for 15 cents, and a ride on a streetcar and a Bonomo's Turkish taffy for a nickel each. Some of the money he was spending was his own, saved from his job as a delivery boy at a small grocery store. Unlike Harold, a stocky lad who walked with a macho swagger and played on the high school football team, Eddie was tall and thin. And Harold confesses to taking full advantage of the privileges of seniority and size.

"I would kick the shit out of him when my mother wasn't around," he remembers. "I was stuck with him as his baby sitter as he was with my sister."

Eddie also had a few scrapes outside the family, and at least once, when he was ten, Harold had to come to his rescue. "I beat up a grown man for him once," Harold says. "The guy was the super of our building and he had a vicious dog that used to frighten all of us. He was beating up on my brother. I was big for my age. I knocked the guy down."

Seymour Bodner, three years younger than his cousin, remembers Eddie as quiet and serious, more interested in reading than in sports or music. The one family quality that Ed shared, Seymour recalls, was a sense of humor. On visits to the Koches' apartment on Milford Avenue, he and Ed would lie on the floor under the family radio and listen to all the comedy shows.

"We were just common, ordinary kids," Seymour says of himself and his cousin.

If Eddie had any sports ambitions, which does not seem likely, they were dashed by a serious accident he suffered when he was twelve. Playing tag, he crashed his left hand through a pane of glass, severely cutting himself. The hand was slow to heal, and, to regain the strength in the atrophied muscles, Eddie was ordered to squeeze a rubber ball as much as he could. For months, the ball accompanied him just about everywhere as he attempted to regain the use of his hand. Eventually, he had to have secondary operations because there was a growing stiffness in the fingers. Even today, his left hand remains smaller than his right.

By the time he entered South Side High in 1937, Eddie had distinguished himself as a student. He was not a genius—school records put his IQ in the average range at 111—but his work had been good enough that he had skipped a grade in grammar school, a common occurrence for bright, hard-working children. He enrolled in South Side's more rigorous college preparatory courses—a program reserved for students who were viewed by others as the school's intellectual elite. He performed well, garnering straight As in English, average grades in math and German, and As in biology, international relations, and economics. He graduated with honors, finishing seventeenth in his class of 299.

During those high school years, Eddie's personality began to take shape. The normal, quiet adolescent remembered by his family came to develop other reputations among his classmates. Virtually all those who remember him paint a picture of a loner, an oddball, an egghead, and most of all, a talker. They recall him as an immature boy whose interests and personality marked him as different. Except for his brief friendship with Bunny, his style was not much of a success in forming relationships. While most boys carried their books tucked jauntily under their arms at their sides, Eddie hugged his to his chest. If he dated other girls, nobody remembers. He was not elected to the student government, dubbed most popular or most likely to succeed or given any of the other designations a senior class confers on its stars.

Because he had been skipped ahead, Eddie had an age handicap in dealing with his peers. He was only fifteen when he began his senior year in high school, making him one of the youngest—if not the youngest—in his class. Some students were as much as two years older than he was. And, although he was already approaching his full-grown height of six-feet-one-inch, his body was thin, gangly, and uncoordinated.

Frances Gendel, who was in Eddie's homeroom, remembers him as a tall, "immature little boy." "He didn't fuss too much with social things," she says. "I don't remember him going to a party."

Gendel and another classmate, Irving Epstein, also skipped grades. Both felt the practice, while common, required a too-difficult adjustment for some youngsters, including Koch.

"I wouldn't advise it myself," Epstein says, adding that the age difference made it particularly difficult for boys to relate to girls. "You had to look up at them like a mother. We had a problem, but I wasn't aware of it until I went into the Army."

Another important factor in Koch's isolation was that he did not share the major interests of most of his classmates. Football and other athletics were popular among most students, but he couldn't care less. Dancing and parties provided entertainment for most kids, but not for Eddie.

"He was an egghead, a square, a loner, and very bright," said Julius Lehrhoff. "He wasn't like the rest of us crazy kids. He wasn't with the dancing and the cars and the running around with girls."

Yet that is not to say that Eddie did not have interests of his own, or that he did not try to make friends. He had already decided that he wanted to be a lawyer—"the Jewish ethic," he has called it—and was one of the few boys in school who registered to take a cooking course. He signed up for numerous after-school activities, including the photography, science, German, and international clubs. In his senior year, he became chairman of the cap and gown committee and qualified for the debating team. Although Max Glassman remembers him having "the gift of gab," Eddie was not able to parlay his interest in debating into recognition. Lillian Altschuler, the debating team captain and the girl voted most likely to succeed, remembers him only as "a face in the class, not as a person." The boy voted most likely to succeed, Zhonta Stapleton, a black, does remember Koch but only as a loner and outsider whom he once debated in the school auditorium. The subject of their debate was the growing troubles in Europe. Koch was assigned to argue for American intervention against Hitler, while Stapleton advocated isolationism.

Another of Eddie's interests was poetry, and several of his meditations, which ranged far and wide, were published in a school magazine, *The Optimist*.

One poem directs an unmistakable anger at, of all things, sand. In hindsight, the verse is rich with irony, given his later-day feelings about Palestine and his strongly pro-Israel viewpoint. Its title is "Sand":

> *You countless grains of sand,*
> *Surging, moving,*
> *Covering the land like a plague,*
> *You dominate this world.*
> *Glorious Babylon*
> *Lies beneath your weight,*
> *Ancient Nineveh*
> *Is crushed beneath you.*
> *Egypt's splendor,*
> *Palestine's glory is covered*
> *By your tumultuous waves.*
>
> *You are*
> *King,*
> *Master,*
> *Lord.*
> *Lord of all but one.*
> *Man.*
>
> *For man whom you crush,*
> *Whose cities you make desolate,*
> *In the end shall*
> *Conquer you.*
>
> *From your wastes,*
> *He will tear fertile acres.*
> *Upon your wastes,*
> *He will build new cities.*
> *Cities upon the sites*

Of those which you
Have destroyed.

So crush,
Desolate,
Cover,
And destroy,
While you can.
For your days are numbered.

If being younger than his classmates and having different interests were not enough to set Eddie apart, his talking finished the job. Never one to suffer in silence, his aggressive, nonstop chatter was viewed as obnoxious by some students. His pronouncements were just that—pronouncements waiting for challenge. And with his brightness and ability to whip off biting, even insulting, remarks some classmates came to view his talking as an attack mechanism, as though he were using the one talent that he surely had both to compensate for his shortcomings and to revenge the rejections he'd suffered.

Judith Mischel found Koch to be "an intellectual snob" who so irritated her that she blocked out most of his chatter. His "cockiness and arrogance," she decided, "must have been hiding something."

"He had a very biting sense of humor," she says. "He was not popular. I think I put him in that stereotype of behavior of an only child. This arrogance—it could have been egocentric. You knew he was there and you didn't much like him. He had this very superior attitude—justified or unjustified—it was there."

Next to the picture of each graduating senior appeared a short statement summing up the impression the student had made, a sort of graduation epitaph.

About Eddie Koch, the yearbook says, "Strong in will to find, to strive, to seek, and not to yield."

Koch graduated from South Side in 1941, at sixteen, and soon moved with his family to Brooklyn where their residence qualified him for a free education at City College. The family lived on Ocean Parkway, in a neighborhood that was predominately middle-class and Jewish. The streets teemed with youngsters who strove to hit a Spaldeen with a stickball bat as far as they could, a distance that was not measured in feet or yards but in the number of sewers between the batter and the spot where the rubber ball landed. Many males, older and younger, were falling in and out of love with either girls or the Brooklyn Dodgers, but Koch was not among them.

"He was kind of a little bit out of it," says Jay Gurfein, whose family lived in the building next door to Koch. "He marched to a different drummer." Instead of joining in the games of other boys his age, Eddie stayed close to his mother and sister, toward whom he was very loving and protective, Harold says. For recreation, the family went to Coney Island.

Koch also landed a part-time job as a salesman in a Brooklyn shoestore called Oppenheim Collins. In an interview with *Cosmopolitan* magazine after he became Mayor, Koch recalled the job in revealing terms. His story of selling shoes is, first, an excellent example of Koch's anecdotal style of humor. Assuming that it's not too embellished for the purpose of being funny, the story is also an example of the elephantlike memory that Koch prides himself on.

It seems that Koch went to work on Thursday nights and Saturdays in the ladies' shoe department and, no expert in women's footwear, quickly found himself overwhelmed by the myriad sizes and styles of shoes he found in the stockroom. During his first two days at work, he tried to memorize them all; then he came back the third day and found, to his horror, that the boxes had been rearranged. As Koch remembers it, he was staring at the new lineup of boxes when "the manager comes in and says, 'Do you intend to go out and sell some?' I said, 'Certainly. That's what I intend to do right now.'

"So I go out and pick out a very elderly woman, thinking she'd be the most kind. And I take off her shoe. Now—stupid on my part, slow learner—I couldn't figure out how to use that whatdoyoucallit? Measuring rod? I couldn't figure out whether you took the number inside or the number outside. So I'm looking. And I say to her, 'What size do you normally take, madam?' She says 6A. I said, 'Well, your foot hasn't grown a bit! You still take 6A.' I said, 'What kind of shoe would you like?' She said an Oxford, and I honestly did not know what an Oxford was.

"Well, I go back to where the 6As are, and I take out ten boxes. Everybody is looking at me. You never take out more than three boxes at a time; it's just not done. I opened the first one and they're about a three-inch pump, and she looks at it and it's clear it's not something she likes, so I say, 'That's not for you.' I did that with each box, and I saw in her eyes she didn't like them. Finally—I opened up this one and see her eyes light up, and I say, 'That is for you.' She says, 'I'll take it.' "

In the fall of 1941, still sixteen, Eddie entered City College with plans to graduate, then get his law degree. But the war clouds that had broken over much of Europe were inexorably moving toward the United States. The student radicalism that had led many young people and intellectuals to embrace communism in the 1930s was giving way to the growing fear of war. Suspected communists had been purged from the faculty by a committee of the state legislature. A young black city councilman named Adam Clayton Powell was complaining that City College had no black teachers, but the administration denied there was any discrimination.

Three months after Eddie took his first class at City College in September 1941, the Japanese bombed Pearl Harbor. America went to war, and the military started draining the country's colleges of men. Koch stayed in school until his turn came in April 1943. At the age of eighteen he was drafted, and the army soon sent him off to Europe to defend freedom and fight Hitler. It damn near got him killed in the process.

4

ED KOCH GOES
TO WAR

A little more than three decades after his parents came from Europe as part of the great wave of immigration, Ed Koch was carrying a rifle on his way to Europe. Clad in fatigues, a duffel bag over his shoulder, Koch boarded the *Cristobal*, a converted passenger liner, at a South Brooklyn pier on August 27, 1944. A fresh-faced member of Company F, 2nd Battalion of the 415th Infantry Regiment—he was a grunt in the Timberwolf Division. It was a warm summer Sunday when the ship, jammed with thousands of GIs, glided slowly out of New York harbor. The green soldiers—kids, really, too young then even to vote in the year's presidential election—gathered on the deck to contemplate the Statue of Liberty. The men of Company F—Walter Bolechowski, Wayne Needles, George Burns, Ken Williams, Al Milwid, Mike Berrigan, Dave Schumm, Tony Hurtado, Bob Cole, Ed Koch, and dozens of other enlisted men— were faces in the crowd. The ship made its way out of the Narrows and into the Atlantic.

Two months later, at the end of a rainy October, Koch, the gawky, unathletic teenager, found himself toting a rifle and marching under cover of darkness across the lowlands of southern Holland. Company F was moving toward the front. They'd started marching in the early morning with what seemed like thousands of other Timberwolf Division troops in two single-file columns stretched out on both sides of a narrow road near the Belgian border. Weighted down with packs and equipment, they were still walking at eleven that night, trudging along a highway that ran west from the city of Breda toward the Dutch coast. Sergeant Bill Dierker rode between the two marching lines in a jeep, dozing lightly. The small towns along the way were a treat for

37

the men, as yet untested in battle. Most of the hamlets had recently been liberated after four years of German occupation, and more often than not, the villagers poured out into their cobblestone streets at the sight of the bedraggled soldiers, waving flags and offering the GIs cookies, cakes, grapes, apples, cider, and pitchers of hot milk with butter floating on top.

The highway cut across the lowlands of Holland, a flat, soggy, open terrain broken occasionally by small canals and dotted here and there with trees. The only moving figures were the marching soldiers, the only sound the crunch and shuffle of their army-issue shoes—they hadn't been given combat boots. A short distance ahead of Company F, the columns were making their way easily through a crossroads. But as the troops trudged along, suddenly there was an unfamiliar sound, a screeching noise that was followed by a thunderous explosion, then another one, then another, and another. Artillery and mortar fire rained down on Company F. The men reacted instantly, some in panic. Like almost everyone else, Koch, Milwid, and Berrigan dove to the side of the road. Face down on the ground and confused, Berrigan lost his rifle. Dierker bolted from his jeep, but moved so fast that he left behind his shovel, a critical piece of equipment for an infantryman under fire. He climbed back up onto the road, retrieved it, and headed out into the fields to dig himself in. An officer the men had nicknamed "Major 88s" because he lectured them repeatedly on the lethal capabilities of the German 88 millimeter artillery was killed by one. Burns, who would later win both the Silver Star and the Distinguished Service Cross, was prone on the ground near a roadside ditch where a group of men were huddled. As the shells dropped nearby, he could hear the wounded, in his words, "screaming like banshees in pain and fear." With many others, he got up and raced out into the flatlands. Koch was out there, somewhere, in the darkness. So were Williams and Milwid. They all hoped to scatter away from the road where the shells were falling, but the Germans had spotters, and the barrage soon began following the troops into the exposed fields. "It was like you had an inhuman being watching you from above and you couldn't get away until it got you," Burns remembers.

Burns and many of the other men eventually found shelter in root cellars and basements of nearby farmhouses. Williams spent the night outside huddled against a farmhouse wall. After several hours, the shelling began to lessen and by the morning it stopped completely. In one night of horror, Koch and his buddies in Company F had learned more about soldiering than they had in their months of infantry training back in the States. They'd grown close during that training but now there was an even deeper bond. The toll among the 180 enlisted men of Company F was nine wounded, and they hadn't even seen the enemy or fired a shot.

Company F had been assembled the previous March at Camp Carson, Colorado, a military base not too far from the foot of Pike's Peak. Many were bright teenagers who had been lifted right out of college into the army, as Koch had. After completing basic training—Koch did his at Camp Croft, South Carolina—they had all been assigned to the Army Specialized Training Program (ASTP) and had been scattered to schools all over the country to learn engineering. Koch and Milwid wound up in mathematics classes together at Fordham University in the Bronx. They stayed there for about six months before it became clear that the war was consuming so much manpower that the country couldn't afford to keep thousands of soldiers in classrooms. The ASTP was broken up and Koch, Milwid, and thousands of others were packed off to infantry units. Koch was dispatched to Camp Carson to join the Timberwolf Division, an infantry unit that specialized in night fighting.

The division had been in intensive training in the mountains and forests of Oregon as well as in the Mojave Desert for almost a year before the green ASTP soldiers arrived in camp. Their much more experienced comrades looked down on the new arrivals with disdain, deriding them as schoolboy soldiers. Partly as a result of that attitude, the schoolboys began to stick together, a small group of friends in a company comprised of men with a wide variety of backgrounds and abilities. The troops of Company F came from forty-seven of the country's forty-eight states. There were Catholics, Protestants, and Jews. Some were functionally illiterate southern dirt farmers. Others—the schoolboys—were much more educated. Some had nearly finished college. One was even deaf, the victim of a local draft board that didn't care. The army homogenized them all—even Ed Koch, the talkative high-school egghead. It made no difference what anyone thought at home. This was a new world, with new standards. Whether you

were handsome, had a lot of girlfriends, or played football counted
for nothing. You were judged by one chief measure—whether
you could be relied on when the chips were down. Koch, like
everyone else, had a fresh chance to prove himself.

There were four platoons in Company F with about forty men
each. With a bunch of the other schoolboys, Koch was assigned
to the 1st Platoon. During the five months at Carson, seven of
them grew to know each other particularly well: Al Milwid, the
scrawny son of an immigrant Lithuanian butcher from Bayonne;
Walt Bolechowski, a Polish Catholic from Philadelphia; Mike
Berrigan, the son of a meat cutter from Williamsport, Pennsyl-
vania; David Schumm, the son of a Milwaukee physician; Bob
Cole, an only child who had been raised in India where his father
was a mining engineer; Ken Williams, the son of a printer from
Saratoga Springs, New York; and Ed Koch, the son of a Jewish
furrier from Brooklyn.

Koch, as always, became known in the platoon for his biting
sense of humor and constant talking. Bolechowski developed a
reputation for forever ranting about the "freakin' " army. It's not
surprising that the two Poles became friends.

"Koch was kind of a politicker," Williams remembers. "How
should I say it? He expressed his opinion and talked very freely."
But the chatter that many of his high-school classmates had found
obnoxious was now viewed as just another quirk of another GI.
Besides, the schoolboys were learning much about the world from
each other, and they spent a great deal of their free time talking.
Koch, the loner who had grown up in a tightly knit Jewish family, was tasting a whole new world. He expressed an interest in
Catholicism, about which he knew relatively little, and explored
it with Berrigan, who was raised in the faith. "And I learned about
the Jewish religion, of which I knew nothing," Berrigan says. "We
spent a lot of time discussing religion."

When they got a pass, the friends would set out in groups for
Denver or Colorado Springs, then a camp town where crap games,
women, and hard-drinking bars were easy to come by. That kind
of entertainment, however, was not for Koch. On that score also
he'd changed little. "Ed enjoyed a nice meal," Berrigan remembers. "At the most he would have one drink—a social drink."
One Saturday night, Milwid and Koch stayed in a Denver hotel
that permitted GIs to sleep in its lobby for free. In the morning,
Milwid rose to go to Mass. "I had to go to church," he remem-

bers, "and Ed said, 'I don't want to hang around here. Can I come with you?' I said, 'Sure, but I don't know why you'd want to.' Ed answered, 'I don't want to be alone.' " The two soldiers went to Mass together.

On August 15, 1944, their training complete, the entire Timberwolf Division shipped out on twenty-four trains for Camp Kilmer in New Jersey. From there, they made their way to South Brooklyn and boarded the *Cristobal*. Thousands of men were on that ship. So many that they slept in bunks stacked no more than two feet apart and had to eat standing up in a walled-in area in the bowels of the ship that many thought had been a swimming pool for the luxury passengers.

On September 7, thankful to be off the ship, the Timberwolves were ferried ashore on Omaha Beach, the site three months earlier of the D-Day invasion. The battling had long since been finished there, but Company F saw the results of war for the first time in the nearby port city of Cherbourg. The city had been heavily bombed and much of it was rubble. Its harbor was clogged with the hulks of sunken ships.

Koch and the rest of Company F were moved inland a short distance and were bivouacked for several weeks in a city of olive-drab pup tents erected in an apple orchard near a small village that had been declared off limits. There were, of course, plenty of apples to eat, and the scent of countless small wood fires used for cooking filled the air. Milwid remembers wondering if what he was doing was like being a Boy Scout. It was a pleasant, almost idyllic experience, and for the first time, two of Koch's personality quirks—his obsession with food and his penchant for trying to strike up a conversation with anybody—came in handy.

"Somehow in his wanderings, Koch had run into a family from the village, made friends, and wangled an invitation to their home," Schumm remembers.

So after dark that evening, Koch, Schumm, Berrigan, and Cole made their way to the house, a small building, surrounded by a low fence. They were welcomed inside by the French family—a mother, her fifteen-year-old daughter, a niece who was about the same age, and her nineteen-year-old son who had been pressed into forced labor by the Germans until the D-Day invasion allowed him to escape.

With blackout curtains drawn, the GIs gathered with the family and drank cider that was brought in from a big wooden barrel kept in a shack out back. The French teenagers, who spoke English, told of their experiences with the Germans. Koch, Schumm, Berrigan, and Cole reciprocated by telling them of their lives in America. As the young people became more familiar with each other, the storytelling became more lively, and Cole, a cheerful nineteen-year-old, took to entertaining everyone by playing the family's piano. The four GIs stayed for several hours and returned to visit the family almost every night for the two weeks that Company F was camped near the town. They brought with them food scrounged from the camp kitchen and on a Sunday came bearing Army-issue blankets, a canned ham, and canned fruit for a picnic. The family brought French bread, cheese, and cider to make the rest of the meal.

The episode enhanced Koch's reputation greatly among his comrades, and was the beginning of his career as the company scrounger. The object in the infantry is to travel as lightly as possible, which is a difficult thing to do when you are loaded down with rifles, packs, gas masks, shovels, food, overcoats, raincoats, ammunition, and sundry other equipment. Along the way, as Company F journeyed through Europe, many of the men began discarding unused equipment to ease their burden. Koch did just the opposite. He traveled like a gypsy, collecting things, anything, as long as it would be useful—extra blankets, chocolate bars, boot laces, toilet paper, and other amenities.

"He just went well supplied, and I guess he didn't mind carrying all that extra stuff," says Schumm. "I don't mean that he went like an itinerant peddler, but he had more stuff than the rest. He bulged out with stuff tucked into his field jacket. Everybody had ammunition belts on, and he would stuff all kinds of things into his pockets."

As for helping the war effort, Koch and the rest of Company F were assigned for a couple of weeks to riding shotgun on slow-moving supply trains traveling between the Cherbourg peninsula and Versailles. It was comfortable, safe duty. The biggest threat was not the Germans but black-market thieves. The time passed easily, but that soon began to change. On October 7, the Timberwolves were designated for combat and on the fifteenth began a two-week journey to the front.

The Normandy assault had driven the Germans from France but had stalled at the western edge of the Siegfried Line for lack of supplies. The logistics problems originated in the territory surrounding Antwerp, the Belgian port. It was under Allied control, but the lowland coastal area to its north in Holland was held by the Germans and was heavily fortified with artillery, making it impossible for supply ships to use the city's harbor safely. The Timberwolves, with other Allied troops, were assigned the mission of pushing the Germans back so that Antwerp could be opened up as a critical supply base.

Company F's trek to the front eventually brought Koch to a crossroads where the troops came under heavy bombardment. All along the long line, there were plenty of casualties, but the schoolboys of the 1st Platoon—Koch, Bolechowski, Milwid, Schumm, Cole, Berrigan, and Williams—came through unscathed. They regrouped, having all learned the same lesson: that it was just the luck of the draw that they were spared while others were hit. The dead and the wounded had been good soldiers—just like them—and they hadn't done anything they'd been warned not to do at Camp Carson. It just happened. The survivors said few words, even Koch. There was no point in talking much about it.

Struggling like everyone else to maintain his courage, Koch began marching again. What Company F was moving into was so terrible that some of the men would soon be driven into frantic, screaming panic. Others would turn their own guns on themselves so they could be carried off the battlefield with wounds that they attempted to blame on the Germans. No one in the company could envision which of them would be killed or wounded. Or who would exhibit courage while others caved in to the terror and death surrounding them. The battles would go on for more than six months, but Koch was luckier than most because his combat tour with Company F would last less than five weeks. Hospitalized with an accidental injury, Koch would be separated from the schoolboys and reassigned to less hostile environs. But that was yet to come.

For now, it was near the end of October and a cold, penetrating rain was falling as Company F moved toward the coast. With the rains, the always soggy Dutch lowlands had been turned into broad seas of oozing mud. From the infantryman's point of view the lowlands were a terrible place to be, not just because they were cold and wet—the men could take that—but because of their terrain. Broad and flat, the lowlands were dangerously open spaces where cover was all but nil. Crossing them made you an easy, certain target. The only breaks in the monotonous flatness were long earthen dikes that rose periodically from the land. The dikes had been built to protect the low-lying country from flooding, but they soon came to serve a far different purpose for Company F. They began to serve as shelter from a rain of incoming shells.

Cold, tired, and wet, the company's 180 men came to rest behind one of the dikes on October 31. A long dirt mound with sloping sides, the dike was about ten to twelve feet high and had a flat top that was of similar width. The GIs spread out along it at intervals of eight to ten yards and began digging into its rear side, carving out foxholes that resembled small caves. The men had good need for the shelter. They were now a front line force in a battle that was being fought largely by artillery. The Germans were seeking to drive the Allies back by bombarding them, and the Americans were attempting to do the same to the Germans. The role of Company F and the rest of the infantry was to withstand the barrage and to move ahead when ordered, taking the territory and not giving ground.

The company was at the dike when the terror that had rained down on them at the crossroads began again. The 88s and the mortar shells came pouring in from an unseen emplacement miles away, screeching through the air, exploding, and pounding the ground with concussions that were powerful enough, when the shells hit close by, to lift the men off the ground. Koch huddled in his foxhole—there was nothing else to do—waiting for the barrage to stop. But it didn't. It just kept going, on and on. For four full days—from October 31 to November 3—it kept up, sometimes intensely, sometimes sporadically. Sometimes it would stop entirely only to begin again at the whim of the unseen Germans. The shelling was often heaviest in the morning and the evening, and it usually picked up when the company cook approached the dike with a five-gallon tub of hot food. That would draw the men out of their holes and into the sights of the German spotters. The screech of the incoming shells would invariably send the men scurrying back to their small caves where they resorted to their cold rations.

There was no way to advance and no question of retreating. The company hugged the dike for dear life and spent so much time in the foxholes that many of the men began to make squirrel dens out of them. With the rain and the high water tables, water constantly seeped into the bottom of the small excavations, making life even more wet and miserable. Many of the men began foraging in nearby farm fields for hay to cover the floor of the holes. Williams even found a mattress at a nearby farmhouse that he dragged into his hole and placed on its muddy floor.

On October 31, the first day of the bombardment, F company suffered its first fatality when Private First Class Wayne Needles took a direct hit from an 88. The word of his death spread quickly, but it was only the beginning. So many were killed on the dike and in the company's later battles that the survivors came to understand the full horror of what had happened only after the war when they looked at a group picture that had been taken at Camp Carson.

"The original bunch just wasn't there. There were so few who I recognized," Williams remembers, his voice trailing off. The shelling continued the next day, November 1, but the casualties were relatively light. The men now looked on that as a major blessing. On November 2, the third day of the barrage, Williams was hit and wounded. And three men—Lt. Henry Bast, his runner Tony Hurtado, and Koch's buddy Bolechowski—were killed.

Bolechowski was hit by shrapnel as he stood atop the dike, firing. A chunk of it ripped through his field jacket and tore into his lungs. Berrigan and others fashioned a stretcher by wrapping a blanket around two rifles. They lifted Bolechowski onto it and raced to a makeshift aid station. The wounded were gathered on one side and the dead on the other. A medic motioned Berrigan to place Bolechowski with the latter. "I couldn't believe it. It took my breath away," Berrigan remembers.

As the casualty rate mounted, the folly of remaining on the dike became obvious, and Koch's platoon was assembled to see if it was possible to advance. Shortly after midnight, the platoon of about forty men assembled around Sgt. Ike Morgan. They were joined by two men from other units, a bazooka specialist for extra fire power and an artillery expert who was being sent to gather intelligence on the German emplacements.

Following Morgan's lead the platoon set out, disappearing up and over the dike one by one. Koch heaved himself up and slid down the other side. Schumm followed him. They crossed the field, crouching low in a staggered line. There was another dike up ahead, at most a thousand yards away, and, beyond that, a road that was elevated above the lowlands on a slight embankment. Koch inched his way out in the slowly moving line. Schumm was on his flank. They didn't get far—the best estimate is between 500 and 800 yards—before the Germans opened up on them with small arms and cannon fire. Koch hit the dirt. Schumm leaped into a crater that had been carved out of the earth by artillery fire. To his horror he landed beside a group of dead and wounded Germans. They were no threat; he let them be and rode out the firing with them in the hole.

At the sound of the first cannon shots, the bazookaman whirled and discharged a round in the direction they seemed to be coming from. But he'd moved too fast. The artilleryman was standing right behind him and was killed by the bazooka's violent, fiery backblast.

The platoon had embarked on a fool's errand. Morgan passed the word they were to retreat, and Koch, Schumm, and the rest inched their way back—often on their bellies—climbed the dike again, and rejoined Company F. After a while—that night or the next morning—Koch spoke with Morgan. There wasn't too much that could be said about what had happened, but in the course of the conversation Morgan said something that made Koch realize that the sergeant didn't know that Bolechowski had been killed.

"Do you know that we lost Bolechowski?" Koch asked him grimly.

"No," answered Morgan, who had come to regard Koch and Bolechowski as inseparable. "Why didn't you tell me?"

"You had more on you then than you could handle," Koch answered quietly.

Morgan looked at Koch, but didn't respond. The tough, thirty-three-year-old Mississippi farmer had come to respect the skinny Brooklyn kid, even if he wasn't much of a shot. Morgan saw him not only as an intelligent guy, but as a smart soldier. Sure, he was always talking, but that was a virtue, too, because Koch had the ability to understand and make himself understood in German. Most importantly, Morgan sized Koch up as a guy you could rely on.

The conversation—a terse battlefield exchange—ended there, and neither man brought the subject up again.

A day or so later, after four straight days of pounding, the barrage abated. The Germans seemed to have dropped back a bit, and the entire company was given the order to advance. Up and over the dike they went, glad to be moving forward again and relieved that the screeching and explosions were over, at least for the moment. Koch, Schumm, Berrigan, Milwid, and Cole pressed on. They were moving warily across the same field the platoon had tried to cross at night. There was no cannon fire this time, but they still proceeded, fearful that the Germans had planted mines. Their immediate objective was to get to the road, cross it, and, if possible, search out and destroy the German 88s.

As they neared the roadway embankment, the company began laying down bursts of fire in an attempt to flush out Germans who might be waiting in ambush. In between the bursts, small groups of men raced to the road and climbed up and over it. When their turns came, Koch, Schumm, Milwid, Berrigan, and Cole took off. They heaved up and over and scrambled down on the other side. They'd made it, or so it seemed. Out of nowhere there was an explosion. Berrigan was lifted off the ground and came down hard. He'd stepped on a mine. The concussion stunned him, but an intense burning pain—a ball of fire at the end of his leg—brought him to his senses quickly. He looked down. Where his foot had been, there was only a bloody ball of flesh. He could see his tattered shoe, with his foot still in it, on the ground in front of him. The company was scrambling to get to him. Sam Burnstein was closest and coming fast. He was running, but there was another concussion. Berrigan saw him lifted off the ground and fall. He, too, lost a foot. A medic scrambled over, ripping out two packets of morphine. He handed one to each man as he tried to stanch their bleeding with wads of four-by-four gauze pads. Nearly blind with pain, Berrigan and Burnstein grabbed at the morphine and injected themselves with it. A Jeep was brought up. In his drugged haze Berrigan watched as Koch and three others lifted Burnstein and him onto the front of the vehicle and raced them to a field hospital.

After less than a week of actual combat, only four of the seven original schoolboys—Koch, Schumm, Cole, and Milwid—were still intact. The next twelve days were relatively quiet for them. With the withdrawal of the Germans, Company F was given a new mission—to fight the enemy along the Siegfried Line battlefront in Germany itself. The line ran north and south roughly parallel to the Dutch-German border. The company was trucked to a spot just east of the German city Aachen, where the men took up positions in pillboxes waiting for the order to advance. They got it in mid-November as the Allies began a major drive to push eastward into Germany, and they soon found themselves under intense fire again.

The terrain was much different than it had been in Holland, and Koch now found himself advancing down the side of a forested hill. At the base of the slope, the woods gave way to a hilly meadow that was about 200 yards wide. On the other side of the meadow was another heavily wooded hill on which German troops were dug in.

Company F was ordered to take a metal Quonset hut in the meadow about fifty yards from the edge of the woods. Getting across the field under German fire was, of course, the problem. They decided the best way to do it would be to dash for it one at a time. So, at dusk, they formed a long single file back into the woods, a line from which they were going to be sent out into the field alone at intervals to run for their lives. Each and every one of them knew that the moment they stepped into the open they'd be entering a gauntlet of fire.

As soon as the first man ran, the Germans opened up with machine gun and rifle fire. They kept it up as new runners burst from cover every ten or fifteen seconds. The casualties were heavy and those who fell were left behind. When it was Koch's turn, he took off bent low and went across the field zigzagging to avoid getting hit. He made it to the hut and joined the rest of the company in the basement, where they hunkered down for three days until the Germans withdrew.

The gauntlet of fire was Koch's last major battlefield encounter with Company F. On December 1—thirty-four days after the bombardment at the crossroads—he entered a field hospital because of a non-combat injury. Like the rest of his combat experience, Koch has remained silent about the accident, even with his closest friends and family. His brother Harold, who also served in World War II, says, "He's never talked to me about it, and I never asked him."*

After his discharge from the hospital, Koch eventually became a denazification specialist in Bavaria. He was attached to a small

---

* This account of Koch's military experience is pieced together from a detailed company diary and personnel records kept by Sgt. Dierker, from the official history of the Timberwolf Division, and from interviews with the survivors of Company F who are now spread all over the country. Army officials say that Koch's personnel records are missing.

military unit near Würzburg where, using his language skills, he purged local Nazi officials from office and confiscated housing and other property for the occupying forces.

One of the few wartime stories Koch has told has a striking similarity to a heroic scene from the film *The Young Lions*, in which a scrawny Jewish soldier is picked on because of his religious background and has to fight to defend his honor. As Koch related the incident to *Playboy* magazine, he experienced anti-Semitism in the army only once—at Camp Croft during basic training. He remembered that 15 to 20 percent of the men in his platoon were Jewish and that many of them were not athletic and had difficulty coping with the camp's obstacle course. As Koch recounted it, "The situation was made worse by this one smart-ass Jewish kid who would always have the answer when the sergeant asked a question. It irritated a lot of people. One guy in particular was constantly making anti-Semitic remarks, and I began thinking, I'm not strong enough to beat him up, but I'm going to build up my strength.

"So I practice, getting stronger, until about the fifteenth or sixteenth week of basic training when he makes another of those brutalizing comments, I walk over, grab him by the neck and say, 'O.K., when we get back to the barracks, you and I are going to have it out.' He says, 'What are you talking about?'—'cause he didn't consider me Jewish. I could do the obstacle course, right? When we got back to the barracks, the Jewish kid who has created the problem now offers to help, and I say, 'Get the fuck away, you prick! It's because of you I have this problem.' So we go out, me and the other guy, and we fight. There was a big crowd, 50 people or more. He knocks me down, I get up. I don't want this to sound like a movie, but he knocks me down again and again I get up. And I hit him. Finally we finish. He's won, of course, but for the next several weeks, there was not one anti-Semitic comment in the whole company. Not one. I felt terrific."

Koch was honorably discharged in early 1946—three years after he was pulled out of City College—and headed home to his parents and the city he would one day rule. He came back to New York a sergeant. He had not been decorated for valor. He did not receive the Purple Heart. He did get battle stars for his time in combat zones. Like so many others who fought longer than he did, Koch was just another dependable soldier, a regular Joe doing an unpleasant job that his country asked of him.

For Koch, as it was for many other soldiers in many other times and places, war was not an altogether unpleasant experience—if you came out whole. He entered the army an eighteen-year-old loner, a tall, gawky kid whose motormouth drove people away. In the army, his commanding officer counted on him, and his comrades trusted him.

Finally, Koch seems to have been as comfortable as any soldier with being on the receiving end of authority. He did his share of sleeping in foxholes, of running across open fields, of stepping gingerly because the ground might explode. And because he survived, he was able to move up the pecking order. In the end, he was the one telling somebody else what to do.

→»» 5 «««—

ONE LITTLE INDIAN

After his discharge from the army, Sergeant Ed Koch, age twenty-one, returned to his parents' apartment on Ocean Parkway. He brought with him two possessions: a boxer dog he picked up in Germany, and a desire to make something of himself. He was not entirely sure what that something would be, but one thing he knew was that he had enjoyed his final army job of purging the Nazis in Bavaria. To be the one who gives orders instead of following them—he had liked that.

But with the rigors of army life and the forced camaraderie behind him, Koch faced again most of the same problems he had encountered before. He was no more handsome than when he left, his personality no more winning, relationships no easier to forge. His family quickly became the focal point of his social life again, and neighbors grew accustomed to seeing Ed walking on Ocean Parkway with his teenage sister, eight years his junior. His dog, aptly named Boxer, was usually nearby and was obedient to Ed's commands, which were delivered in German.

Searching for companionship, conversation, some niche to fit into, Koch soon followed young singles in the neighborhood to a social group organized by the Flatbush Jewish Center, the conservative temple where his family worshipped. The group, called the Senior League, was essentially a forum set up to help young Jewish men and women meet potential mates on organized outings to Coney Island, the theaters, and bowling alleys. But, as happened throughout his life, Koch did not form any lasting romantic relationships. That is not to say, however, that he was not looking for a mate.

"He went to all the dances, the clubs, the weekends," says

Harold Koch. "He did what all nice Jewish boys are supposed to do."

Bruce Bayroff, then a young law student, double-dated with Koch.

"We used to go out," Bayroff says. "He wanted to meet nice girls with the idea that he would get married and have a family. At that time, I would say that he thought of getting married, while I thought I'd be a bachelor. As it worked out, just the opposite happened, and I'm not sure why."

Perhaps more important to Koch than romance was a career. The military had taken nearly three years of his life, and he was anxious to fulfill the ambition that he had harbored since high school—to be a lawyer. Although he had not graduated from City College before being drafted, Koch was able to go to law school by taking advantage of an educational credits program that allowed some GIs to enroll in graduate programs without having college degrees. The program was designed to help returning soldiers catch up to those who had not had their career paths interrupted, and Koch enrolled at the New York University Law School the same year he was discharged from the army.

Now a highly regarded school, NYU at the time was a second-rate institution that opened its doors to veterans. The returning GIs flooded the school, thankful for the opportunity, and attended classes year round so they could graduate in two years instead of three. Koch was one of them and, like many of his classmates, commuted to the school by subway. When not in classes or the law library, he spent some time in the Greenwich Village area, where the school is located. He was an average student, and became friendly with a handful of his classmates who rotated a weekly card game among their homes. Arnold Kronish, one of the regular card players, remembers Koch as outspoken but says he saw no indication that he was politically inclined. He does, however, remember him as liberal and caring. "He was the kind of guy who got kind of sick when he saw an old lady homeless in the street," Kronish remembers.

In 1948, Koch graduated without distinction and was admitted to the bar the following year. Starting out on his own as a lawyer was difficult for Koch. Some of the larger, prestigious firms did not hire Jews in those days, and most firms did not hire anyone from schools such as NYU, especially average students lacking bachelor degrees. So Koch bounced around in lower Manhattan, working first out of an office on Park Row, across the street from City Hall, and then out of one at a better address on Pine Street. Eventually he would move up to an office at 52 Wall Street, which impressed the folks in Brooklyn because he could now, technically at least, call himself a Wall Street lawyer. But in truth the only thing blueblooded about his practice was the embossed stationery with his name on it. There was certainly nothing fancy about his office. Located at the end of a long, dreary hallway, it was the kind of place where the tenant's name was stenciled on the door in removable paint so the landlord could easily scrape it off if the rent wasn't paid.

Ed Koch, Esq., was forced to scramble for both clients and partners. Kronish remembers visiting him soon after graduation, when all the newly sworn-in lawyers from the class were trying to make a go of it. "Since most of us were single practitioners or working for somebody in a firm where we didn't want to ask the boss a question, we'd talk to each other," he says. "I was up to Eddie's office shortly after we graduated. All I can remember is a dark background and discussing where we were headed. I was working for a guy at that time. Ed said, 'Let's go into partnership.' I said, 'Ed, I'd love to, but I don't see how. I don't have clients. I'm working for a guy. I don't come from a business family.' Then I said, 'Do you have any clients?' and he said, 'Sure.' So I said, 'Who have you got?' 'I've got my father,' he said."

Eventually Koch's business consisted of small, run-of-the-mill matters—wills, minor negligence cases, and the like. He was better at some than others. From the description of a later law partner, he disliked the haggling over money that goes along with negligence cases, but thrived on handling matrimonial matters. He had the perfect personality for it. "It is a field where people use the lawyers to punish the spouse, and Ed was very effective at that," remembers the partner, Victor Kovner.

Given the nature of his practice, it's no surprise that Koch made little money. He continued living at home in the Brooklyn apartment ruled by his mother, who was glad to have him, even if she did complain now and again about having to care for Boxer. The rent was cheap and the surroundings comfortable and familiar. It's a good thing, for Koch's law practice never really caught fire. Even after a decade, more successful lawyers visiting his office would be surprised to find him, and not a secretary, hunched over a typewriter drawing up his own legal documents.

Despite the frustrations of trying to establish himself, Koch harbored grand dreams of success, dreams that were not limited to being a successful lawyer. At times, he talked to family members and acquaintances of going into politics, saying he believed he could do well. Many of those who heard him accepted his talk with a tolerant "he-can't-be-serious" response. A struggling, talkative Jewish lawyer from Brooklyn seemed to have about as much chance of making it in New York politics as the neighborhood milkman.

That Koch should consider a political career was not entirely illogical. In the days before the Vietnam War, Watergate, and the cynicism of the 1970s, politicians were revered figures in American society. Leaders such as Franklin D. Roosevelt were not just famous—they were heroes, looked up to by many families not just as the embodiment of success but also as the embodiment of what is good and right. They were living proof that the American dream could come true. Moreover, for the young Ed Koch, if he was interested, there were role models to look to. Meyer Ellenstein, the flamboyant mayor of Newark for much of the time the Koch family lived there, was the first Jew to head that city's government. To have one of their own make it to the top, the leader of the entire city—there could be no clearer proof for Jewish immigrants that America was a different world than the bigoted Europe they had left behind.

Fiorello La Guardia was an important influence on Koch. First from Newark, then from Brooklyn, the Koch family had taken in the Little Flower's exploits: smashing pinball machines with a sledge hammer, reading the comics to children over the radio, and creating an international incident by recommending that a likeness of Hitler be put in the "chamber of horrors" at the 1939 World's Fair. That La Guardia, the son of immigrants, was half-Jewish was not unnoticed in the Koch household and Ed has often said that La Guardia "set the standard" by which mayors are judged.

Yet these childhood and adolescent recollections would not have taken shape inside Koch had it not been for his experiences in Greenwich Village. Located toward the southern end of Manhattan, the Village, as it is known, is one of a handful of primarily residential communities sandwiched between midtown Manhattan and the government and financial districts at the island's tip. For decades the area, with its European-like narrow streets lined alternately by gritty tenements and elegant brownstones, had been a solid, blue-collar community of Italian and Irish families. It had also been the long-time home of an influential community of artists, radicals, and bohemians.

In the 1950s, in ever-increasing numbers, young, curious, restless Americans flocked to New York, and especially Greenwich Village. Many were struggling creative people—actors, painters, dancers, singers—who migrated to the Village's low-rent tenements and walk-ups. Some were students at NYU. There were coffeehouses, jazz clubs, poetry readings and folk singing. The Bohemian movement thrived in the Village as did the beatniks, with their berets, beards, and endless talk. Characters abounded— Allen Ginsberg, Jack Kerouac, Lenny Bruce, and Bob Dylan all passed through the area, absorbing its energy and leaving some of their own behind. It was a place were nonconformists were the norm, where new ideas and new ways of living were debated and tried. To live in the Village was to be on the cutting edge of change. To know what was happening—to be a hipster— you had to be able to circulate in the Village. There was also a sizable homosexual population, one more open about its sexual lifestyle than homosexuals in other parts of the city.

Other types of newcomers were also being attracted to the community. Many were young single professionals—lawyers, accountants, teachers—who had adopted liberalism as their guiding philosophy. More traditional-minded than the radicals, who stood on the street corners and espoused revolution, communism, and socialism, and more mainstream than the avant-garde artists, they nonetheless thrived on new ideas and welcomed calls to change the establishment, to improve it, to make it better. They found in the Village like-minded people who shared not only their concerns about the world, but also common experiences in their careers and lives. The social life wasn't bad either.

On the fringe of this chaotic and creative energy was Ed Koch. He had become familiar with the Village during his law school days, and he knew the area because his law office was nearby in lower Manhattan. Though he did not look the part of the Village hipster—already balding, dressed in a jacket and tie, and loaded down with legal papers—Koch was attracted to the Village. He liked it so much so that in 1956 he moved out of his parents' home and into an apartment of his own there. With a roommate named

Bill Sommer, he moved into 81 Bedford Street, a building full of sociable young singles who had also migrated to the Village. It was about time. Koch was thirty-two then and had lived at home with his parents for a full seven years after becoming a lawyer. His father, some years later, said that Ed left when his mother kept pestering her son, "get married, get married." So Ed apparently had a choice—leave and get married or just leave. He chose the latter.

Koch's move coincided with the 1956 Presidential campaign, which pitted Democrat Adlai E. Stevenson against President Dwight D. Eisenhower. The race was a rematch of the one four years earlier, with Stevenson, the articulate and witty former Governor of Illinois, once again depicted as the "thinking" voters' candidate. Eisenhower, on the other hand, was still the popular hero from World War II who was guiding the nation through an unprecedented rise in the standard of living.

Koch, like many Village Democrats, had embraced Stevenson's cause in 1952, and did so again, to a far greater extent, in 1956. He recalled years later that he was inspired by Stevenson's speeches. "Ones you loved to read, not junk like most politicians write," he said. But Stevenson's oratory alone does not account for the change that Koch underwent in the years following his graduation from law school. As the years progressed and his law practice failed to take off, Koch's interest in politics grew steadily. And by the time he moved into the Village in 1956, Koch's dreamy talk about a political career had been replaced by a certain ambition to have one. Having failed to make his mark as a lawyer, Koch was determined to get ahead in politics instead.

During both of Stevenson's campaigns, a maverick group—New Yorkers for Stevenson—sprang up in the city to support him outside traditional Democratic Party channels. Nowhere was the group more active than in the Village, with its eager corps of liberal young newcomers. Some of them rang doorbells, stuffed envelopes, and made phone calls. Koch pitched in with the one talent he could reasonably lay claim to—talking. Throughout lower Manhattan, in parks, on street corners, anywhere people passed or gathered, Ed Koch could be seen on a "soapbox," clutching a small American flag and bellowing out the virtues of Adlai Stevenson.

Without success, of course, for Eisenhower defeated Stevenson again. The reasons were obvious. The country was at peace, now that the little "police action" in Korea was over, and many American families enjoyed a growing prosperity. Families that had struggled for generations found themselves with enough money to make a down payment on that dream house in the suburbs. There were new gadgets in the kitchen to make cooking and cleaning easier, a television in the living room to pass away all those leisure hours, and a car in the garage for trips to the seashore. Inflation and unemployment were both low and the Misery Index was still a generation or more away. There was some grumbling that Eisenhower spent too much time playing golf, but the malcontents were a minority and the incumbent was swept into the White House for a second term on a tide of "I Like Ike" buttons.

Although the city's Democratic Party organization had supported Stevenson in name, the maverick Stevenson loyalists were angry. They believed the regulars had not thrown their full weight and muscle into the fray and said so. The regulars protested, but could not deny that some of their ranks resented Stevenson's artistocratic bearing and saw him as more of a threat to their way of life and politics than Eisenhower was. They were comfortable with the General, and so they had channeled their energies into electing Democrats to local posts.

The Stevenson loyalists vented their anger at one of the most powerful political machines in America, Tammany Hall, the heart and soul of the city's Democratic Party. Founded as the Patriotic Society of Tammany in the days of George Washington, the machine became notorious in the late nineteenth century under the reign of William Marcy "Boss" Tweed, who plundered the city treasury for the extraordinary sum of $30 million. After the turn of the century, George Washington Plunkitt, expounding from a courthouse bootblack stand, rose to become the machine's resident philosopher. His were the simplest of nostrums for gaining political power, and, of course, using it to best personal advantage. "To hold your district," he advised, "study human nature and act accordin'." As for how he got rich, Plunkitt explained breezily, "I seen my opportunities and I took 'em."

Tammany dominated the city through a network of local clubhouses, all graced with American Indian names. The stronghold in Greenwich Village, Koch's new neighborhood, was the Tamawa Club, a big open room one flight up from the street on 88

Seventh Avenue South. The old regulars from the neighborhood—mostly working-class Irish and Italians—gathered there a few nights a week mostly to play cards and talk. They talked about everyday subjects—jobs, kids, weddings, births, sickness, and death. But they talked business, too, and the business of the club was getting the party faithful elected. They would do it honestly if possible, but they would not shrink from stealing an election if they had to. Good Tamawa braves were not shy about forging signatures on election petitions, nor about swapping stories of how a friendly election inspector could slip bits of lead under his fingernails so that he could secretly deface an opposing candidate's ballots, thus invalidating them.

But nobody—or very few—did anything for nothing at the Tamawa. Lawyers from all over the city joined and worked for the club's candidates, gathering in a separate section of the club, a few feet from the blue-collar neighborhood men. Their reward, if they were lucky, would be a lucrative appointment for legal business in the city's patronage-ridden court system. Minor grafters sometimes walked openly among them. One was the law clerk to a judge, a patronage post he'd won through the club, who was in the custom of accepting $150 payoffs from attorneys who were anxious to have him speed their cases through the badly clogged courts.

"The guy openly complained in the club that he had a lousy month, that he had only made a certain amount of money," remembers George Delaney, a lawyer who joined the Tamawa in 1955. "We're talking about thousands of dollars."

Toward the front of the club, there was a small raised platform with a table and chair. Sometimes the chair was empty, but on Monday and Thursday nights, Thomas I. Fitzgerald, a roly-poly, jovial man, sat there. He was the club secretary and when he was on duty, business was conducted. He was there to help people—to find them jobs, straighten out disputes with their landlords, get them free legal help from one of the assembled lawyers. People trudged up the stairs to see Fitzgerald and waited sometimes for hours in the club's big room, a hall forty to fifty feet long, bedecked with pictures of Democratic presidents, governors, and mayors. "Whatever affects human beings, they came in with," Fitzgerald remembers.

Joseph O'Connor went up to the Tamawa as a boy of fifteen, hoping like so many others that the club could help him find a job. His dream was to work in the Post Office at Christmas time. O'Connor's family lived at 47½ Morton Street, a solid Democratic building—so solid that it was known as Little Tammany Hall because the voting rolls for the tenement listed far more registered Democrats than the number of people who lived there.

"There were about forty people on line to see Thomas I. Fitzgerald," O'Connor remembers. "I was a kid. I said, 'Mr. Fitzgerald, I'd like to get a job in the Post Office.' He sits there and writes it down and that's all. Then every night seven to 10:30 I come back and wait on line, and every night he writes down 'post office.' Everybody on line used to joke that he had a pen with disappearing ink. I never got that job, but for two years he did get me a job at Christmas in Lord & Taylor, the department store."

Fitzgerald's political contracts were the bread and butter of the club. He would provide help, and at election time, the grateful recipients would return the favor by voting for the candidates lucky enough to receive the Tamawa designation. Judges, city councilmen, state legislators, congressmen, mayors, senators, even presidents—Tamawa was involved up and down the line.

"The club captains would know who we helped in some way, and at election time we'd see that our friends came out," Fitzgerald remembers. The issues, or who stood on the left or right, made little difference to the machine leaders. It was, instead, the politics of self-interest—one hand washing the other. In simple, crude terms, it was buying votes with jobs and other favors. That was the way it worked all over the city, with Tammany Hall making or breaking the careers of would-be public servants.

The leader of that fiefdom was a courtly, forty-eight-year-old gentleman with a taste for finely tailored silk suits. Because of his unquestioned authority, some called him "The Chief." Others, noting his manner of speech—softly modulated with a tone a prelate might use with a parishioner in a cathedral—dubbed him "The Bishop." His name was Carmine Gerard DeSapio. And he was on a collision course with Ed Koch.

Born in the Village in 1908 to parents who had immigrated from Sicily, DeSapio entered politics as a teenage laborer for the Huron Club. During cold weather, his job was to deliver coal to families who needed it to fire their tenement stoves. In the summer, he carried ice. At Thanksgiving and Christmas, he delivered holiday goodies, including turkey dinners, to the most faithful of the poor. All courtesy of the local political club.

Such soldiering in the army of Tammany was expected and rewarded. Young Carmine worked steadily and reliably in jobs given him by the party, and climbed through the ranks of the machine. In 1937, he felt strong enough to wage a power struggle with the leaders of the Huron Club, and broke away to form the Tamawa Club. By 1943, he had become a district leader; in 1949, the boss of Tammany Hall.

The machine he took over had long ago left innocence behind, and corruption was taking place on a far grander scale than the card players who gathered on Monday and Thursday nights at the Tamawa could know. A lawyer could guarantee himself a judgeship by paying a hefty fee. Those who couldn't pay had to show their sincerity and devotion to Tammany by bowing, scraping, and genuflecting before the most minor hacks.

DeSapio had risen to the top of Tammany without ever being personally linked to the corruption, yet the aura, the suspicion, surrounded him. The public expected it of its political bosses, and he accommodated by looking the part of a crook. Afflicted as a teenager with iritis, a rheumatism of the eyes, DeSapio always wore dark glasses. What more sinister stereotype could there be than a polished, powerful, middle-aged Italian in tailored silk suits and dark glasses? He was the Hollywood image of a Mafia don. The image became reality for many when, in 1957, a cab driver found an envelope stuffed with $11,200 in soiled fifty- and hundred-dollar bills on the back seat of a taxi DeSapio had just climbed out of. The Chief denied that the money was his, and no claimant ever stepped forward for it.

But DeSapio was by no means an out-and-out thug, and his courtly manner and support of good government, nonmachine candidates, such as New York Governor Averell Harriman, had the salient effect of making him appear both boss and reformer at once. It was a talent that enabled him to become the single most influential Democrat in the state and a necessary ally for would-be judges, congressmen, mayors, governors, and senators. It was DeSapio, for example, who, along with the Bronx organization, put Robert F. Wagner in City Hall in 1953 over the objections of some party leaders satisfied with the incumbent, Vincent Impelliteri. DeSapio was not ignored in presidential elections, either.

As DeSapio's influence grew in the city, across the state, and nationally, he began spending less and less time at the Tamawa.

So little, in fact, that to many it seemed that he rarely came around anymore. More often he was to be found uptown in meetings at the Biltmore Hotel, the base from which he dealt with the high and mighty. When DeSapio deigned to return to his old stomping grounds, to climb the stairs to the Tamawa, he was treated with reverence.

"When he did come to the club, it was like God was coming, the emperor," remembers Robert Fine, a lawyer who became a club captain. "You wanted to touch his robes."

The visits were not only ceremonial, for DeSapio knew he needed the Tamawa. Without it, without the allegiance of his neighbors in Greenwich Village, he would have nothing. These people—the bakers, the dock workers, the bus drivers—had elected him as their grass-roots Democratic Party official. He was their district leader. In most cases, being a district leader meant being a minor party functionary. But to DeSapio the post was of crucial importance because without it, he could not be the boss of all. According to party rules, only a district leader was eligible to be the Lord of Tammany Hall.

The basic political subdivision in New York is the assembly district. In each district, members of the various political parties elect two people—one male and one female—to represent them as their district leaders. The assembly districts are grouped by the county in which they are located, and the district leaders are organized into a ruling county committee. This committee chooses one of its own as chairman. In Manhattan—officially New York County—DeSapio was chairman, the county boss, the head of Tammany Hall. But it was his post as the male district leader of the First Assembly District South that made it all possible and opened the door for him to deal with presidents. Take that away, and Carmine's house of cards would have fallen in a heap.

DeSapio's strength in the Village rested with the community's old-line residents. Despite the free-thinkers and upwardly mobile professionals who were moving in, at its heart the Village was a working-class neighborhood. The Irish lived primarily on the west and the Italians on the east side and in the area known as the South Village. The Irish had come first, settling initially in the South Village and then migrating westward a few blocks for better housing. Behind them came the Italians, moving onto the streets with Irish names—streets named MacDougal, Sullivan, and Thompson.

Peter Canevari, who became a captain in the Tamawa in the 1950s, grew up in a building his family owned on Thompson Street. Like all the other buildings it was a walk-up. There were twenty-two apartments. "Maybe three apartments were non-Italian in the whole building," he remembers. "They were artists and writers and didn't have the workaday pursuits of the Italian people."

Most apartments in the community were, at best, modest. Families were large, and the accommodations crowded. "There were five, six, seven people in an apartment. The Italian families were big," remembers Anthony Dapolito, who headed the Greenwich Village Association, the community's largest civic group. "A lot of people lived in the buildings and took care of them, really took care of them. I mean clean."

Dapolito was then—and is now—a baker, the owner of a small shop where he bakes Italian breads and rolls in a coal-fired brick oven. He knew Carmine DeSapio well. On Easter Sundays in the 1950s, The Chief's family—his mother, father, and uncles—would descend into Dapolito's basement to bake Easter bread. Surrounded by such friends and familiarity, DeSapio's machine seemed to be on cruise control with no real obstacles in sight. Anybody who would have predicted that things were not going to go on like that for a long time would have been laughed out of the neighborhood.

But the unhappy band of Stevenson loyalists was angry enough over the election debacle to begin plotting DeSapio's downfall— to begin pushing for political reform. And they had a powerful ally—time. The Village was changing rapidly now, and in their favor. The Chief's army was being replaced by the young professionals, many of them Jewish, many of them educated and liberal. The newcomers were moving in, while the Depression-era children of the Irish and Italian families, grown up by the early 50s, were leaving in search of something better. Few wanted to live and raise their own families in the cramped tenements they had themselves been raised in. Better apartments beckoned in Brooklyn and Queens. So did the opportunity to own homes on Staten Island and in the suburbs. Anthony Dapolito was one of five brothers. He is the only one who stayed in the Village, a phenomenon that was repeated in many families. And those who left took their votes with them.

Waiting in the wings were the angry Stevenson loyalists. They had been excluded by DeSapio's brand of politics, and they suddenly found themselves caught up in a movement that was germinating in many neighborhoods. The city as a whole was losing patience with boss-ruled government and all that it entailed: patronage, deal-making, back-room politics, and corruption. Respected public figures, most notably former U.S. Senator Herbert Lehman and former First Lady Eleanor Roosevelt, were beginning to work for change. And the idea of reform—Reform—was becoming a movement fueled by new recruits every day.

Nowhere did the movement blossom more fully than in the Village, but even there the reform troops had scant resources and little practical experience. In many ways they were a comical bunch, united not by self-interest but by principle. In short, they were about as improbable and naive a political group as one could imagine.

Struggling to hang together after Stevenson's defeat, the budding reformers gathered to plan their future. The immediate question was whether to open a political club to compete with the Tamawa for power. On one side were those who found DeSapio and all he stood for revolting. They called for a new order of patronage-free politics based on vigorous, intelligent debate on the issues. The other side—the losing side—argued for a strategy of joining the Tamawa and working for change from within. Out of the debate was born a new club—the Village Independent Democrats, more familiarly known as the VID. Koch was one of those who argued against founding the VID. His position is one of the great political ironies because the club would eventually become the base from which he succeeded in politics.

"I opposed forming the new club, so did Koch. I was brought up in an era when you did things through the organization. Insurgency wasn't promoted," remembers George Delaney, the lawyer who joined the Tamawa in 1955 but also worked as a Stevenson volunteer. "There were plenty of pragmatic people who would say, 'How the hell would we ever win?' "

Once the idea of forming the VID was settled, a struggle for control of the organization developed between two factions. Koch aligned himself with the group that lost. Seeing no chance to advance in the new club, and doubting that it would be successful, Koch took a step that was the first signal of one of his primary political characteristics: absolute pragmatism. He walked over to 88 Seventh Avenue South where he climbed the well-worn flight of stairs into DeSapio's Tamawa wigwam. The reformers were fighting for a cause. That interested him, but, after struggling as a lawyer for nearly a decade, he was in too much of a hurry to wait for the revolution to take its course. As had so many others before him, Koch thought he saw opportunities for personal and political advancement in the Tamawa and was prepared to take them. This was 1957, the year the cash-stuffed envelope was found in DeSapio's taxi.

"He just figured that we were a ragtag group without any chance. I think he had ambition then and felt he had a better chance of moving ahead in the DeSapio organization," remembers Edward Gold, who later became president of the VID.

Richard Kuh, who became the club's first president after leading the faction that won control, also remembers Koch's defection to the Tamawa, but Kuh believes that it wasn't the first time that Koch had been to DeSapio's lair. His recollection is that Koch actually joined the Tamawa before the Stevenson campaign and then left it temporarily to work with the volunteers on the street. "There were factions as we started the VID. I was in the dominant faction," Kuh remembers. "As soon as Koch's faction lost, within a week he was back at Tamawa. That suggested some opportunism rather than some deep-seated conviction for reform. I and many others saw it as two-faced."

Koch was joined at the Tamawa by three other lawyers who had worked for Stevenson—George Delaney, Robert Fine, and Ed Hale. The idea of getting ahead professionally was important to all of them. "In that respect, I think that joining the Tamawa was a sensible thing to do," Delaney remembers. "The idea among young lawyers in the City of New York was that if you wanted to get ahead politically or get an edge professionally, you joined the local political organization."

To join the Tamawa club, you had only to walk up the stairs, take a place inside, and start passing the time. It seemed simple but Koch had miscalculated. The old regulars who had been with DeSapio as he climbed through the Tammany ranks were a closed circle. They did not accept strangers easily, even if they were born and raised in the neighborhood. "I lived in the Village all my life, but I was almost like an outsider when I went up there," remembers Carmine Cardone. "Unless you were in the club for, say, fifty years you weren't accepted. When you take a guy growing up in the neighborhood not being accepted, you can imagine what happened when people who just moved in tried to join."

Particularly if they dressed differently—in a suit and tie—talked "funny," perhaps were Jewish, and were aggressively looking either to change the system or to grab personal political power quickly. To the Tamawa braves, the outsiders even had peculiar ideas about how a club should run.

"Koch and his kind of guys stood out because they were young and Jewish," remembers Joseph O'Connor, the teenager who got Christmastime jobs at Lord & Taylor and later dated DeSapio's daughter. "And they didn't understand how the club worked. The club had no formal membership. Carmine wouldn't have the balls to ask a member to join and pay a fee. As bad as politicians were in Tammany days, it was ludicrous to ever ask the people to pay money. The politicians probably made so much money on the side, it would have been like a guy running a whorehouse charging admission. The reformers would come up and they couldn't understand that. They'd ask for membership applications. They'd say, 'Would you please give us membership applications?' We'd say, 'We don't have any.' Then they'd get all indignant and storm out saying, 'They're refusing to give us membership applications.' "

Given the informality of the Tamawa Club, it is impossible to pinpoint how long Koch remained a member, although Robert Fine, one of the lawyers who joined Koch there, recalls one memorable conversation between Koch and two stalwart Tamawa chiefs—George Tombini, DeSapio's uncle and a gruff stevedore of a man, and Tom Chimera, a short, fat, cigar-chomping judge who made it to the bench through the club. The conversation may have been Koch's last at the Tamawa.

"Koch came over," Fine remembers. "Tombini was not particularly articulate. Chimera, you couldn't shut up. Ed says, in effect, 'What's in it for me?' Chimera says, 'Take me for an example. You come down here and give neighborhood advice, you help the people. If you do what I did and meet people, someday you can become a judge.' "

"How long will that take?" Koch asked.

"Twenty years," Chimera answered, reflecting the wisdom of his experience.

"I don't want to wait that long," Koch answered.

Soon after that, Koch left the club.

For a struggling thirty-two-year-old lawyer in a hurry to get on with his life, the Tamawa was a dead end. At the same time, the VID didn't seem to have a prayer of becoming an effective political force. Frustrated, Koch dropped out of politics for more than a year and returned to trying to make a go of it practicing law. It was another miscalculation. While Koch sat on the sidelines making little progress in the legal profession, the VID evolved into a functioning, bitterly competitive organization, churning with factions and liberal ideas. It met on Tuesday evenings in a storefront at 224 W. 4th Street—physically just a few blocks from the Tamawa, but emotionally and politically, light years away. VID meetings were conducted by *Robert's Rules of Order*, and there really were meetings, as opposed to the card-playing and bull sessions at the Tamawa. The members gathered at a prescribed time and spent most of the night, hours on end, heatedly debating the great liberal world issues of the day. It was not uncommon for the debates to escalate into arguments and to drag on well past midnight—until the entire crowd finally gave up from sheer exhaustion. "To an extraordinary degree, they devoured one another," says U.S. Senator Daniel Patrick Moynihan, who was a member of a nearby reform club and who studied Village politics of the day. "They just used up their energy in arguments that went on all night."

But as tumultuous and combative as the meetings were, the club was solidly united behind a single principle: that the old way of doing political business—patronage—was nothing short of evil. In that respect, the VID resembled a cult more than a club, and its members competed to outdo each other in the zealotry they brought to the fight against old-line politics. Although they championed open, free debate, they brooked no dissent on the issue of patronage. It was bad, bad, bad, and so was everyone who felt otherwise. They viewed themselves as pure. "The driven snow was mud compared to the leadership of the VID," remembers Herbert Rosenberg, an active member.

So sure were they of the rightness of their position that many came to disdain those who didn't agree with them—including the less-educated, lower-income Irish and Italian residents who seemed perfectly happy under DeSapio's form of government. And so smug were they that they concluded that the Irish and Italians didn't agree with them simply because they hadn't been afforded the necessary educational and cultural opportunities for enlightenment. The VID people were just, well, better.

The membership was roughly divided between men and women, most of them young singles who came to view the club as both a political and social outlet. Inevitably, many began to date and several had open affairs. Rosenberg recalls that many of the women joined partly because "this might be a place to meet a man similarly motivated, and for the men I think it wasn't so much to meet a woman for marriage, but to meet women just for sex, whatever."

"It was quite a social group, many singles. We had some virile studs who made out very well," remembers Ed Gold.

The political and social energies of its members soon propelled the VID into the forefront of a reform movement that had started to sprout in similar clubs in other neighborhoods. The rallying cry for all of them was that DeSapio had to be dethroned. Spurred on by his proximity, none felt this more strongly than the VID. They decided on a strategy that was quite logical. If DeSapio could be defeated in a race for his lowly post as the Village district leader, he would no longer be eligible to rule Tammany Hall. The VIDers began to fancy themselves giant killers.

Still inexperienced in the nuts-and-bolts of running a political campaign, the club fielded its first candidates against DeSapio and his female coleader in 1957. Not surprisingly, they lost. Buoyed by his traditionally strong support in the South Village, DeSapio trounced them, pulling in 64 percent of the vote. But the VID was still encouraged. The club had hoped at best to get 30 percent of the vote and wound up topping that by six points. "We were licked but for a first effort versus a national figure we made a good showing," remembers Kuh, the club's first president. "And I think that everybody began to see the VID as the wave of the future."

There were many reasons for optimism. In addition to the continuing growth of the reform movement and the changing demographics of the Village, DeSapio, the silk-suited kingmaker ensconced in the Biltmore, was beginning to lose touch with the old neighborhood. He rarely came around anymore and the voters once solidly his had been turning out less and less. As the election of 1959 approached and the VID prepared to challenge

DeSapio with new candidates, a trend was becoming obvious, even to many of the Tamawa braves: sooner or later the VID was going to win.

"In 1959, I was still at the Tamawa," George Delaney remembers. "I went out to get petition signatures for Carmine's race and I discovered that I had to bust my ass because people were getting hostile to him. It was very rough."

As the election neared that year, Koch's interest in political activity was rekindled. Ever the pragmatist, he was no doubt attracted by the club's brightening prospects and enrolled himself as a member of the VID. For someone seeking political opportunity—and maybe a social life—in the Village, it was the right thing to do. George Washington Plunkitt would have been proud of Koch. But not so the VID. He was seen by many there as a shameless opportunist, far more concerned with his own political ambitions than the principles of the reform movement. Worse, in going to the Tamawa, he had gone to bed with the devil. In the club's near-religious fervor, he was viewed as unclean.

Despite the animosity he was facing, Koch plunged into the VID. So much so that after the 1959 race against DeSapio—in which the VID tally rose encouragingly to 47 percent of the vote—the apostate stunned the club by running for president and then vice-president in separate elections. He was defeated badly both times. Ed Gold ran against him for vice-president. "We both made awful presentations to the club," he remembers. "His speech was that he was not going to apologize for leaving the club and going to the Tamawa. He said, 'I'm not going to apologize. I thought it was an opportunity so I went.' The issue in a facetious sense was who was closer to God."

Undeterred by his losses, Koch became a fixture at the club and in the Village. While most everyone else spent what seemed like thirty-six hours a day talking, he worked that long. If someone was needed to run the mimeograph machine, organize a fund-raising dinner or supervise the preparation of petition papers, Koch did it. When the Parks Department—supported by many of the old-line Italian residents—issued an edict banning folk singing in Washington Square Park, Koch organized a successful campaign to allow the growing number of guitar-playing, bongo-tapping performers to continue to use the park. During campaigns, Koch eagerly took to the streets to deliver curbside orations. He spoke loudly and as often as he could on behalf of VID candidates and he even volunteered to form a one-man sidewalk speakers bureau for a reform candidate running for Congress on Manhattan's Upper East Side. On Wednesday nights he could be found in Judson Memorial Church, the moderator of a bizarre series of forums that could only have taken place in the Greenwich Village of the early '60s. It was called the "Hall of Issues."

The church opened one of its rooms to avant-garde and pop artists so that they could display their works and stage what were then called *happenings*.

"There were paintings, collages, sculpture, but it was all that early '60s stuff," remembers Howard Moody, senior minister of the church. "Some of it was really weird, crazy, satirical, and funny, like a bomb as tall as the ceiling. The artists also staged happenings that were part painting, part people acting. Many times they were very political."

On Wednesday evenings the public was invited in to debate art and politics with the artists and one another. Koch became the moderator for the packed, tumultuous sessions. "They were a bunch of crazies and he was a middle-class square," Moody remembers. "But he was fairly good at moderating because he used his sense of humor to break the tension and lead the discussion in new directions."

The Hall of Issues ended when it came to be dominated by a faction that argued seriously that it was permissible to engage in sexual activity with children. "It was complete and sheer craziness," Moody remembers.

By day Koch put in whatever hours he had to as a two-bit lawyer, but at night and on the weekends—whenever he could—he devoted himself to the club. He was not universally liked. Many describe him in the same terms as those who knew him in high school—abrasive and egotistical—and they remember his tendency to launch into scathing *ad hominem* attacks when debating other club members. It was through the VID's constant debating, however, that Koch began to forge both his opinions on issues and his contentious political style. Even those who found him personally distasteful accorded him grudging respect because of the enormous time and energy he was putting into the club. Slowly, through single-minded determination and slavish hard work, he began to emerge as a force in the VID.

Koch's career was finally on the move, but his advancement was not coming without a price. As a bachelor in his midthirties in Greenwich Village, this was a time when much should have been happening for him: dating, perhaps marriage, new friends, and expanding social horizons. They were all within his reach, but Koch turned his back on them. By now the idea of getting ahead in politics was no longer just a vague ambition. It had become the driving force of his life, an obsession that precluded intimate relationships and would eventually dominate his whole life. Politics, with its chances for ego gratification and power, would fill a void left by his social failures and offer him the possibility of real success.

A loner since childhood, he stayed alone in the VID despite its thriving social atmosphere. When friendships developed, they were relationships of utility, premised, as far as he was concerned, on advancing his career and easily cast aside when they didn't. Awkward with women since even before his painful experience with Bunny Persky, he let pass virtually every chance for a romantic or sexual relationship.

Koch's decided lack of interest in the opposite sex was particularly noticed by the women in the VID, and especially by those who would have liked to date him.

"I knew at least one gal who would have flipped her lid for him, but that wasn't his style," remembers Bernice Singer, who grew friendly with Koch in the VID. "I don't think the male/female bit was his thing, for whatever reason. We had lots of social affairs; he never came with a girl. Certainly, all the women talked about it, 'How come he's not married?' "

For a time, Koch appeared to some VID members to be dating one woman fairly regularly. Then that ended. Occasionally, he asked others out, but it was frequently as part of a group and the results were often poor. "The reports were all the same," recalls one VID member. "He was charming, witty, delightful, but totally self-absorbed. He only talked about himself." Phyllis Yampolsky was a young Village artist when Koch asked her out to brunch on a Sunday and took her to the Bronx Zoo. She had a pleasant time, but he never asked her again. Micki Wolter, then a young psychiatric social worker, grew to know Koch in the VID and briefly thought she detected in him a spark of interest in her. "There were times in the early years I thought he might be interested in me, but it wasn't the case," she says. "He was friendly—and the way he looked at me, we were of an age when one thinks that kind of thing." Several times Koch asked Wolter out but it was always with a group, and the closest they came to a real date was the time he invited her to a play with him. They went with another couple with whom Koch was friendly. "I remember he called me up," she says. "As I recall, it surprised me. I supposed I hadn't thought of him then having a dating interest in me, and I'm not sure that he did. Maybe he just wanted a friend along when he went out with this other couple."

Koch's limited contacts with women—and their chasteness when they did occur—inevitably led to a question that was to haunt him throughout his political career: Was he a homosexual? The issue was frequently discussed among his friends, and when he eventually began running as a candidate against DeSapio, the Tamawa troops mounted a whispering campaign about it. As a Greenwich Village bachelor who was rarely seen with women, it was easy enough to portray him as a homosexual, particularly to many of the old-line Village residents who viewed him and the rest of the reformers as effete. The political damage that it could cause him was obvious.

Wolter remembers talking with Koch about his fears that homosexuality would be raised against him.

"He was concerned," she says. "We used to talk about him not being alone with some man in his apartment where someone could make an accusation."

The attitude of the old-line residents is best summed up by an incident that happened at a polling place where Mary O'Connor, a DeSapio loyalist, was serving as a Board of Elections worker. One of O'Connor's jobs was to see that voters placed their signatures on a record card. As they signed, she was supposed to cover their previous signatures to prevent attempts at forgery. Koch was watching the polling place for the VID to keep everything on the up and up when John Forrest, a longtime neighborhood resident, came in to cast his ballot.

"I'd known Mr. Forrest all my life. I'd lived in the same building with him. I knew he wasn't an impostor, so I didn't cover up his signatures," O'Connor remembers. "Koch was a nervous nellie, and said I had to cover the signature. I said, 'I know this man.' He said, 'I don't care, you can't do it.' So he called a lawyer down from the attorney general's office, and they said I had to do it. We went back and forth and I made a few remarks about the types that belonged to Koch's club. I told him I didn't think any of them were normal men. You can take it from there."

Both those who knew him in the VID and those who know him as mayor say that they've come to view him as neither heterosexual nor homosexual, but as asexual, as a man who sublimated his sexual desires, along with many other elements of his personality, in his singleminded quest for political power. "He was totally dedicated to politics," remembers Michael Harrington, the socialist and author of *The Other America*, who became friendly with Koch in the VID. "His idea of a sexual kick, I think, was to go out and shake hands at a subway stop. That's his greatest erotic encounter."

Koch's singleminded drive to become a political success is virtually unbroken from the time he rejoined the VID. Nevertheless, in the early 1960s his career did take one small and little known sidestep—that of becoming an inventor and entrepreneur. Struck by a bolt of inspiration, on March 13, 1961 Koch applied for a patent on a creation that he hoped would not only bring him wealth but would also bring happiness to children. The application papers were highly technical, covered as they were in detailed drawings and schematics, and the description of the invention was perhaps best understood by a trained engineer. Its formal name was the Simulated Vehicle Toy, but it was more familiarly known as the Boxmobile. One small portion of the application reveals just how complex an idea it was. The application explained that: "Flaps 16–19 are joined to panels 12–15, respectively, along the top edges thereof. Side flaps 18, 19 are first inwardly folded to lie in planes parallel to the planes of side panels 14, 15. Thereafter rear flap 17 is inwardly folded to lie substantially parallel to rear panel 13 and front flap 16 is inwardly folded to be obliquely positioned for a reason to be hereinafter described. . . ." No one had ever thought of that before and on July 30, 1963, the U.S. government issued Patent No. 3,099,443 in the name of Edward I. Koch, inventor.

Quite simply, Koch had invented nothing more than adhesive decals that could be placed on the front, sides, and rear of cardboard boxes so that the boxes would look like either a car or a locomotive. And inside the box, another decal would simulate the control panel of the car or train. He'd gotten the idea for the Boxmobile watching his sister Pat's children at play and decided that it would not only bring joy to children, but that it would also be inexpensive and would raise a parent's stature in the eyes of the child. As the inventor explained it to the government, this was all possible because:

"This invention relates to children's playthings in general and more particularly to a simulated vehicle toy which is inexpensive to construct in that the most costly element thereof is free.

"Young children in the process of growing up pass through a stage where they experience a strong urge to be in control of vehicles such as automobiles, boats, tractors, fire engines and space ships. As a practical matter this is not possible, so as a substitute toys are made to simulate these vehicles. . . .

"It is well known that a child of tender years is not impressed by the degree to which the details of an authentic article are simulated but is more impressed by the overall appearance and a construction which enables the child to utilize the toy with reckless abandon. That is, without being restrained by the parent. . . .

"The simulated vehicle toy hereinbefore described is so inexpensive that the parent will not be concerned about destruction thereof. In addition, the toy, being constructed of relatively yieldable material, is not likely to damage household furniture nor is the toy likely to injure the child or his playmates.

"Further, the construction is so simple that even a parent having no mechanical leanings whatsover can readily assemble the toy. While the parent may not receive the direct satisfaction of achievement since assembly is so simple, there will be considerable satisfaction resulting from the child's statement to the effect 'see what Daddy built for me.' "

The patent in hand, Koch put the Boxmobile into production, distributed some to friends and family and placed them on sale in at least one Manhattan store. The idea bombed.

If Koch's attempt at invention and entrepreneurship was less than a roaring success, his political adventures and career were moving onward and upward. In 1960, the VID fielded candidates for a secondary race for slots on the state Democratic Committee. DeSapio wasn't running, but he backed a slate of his own. Both sides saw the election as a test of their local strength. Koch, by dint of his incessant hard work, had by now risen to a post as the club's law chairman, and his role in the election was to oversee the preparation of the signature petition papers that were required for the VID's candidates to appear on the ballot.

He set about the task quite diligently, but, as he was still newly converted from Tamawa, DeSapio and his henchmen struck dread in his heart. Who knew what those villains might try, or where they might be lurking! What if they were to try to steal or destroy the petition papers! The fears came to a head when the crucial petitions were finally bound for delivery to the Board of Elections. Koch and Wolter worked late into the night getting the valuable papers ready, and, the job completed, they faced the question of what to do with them. They decided against leaving them in the club. It would be too easy, they thought, for the DeSapio forces to burglarize the place and make off with them. Better to bring them home. But was it safe even to walk the streets with the papers? Koch and Wolter decided to chance it.

"We took the petitions and walked to Koch's car," Wolter now says with a laugh. "When we got to it, we even looked in the back seat to see if anybody was hiding there."

There wasn't. Koch and Wolter got into the car, a run-down hulk with a hole in the floor large enough that Wolter could see the street through it. They pulled up at Wolter's apartment so Koch could drop her off. They looked at each other. Wolter could see that Koch was nervous.

"Would you be more comfortable if I accompanied you home?" she asked.

"Yes," he assured her, he would.

Wolter escorted Koch to his door with the papers and left him there.

"He told me later that he slept that night with a baseball bat next to him," she said, amused.

When the election was over and the votes counted, the results were a surprise to many people both in the Village and throughout the city's political establishment. The VID had gone head-to-head with DeSapio and for the first time the club's candidates had won.

The real test, however, did not come until the following year, 1961, when the VID matched up against DeSapio directly for the district leadership. The club entered the contest more confident than ever. In addition to a growing number of recruits, an odd conglomeration of political heavyweights, including then-Mayor Robert F. Wagner, Senator Lehman, Mrs. Roosevelt, and indirectly, President John F. Kennedy, suddenly offered to help. The club's candidate was James Lanigan, a lawyer and political neophyte who was imposed on the VID by Lehman.

The story traces back to the 1960 Democratic convention in Los Angeles. There, DeSapio—the most powerful Democrat in New

York State—had supported Lyndon Johnson as the party's candidate over JFK. The Kennedy family felt that DeSapio, a man they viewed as corrupt, had betrayed them. After the election, they set out to right the wrong with Lehman's help. According to Lanigan, Lehman was summoned to the White House where he met with the President and his brother, Attorney General Robert F. Kennedy. "Lehman reported to all of us that the Kennedys had asked him to find a way to remove DeSapio from power," Lanigan remembers.

Lanigan had never belonged to the VID. In fact, he didn't even live in the Village. But Lehman and Mrs. Roosevelt both knew him and decided that they wanted him to run against DeSapio in 1961. Lehman presented him to the VID. "He got up and said, 'All right, my candidate is Jim Lanigan, and I'll arrange the financing for him. If you don't want him, I'm not going to be involved.' Which was blackmail in a way. They didn't like it, but they accepted it because they couldn't function without Lehman's financial support."

At the same time, in other neighborhoods in the city, the fractious reform movement was beginning to elect other candidates of its own. Among the first was William Fitts Ryan, who defeated an incumbent Tammany-supported congressman in 1960 largely by branding him "DeSapio's Candidate." The lesson of that election was not lost on the city's major political leaders, including Wagner, who had held the mayoralty for eight years in close alliance with DeSapio. Wagner was up for reelection in 1961, and astute politician that he was, he couldn't afford to take lightly the public's antipathy toward the power broker who helped make him mayor. Nor could he ignore the fact that Lehman and Mrs. Roosevelt had placed toppling DeSapio on the top of their agenda. Both were popular, savvy, well-financed, and, as far as the public was concerned, fighting on the side of the angels. The result was that Wagner broke with DeSapio to run a remarkable anti-boss campaign of his own, and the VID urchins suddenly found themselves courted and supported by Mr. Inside himself.

Lanigan was joined on the VID ticket by Carol Grietzer, a young housewife and mother, who had been among the founders of the club. The key issues in the race were, of course, bossism and a banishment of patronage from city government. The VID, however, had also begun to move vigorously on community issues in an attempt to preempt the area in which DeSapio should have been strongest, what with his ready entree to the city's commissioners. Lanigan and Greitzer called, among other things, for strengthening the city's rent-control laws; battling drug abuse; and closing Washington Square Park, the recreation spot at the heart of the Village, to all traffic. This last hit a particularly responsive chord. For years, the city had permitted buses to drive through the park. The community had long been angry about it, but no one had ever been able to change things.

The VID also picked up on an issue that might help them make inroads into the predominantly Italian South Village, but it was only with Wagner's aid that they were able to use it, ironically because of a bosslike, behind-the-scenes decision.

The issue was the revival of a long-dormant plan to build a new street called Verrazano Street in the Village. The plan required the bulldozing of a group of apartment buildings—all occupied by solid, old-line Italian families. Some of the residents appealed to Anthony Dapolito, head of the Greenwich Village Association civic group, to mount a last-ditch effort to save their homes. Dapolito took their case to the highest official in Manhattan, Hulan Jack, the borough president.

"He said, 'The darn thing passed a couple of years ago. It is pretty hard to rescind the whole thing,' " Dapolito remembers. "Now it looked like the people had no place to turn, but they did, and who would have believed it, it was the VID."

The club brought the issue to Mayor Wagner.

"So what does Wagner do?" Dapolito asks. "He stops the street."

All of a sudden, the VID and not DeSapio had delivered. And the club had done it for the Italians. "That was a great way to infiltrate the community," Dapolito remembers.

Koch took to the streets in the campaign, as always a sidewalk orator. And it was then that there occurred the little-known incident of his arrest, and, by one account, handcuffing to a police car.

The key players in the piece are Koch and Joe O'Connor, the loyal Tamawa brave. This is how Koch told the story a few years ago, when he addressed the annual dinner of the Friendly Sons of St. Patrick.

"I was very active in politics in Greenwich Village, which at that time was in a district that was being run, very insistently, by Carmine DeSapio. I was Mr. DeSapio's opponent—which was considered to be a rather courageous thing to do—and one of DeSapio's district captains was a man by the name of Joe O'Connor.

"Now, Joe billed himself as the last Irish district captain in the Village, and he was a man who knew how to win an election.

"Well, one day I was out on the street shaking hands when word reached me that someone was ripping down my campaign posters. It didn't take long for me to follow the trail of torn paper, and there, standing at the end of the trail, was Joe O'Connor.

"O'Connor was certain that we could talk things out. However, I came from the Talmudic branch of Irish politics, and I wanted to invoke the power of the law.

"Our debate grew louder and louder, and suddenly who should appear on the scene but a large man in a blue uniform. My prayers were answered. Or so I thought.

"The officer got us both calmed down, and he asked us for our names.

" 'O'Connor,' Joe said.

" 'Koch,' said I.

"The officer nodded wisely, and then issued a formal statement: 'Mr. Koch, my name is Riley, and you are coming along with me.'

"And off I went to the local police precinct in the firm escort of Officer Riley."

It's a very funny story as Koch tells it, but no one else remembers it even remotely that way. First, when the arrest occurred, Koch wasn't running for office. Second, it didn't take much courage to run against DeSapio, although sleeping with a baseball bat could be reassuring. Third, what really happened was a minor brawl one night in Sheridan Square, a Village crossroads and a favorite spot for political speeches involving Koch, O'Connor, and Ed Hale, one of the lawyers who had joined the Tamawa with Koch but had also switched to the VID. And fourth, . . .

Let O'Connor tell the story.

"I was on one side of the square up on the tailgate of a station wagon with a microphone and loudspeaker," O'Connor remembers. "Hale was across the square with another microphone, and Koch, I guess, is standing there. Hale is talking about Tamawa hoodlums and patronage. I'm letting him talk, letting him finish.

He went through his speech, then I spoke. I said, 'Yes, Ed Hale, you tell the people the reason you quit the Tamawa club is because we wouldn't give you any patronage from Surrogate's Court.' So what does Hale do? He jumps down and starts running across the avenue with Ed Koch behind him and a policeman in between. I started calling it like a horse race. I say over the megaphone, 'Here comes Ed Hale, running across the street.' I wanted to bring attention to him. I was a little surprised that he was coming at me because I always thought the reformers were not physical, that they were lightweights. When he gets up close to me, I was above him on the station wagon. I leaned back and kicked him in the stomach. He goes right down. I'll never forget because he lost his glasses. They went underneath another car. When he got up, the cop was arresting him. I never expected the cop to arrest him, but I guess he saw the guy jump on top of me. So Koch comes running over and starts breaking the cop's balls. I said, 'He was with him. He's the guy that was fighting. He's part of the other gang.' A crowd started gathering. The cop was a young cop and he really panicked. Koch started to yell at him, and he [the cop] got like annoyed that the Jewish lawyer was shouting at him. So, boom, the cops says, 'You're under arrest,' and he handcuffs him to a squad car. The cop was crazy to do such a thing. It wasn't long, but Koch was handcuffed.''

That's even funnier, but is it true? Hale agrees with most of it, but he remembers besting O'Connor by wrestling him to the ground. He also questions whether Koch was even there. O'Connor, however, insists that he was. In fact, he continues the story. According to his version, the whole crew—Koch, Hale, and O'Connor—wound up in the Charles Street station house. O'Connor was pressing charges against them, and they were cross-complaining against him. Then, through an emissary, O'Connor says he received word that DeSapio would like him to drop the matter. O'Connor did, and so did Koch and Hale. But before he left the station house, O'Connor says that he extracted a concession from Koch—and a remarkable one considering Koch's personality.

"I made Koch give me a promise that he would go back and apologize on the sound truck for an attack on me," O'Connor remembers. "He did. He walked back to where the incident happened and got up very scholarly and told everybody, 'There was an altercation. We're embarrassed. We're sorry.' ''

In the end, Lanigan beat DeSapio decisively and the dragon was slain. That night the delirious reform troops gathered to celebrate. The newspapers were there. The victors were photographed and interviewed. One picture shows Lanigan and Greitzer smiling jubilantly with their arms raised in victory. Koch was standing a few steps away, gazing at them with ever so slight a smile on his face.

"He looked wistful," Greitzer remembers. "It was almost as if he were thinking, 'Someday, this is going to be me.' "

The next year, 1962, Koch got his first chance when the VID chose him to run for a seat in the state Assembly against William Passannante, a liberal incumbent who was allied with DeSapio. Koch designed his own campaign and it wound up being one of the most liberal ever devised. Three of his main planks called for repealing state criminal laws against sodomy, relaxing prohibitions on abortions, and making it easier to get divorced. Sodomy. Abortion. Divorce. Behind Koch's back, the campaign became known as the SAD campaign. And indeed it was.

"You couldn't have come up with three more controversial liberal positions," says Micki Wolter, who remembers meeting with Koch and several others as he planned his campaign. "Those were his ideas, the issues that he thought ought to be raised. We reacted with shock, not because we didn't agree with them, but because we felt they were so ahead of the time that they wouldn't get votes. Certainly we felt that way about the sodomy issue."

At the same time, many in the VID were unhappy that Koch was even running against Passannante. Some feared that the effort to unseat Passannante would be seen as anti-Italian. Others felt that despite his association with DeSapio, Passannante had been a good representative. The result was that Koch found to his horror that, after investing so much time and energy in the club and finally getting his shot, many in the VID refused to work for him. And matters were only made worse when Wagner, the Citizens Union, a good government group, and the great Senator Lehman all backed Passannante. Of the major reform figures, only Mrs. Roosevelt supported Koch—and she only did it because he was battling a DeSapio ally.

At one point in the campaign, Koch was delivering a speech from a stepladder set up on a corner near Washington Square Park. As he spoke, Mrs. Roosevelt pulled up in a car. She emerged and was escorted to the ladder so that she could mount it and address the crowd on Koch's behalf. But as she was about to take the first step up, she turned and whispered discreetly to one of the VID leaders.

"What is the name of your candidate?" she asked him.

"Ed Koch," he answered in a whisper.

Mrs. Roosevelt nodded, stepped up onto the ladder and delivered what the VID leader remembers was a "stirring speech" for Koch.

Koch reacted angrily to what he saw as a betrayal by Wagner and Lehman and denounced them as bosses. And when he lost the election—his only electoral loss until he ran for governor twenty years later—he wept, declaring, "I'll never run again. It is a filthy business." Horribly depressed, he drank himself sick at a party a few days later, Wolter remembers.

Koch's fury was not directed only at Lehman and Wagner. The club, he seethed, had been disloyal to him—a cardinal sin as far as Koch is concerned even to this day. "Ed was furious. He was very upset with anybody who wasn't 100 percent for his candidacy, and he kept getting the club upset because he spent so much time denouncing people and blaming them for his loss," remembers Ed Gold.

Steve Berger was one of those in the VID who didn't support Koch. Years later he would play a significant role in boosting Koch's political career, yet even today Berger believes that Koch has not forgotten his failure to back him more than two decades ago in the Passannante race.

"When Ed ran, many of us didn't help him," Berger remembers. "And I think in his heart he never forgave any of us. You know Ed and his memory."

Filthy business or not, Koch's ambition soon got the better of him and he was back in politics. In 1963, he battled his way to the presidency of the VID and when Lanigan broke with the club, Koch was selected to run in his place against DeSapio, who was mounting a comeback try. Reform, patronage, bossism, and the evil-looking man in the silk suits were again the focus of the campaign. Koch and Greitzer found themselves backed wholeheartedly by the establishment. Wagner and the new head of what was left of Tammany Hall, Edward Costikyan, were determined to keep DeSapio in his grave.

"We were all walking a tightrope to try to hold the party together," Costikyan remembers. "They were running against Carmine by trying to get every reformer in town involved. But we had a poll that showed that everything that Koch was doing was wrong. The people in the Village resented the outsiders coming in, and they didn't care about reform and the leadership fight. They were more interested in local control and issues."

Costikyan read Koch the poll and was surprised by the absolutely pragmatic way that Koch responded to it. "Instead of patronage, he talked potholes," Costikyan remembers.

The VID pulled out all the stops, canvassing the neighborhood and delivering speeches on behalf of Koch and Greitzer. Early in the race, Koch and DeSapio encountered each other in a hallway at the Board of Elections and with reporters present engaged in an impromptu debate. Koch was then a smoker, and as he puffed on a cigarette, DeSapio drew most of the attention with a witticism. "First, I'd like Mr. Koch to remove the cigarette because I am not accustomed to smoke-filled rooms," he quipped.

DeSapio's supporters included an animal lovers group who announced they were backing him because he had both a dog and a cat and was against the ban on pets in the city's public housing. Koch responded by announcing that he too supported lifting the ban and demonstrated his credentials as a pet lover by telling of his dog Boxer, who had since died at the age of ten. All of that was trivial, however, compared to the blessing that Costikyan and Wagner bestowed on Koch shortly before the election: the long-sought closing of Washington Square Park to traffic.

"We persuaded Wagner to close Washington Square to traffic—at Koch's request, of course," Costikyan says. "It was real cute."

The night of the election, the VID troops rang doorbells and climbed stairs to pull as many voters as they could to the polls; some were even brought in their pajamas. Koch wound up winning by only forty-one votes. He was ecstatic, and later that night Anthony Dapolito, the civic leader who baked Easter bread with the Chief's family in the basement of his bakery, met Koch on the street. They walked together for a while and talked. Koch struck Dapolito as philosophical. Elected to his first official position, a lowly Democratic Party post, Koch reflected on what he thought the future would hold for him.

"This is the way it is," Koch said. "In ten or fifteen years they'll be running against me and saying I'm a boss. That's the way it is. Somebody will be calling me a boss and looking to get me out."

CLIMBING

Tony Dapolito would have been astounded had he known what Ed Koch had in mind. The VID had worked long and hard to defeat DeSapio, and now that they'd done it twice, many in the club exulted at the resounding blow they'd struck for the reform movement. But achieving the political goal that had been their *raison d'être* for so many years had its downside, too. It was almost as if a bunch of rookies had made it to the big leagues on an expansion team and won the World Series. What more was there to do? Many in the VID pondered that question, but not their president and district leader. Dethroning DeSapio had never been an end for him. Rather, it was but the first item on a long, detailed personal agenda. For by now, Koch was burning with ambition to climb—to be somebody—in politics. And just how far he wanted to go surprised everyone. "I'm going to run for Congress. I hope you'll support me," he told Bernice Singer, one of his campaign managers, shortly after his victory over DeSapio. It was hard to imagine that he'd ever make it that far, but to Koch even that was just a way station. Still tottering from his first baby step in politics, what Koch was referring to that night as he walked with Dapolito was his ultimate goal.

"What he wanted to be was the Mayor of the City of New York," remembers Michael Harrington. "That was from the very beginning, and my wife and I used to joke when he became district leader that Ed was not your charismatic politician. We thought, that was about as far as he would go."

There was good reason to doubt. On its face, the idea was absurd, almost delusional, particularly coming from an individual who was graced with so few apparent political gifts; whose career as a lawyer was still foundering as he approached forty; whose personality was at best difficult and who comported himself as an ultra-liberal. Harrington's wife Stephanie was a writer for *The Village Voice* then and remembers her thoughts about Koch and his street-corner orations in Sheridan Square. "I was sitting there typing one night, sort of half listening to what was going on in the square and just kind of marveling at the fact that Koch had this enormous confidence," she remembers. "I used to wonder why. He certainly was not an imposing person. He was the kind of person that you could see being heckled."

But Koch was serious about a career in politics. So much so that he soon convinced himself that there was no question that it was going to happen. And he began telling his friends not just that he hoped to be Mayor, but that he was definitely going to be Mayor. One of those he told was Allen Schwartz, who became Koch's law partner in 1965. In April 1966, the two men sat in their law office at 52 Wall Street, a few days after Schwartz's first son David was born. "He will have his bar mitzvah in Gracie Mansion," Koch predicted flatly. Schwartz thought he was crazy, but thirteen years later the prediction came true.

Koch's ambition to become Mayor was so overriding that it is the prism through which most of his mature years have to be viewed. The goal was at once so distant and so alluring for him that the outlines of the rest of his life were set once he fixed his gaze upon it. He'd come into the VID distrusted and disliked— an outsider as he'd been virtually all his life. And over four hard years he'd battled his way not just inside, but to the very top, working night and day and living a life—whether by choice or not—singularly devoid of love, affection, or intimate companionship. Those friendships that Koch did develop were usually relationships built on advancing his career. Their primary component was political loyalty. And those who did not hew to that one-way standard ran the risk, as David Brown, his congressional chief of staff and later deputy mayor, put it, of being "thrown out into total darkness because Ed could do that to you."

This pattern is important to understand because it repeats time and again in Koch's career. At every step of his climb—from district leader, to the City Council, to Congress, and the mayoralty, Koch was the outsider, the ugly duckling, the long shot, the poor, underestimated, working-class kid with his nose pressed to the glass of the toy store window. Others had political connections.

Others came from money. Others were born to blueblood families and grew fat in white-shoe law firms. Not Koch. No, he had to fight for his breaks—to work for every last one of them while others were given every advantage. He hated it, and them.

Ambition. Exclusion. Resentment. Those are the touchstones of Koch's career. Constantly mixed and remixed, raised to a boil and cooled to a simmer, they reacted in him to produce unique and unexpected results. They account for his cold, calculating pragmatism. For his tendency to personalize every political argument and slight. For his lust for public approval and his passion for getting even once he's on top. They nurtured the development of the extraordinarily sensitive antennae by which he grew able to read the public's mood—and lead it where it wants to go.

The gargantuan proportions of the climb facing Koch the night he walked in the Village with Dapolito insured that his stunted social development would remain so—a necessary tradeoff, in his mind, for the enormous psychic rewards that success would bring. The most casual of social settings—vacations, summering at the beach, dinner parties—which offered the opportunity for social interchange and new relationships became work at best for Koch. At the worst, they were annoying distractions.

During the summers, many in the VID shared rented homes in the various small oceanfront communities of Fire Island, a pristine, white-sand barrier island off Long Island's south shore. Far from the asphalt and crowds of Manhattan, they ate, they drank, they sunned themselves and swam. Some of the singles—even some of the marrieds—paired off. Koch took to the beach too, eating, drinking, swimming and sunning himself after a fashion, but nothing more. He seemed no more interested in women on the beach than in the Village and lying still on a sandy blanket seemed a trial. More often than not he could be seen darting about the beach talking with whomever, ever ready to whip out the pen and small notebook in his pocket to jot down people's concerns.

One summer he journeyed as far from New York City as Lake Placid to visit his friends Gene and Miriam Bockman. Koch had met Gene and Miriam separately before they were married. Gene had been part of the reform movement in the Bronx, which was trying to topple that borough's boss, Charley Buckley. Koch and Gene had occasionally shared the experiences of their battles over dinner. Koch had met Miriam even earlier—within a year or two of his moving into the Village—through friends that she had in his building at 81 Bedford Street. They grew friendly enough that some thought they had a romantic relationship, but, according to Miriam, they were "just friends. We had just a good personal relationship." She adds, however, "He is someone who does not let people get close to him. He was always good in conversation in terms of substance and government, but in terms of personal things he was not an outgoing person."

Gene and Miriam fell in love, married, and in 1965 took a summer place in the near-wilderness beauty of Buck Island, a small chunk of land in Lake Placid. It was rustic and quiet—an atmosphere about as different from Manhattan as one could find. Gene, an avid fisherman, loved it, and when Koch visited the Bockmans, Gene invited him to partake of the tranquil pastime with him. Early in the morning they loaded their poles, hooks, and nets into Gene's fifteen-foot outboard and sliced away from the shore on the shimmering surface of the lake. Casting their lines, they began trolling for rainbow trout and smallmouth bass. Gene settled back to wait, lulled by the gentle slap of the lake against the boat's hull. The morning sun beat warmly on his face. It was paradise. Koch watched the lake where his line entered the water. There was no sign of a bite, not even a nibble. He shifted in his seat. He looked at the sky, the water, the shoreline, the trees. Nice, but how long can you keep that up? He tapped his fingers. He shuffled his feet. Five whole minutes and nary a bite. Across the lake he could see the village of Lake Placid. Civilization. Surely they'd have the newspapers, maybe even the New York City papers. Koch had to get over there to find out what had happened in the world since he was gone. Gene saw there was no sense in fighting. Koch was so fidgety it wouldn't have been a complete surprise if he had jumped in and swum for it. Gene nosed the boat toward Lake Placid and ferried Koch over. He found the *Times* and rode back across the lake absorbed in the day's political news, enjoying himself immensely.

Koch found his political lessons everywhere. One year, the VID organized a group vacation to Europe. Koch joined the bunch, traveling from city to city and country to country sampling the local cuisine in as much quantity and variety as possible. But it was in Copenhagen that he hit his stride. He was on a tour bus with Miriam Bockman and others when they came upon the building that houses the Danish Parliament. Government! Koch's interest perked up immediately, and as the bus passed, he spied a group of demonstrators picketing the building. That was too much for him. Leading Miriam, Koch leaped off the bus and ran to the picketers.

"Immediately he was down there, trying to find out what was stirring the people up," she remembers. "It was crazy. We ended up in the Parliament listening to the session in Danish. We couldn't understand a word of it."

The demonstrators were kindred spirits to Koch. No matter what the issue, they were battling from the outside to assert power, a position that Koch understood viscerally. Protesting at the drop of a hat was a way of life for him. In fact, Victor Kovner, his former law partner, remembers a personal sit-in that Koch staged in the elevator of the building that housed their law offices. There were, of course, many other tenants in the building, most of them much more prosperous than Koch and his partners. One of them—the major law firm of Cleary, Gottlieb, Steen & Hamilton—occupied plush, dignified offices on several floors of the building. The firm was such an important tenant that the landlord agreed to dedicate one elevator in the building for its exclusive use. Arriving at the building one morning, Koch boarded the elevator only to be told by its operator that it would not take him to the floor his office was on. This did not sit well with Koch. He wouldn't stand for it.

"Ed came in and didn't notice the new sign," Kovner remembers. "He gave the elevator operator the floor number, but the elevator operator said no. Ed said, 'It took me yesterday, it will take me today.' The elevator operator said, 'I can't do that.' So Ed said, 'I'm sitting down in here until you take me.' He did it."

Socially, matters were about the same. The trait Miriam Bockman noticed in Koch—his seeming inability to talk about anything but government—became painfully apparent at small gatherings and parties. He would often find himself standing alone in the corner, nursing a drink, unable to mingle and circulate with the crowd. Small talk seemed impossible to make. Years later, guests at parties thrown by such hostesses as Mary Nichols, who met Koch and grew friendly with him as a reporter for *The Village Voice,* could expect to be urged to go over and "say hello to Congressman Koch." Those who did often reported back that they had been driven away—either by a boring, self-centered political monologue or outright hostility.

Even among those who often considered themselves his closest friends, Koch confined his conversation to the concerns of the
moment—usually politics. Ask these friends if he ever talked about
earlier phases of his life—about his boyhood and adolescence,
about his years in the service, about his love life—and they will
answer that he shared next to nothing with them. At best, they
will speculate without evidence. That there's a well-hidden sexual indiscretion in Koch's past. Or a long-lost love who spurned
him painfully, driving him from romance for good. The one exception to his silence regarding personal matters was the death
of his mother from cancer in 1960. With his sister Pat living north
of the city in a suburban town and his brother Harold in New
Jersey, Koch visited the hospital every day where he witnessed
the irrevocable decline of the strong woman who had held the
family together through tough times and pushed him to succeed. To many of his friends through the years he spoke in moving terms about her death and how the whole family had suffered. When she was first diagnosed, a doctor had told them that
she would die in three months and there was nothing anyone
could do about it. Yet Louis and his children dragged her from
doctor to doctor, looking for a miracle. Koch remembers the family's desperate need "to do something. It's ridiculous," he said.
"You can't let somebody die."

But nothing worked. The doctor had been right.

"She died to the day, three months," Koch said. "That is what
is so incredible."

Successful in the VID, as he never could have been in the Tamawa, Koch was now the reformer's reformer, as religiously certain as anyone of the need for a clean-as-a-hound's-tooth, patronage-free political system. He also conducted himself as a
liberal, championing the VID's progressive agenda. But there is
plenty of evidence that Koch was not the liberal he seemed to
be, although it would be years before the political climate would
make it safe for him to show his true colors. One of his closest
friends from those days describes Koch in terms that would fit a
chameleon. He believes that although Koch subscribed to much
of the VID agenda he was never as far to the left as the club was.
"He took on some of the coloration of the particular surroundings," the friend says. "In a very liberal environment, he may
have been perceived as more liberal than he really was." If that

was so, Koch did nothing to dispel the idea. For doing that would have severely damaged his standing in the VID. Stephanie Harrington, who grew close to Koch for a time, viewed him in those early days as a "maverick liberal who would take a position regardless of the consequences if he felt it was right." In retrospect she sees him much differently—as a man who entered politics without "any kind of vision of the kind of society he wanted to live in," and who merely reacts viscerally and pragmatically to issues.

"What I see fueling his engines is not a vision of society but personal success in his chosen career," she says. "That is not evil. A lot of people go into politics for that reason. But it is something I did not realize at first."

A major issue for the VID in the early 1960s was civil rights. The Supreme Court had already handed down *Brown* v. *Board of Education*, the landmark civil-rights decision that helped open the country's eyes to the two-tiered racial society that had been taken for granted, not just in the South but in many northern cities as well—the kind of society in which Koch had lived for ten years as a youth in Newark. Television was broadcasting the images of Martin Luther King, Jr., Medgar Evers, James Meredith, Bull Connor, Rosa Parks, George Wallace, police dogs, and water cannons. The desire to help Negroes—they were not called blacks then—was adopted wholeheartedly by the white reformers in the VID.

At the same time, the rage generated among blacks by the slow pace of change spread to American's northern cities and long, hot summers became part of the fabric of life in the country's urban ghettos. Like Watts, Detroit, and Newark, New York City was racked by its share of racial rioting. In 1963, looting and burning broke out in Harlem and the Corona section of Queens, and in the summer of 1964 the streets of Harlem and Bedford-Stuyvesant exploded with violence after an off-duty police officer shot and killed a black youth.

Koch was at the forefront of the civil-rights crusade in the Village even before rioting broke out in the city. He did legal work for the Congress of Racial Equality (CORE). He mediated a dispute between black workers at a local Howard Johnson's and the restaurant's management over the workers' claim of racial discrimination. He led the VID in collecting food and money to send to civil-rights workers in Mississippi. He took part in a local protest to maintain integration in the Village's main elementary school. And in the wake of the rioting, which sparked many allegations of racially motivated police brutality, Koch supported a highly controversial drive to create a civilian review board to investigate complaints of police misconduct.

In 1964, a delegation from the VID, Koch included, made an exhausting day trip to Alabama to join a civil-rights protest march in Selma. "I think we all at that point were emotionally involved in what Dr. King was doing," says Miriam Bockman. "We felt we had to bear witness." The group dressed as middle class as they possibly could—the men in jackets, ties and hats, and the women in skirts and sweaters—and flew down on a charter flight to join the march.

"We walked together and talked together, and there was one point in which the marshals wanted us to run to catch up," Bockman remembers. "Koch said, 'Somebody tell that marshal we are intellectuals, not athletes.' "

Koch and several others from the VID returned to the South, to Mississippi, for eight days to work with the Lawyers Constitutional Defense Committee, which was organizing attorneys to represent blacks who had been arrested. "We were put up by black families at different houses," remembers Henry Stern, one of those on the trip. "Ed, because he was a trial lawyer, was sent to defend blacks who were accused in court. At that time there were only three blacks who had been admitted to the Mississippi bar, and no white lawyers would take the cases . . . Ed argued for these people in these tiny towns."

The atmosphere was threatening, the hostility of many Southern whites palpable. "I remember thinking to myself, 'Here is a big, obviously Jewish person, and they don't like Jews very much down here, arguing in court for these people," says Stephanie Harrington. "Ed really impressed because of that. I thought that was very gutsy."

Many of the northern lawyers returned with tales of great danger, and wore the stories like stripes of great liberal honor. "I and everyone else made great heroes of ourselves," says Martin Berger, one of the earliest of the VID lawyers to work in the South.

Koch's liberal and reform credentials stood him in good stead both in the VID and with the progressive leaders of the Village.

He became the darling of the community's newspaper, *The Village Voice,* then a small, struggling weekly that served as the area's intellectual bulletin board. In many ways, the *Voice* and the VID had a symbiotic relationship. As one grew so did the other. The paper covered Koch's every move—with few exceptions, favorably—and on Friday afternoons he and others from the VID dropped by the paper's office to gossip and discuss local and world affairs. Koch grew friendly with its writers, including the well known liberal commentators Jack Newfield and Nat Hentoff. He also began a long, close relationship with the paper's soft-spoken cofounder and editor, Dan Wolf. He consistently supported Koch with strong editorials, describing him in 1966 when he ran for a seat in the City Council as "a front-line urban fighter, and in a sense . . . the best example of the new, effective urban politician." And although Wolf has long since left the paper—he is now perhaps Koch's closest advisor in City Hall—in the *Voice* offices there is still a framed copy of a similarly glowing editorial that Wolf wrote supporting Koch in his 1962 race against Passannante. Koch had the editorial mounted and presented it to Wolf with this note:

> Dear Dan—
>
> Please forgive my apparant (sic) immodesty in framing your editorial. It, notwithstanding the forces arrayed against us, by its brilliant exposition, would have won the election had we the time to distribute it to the electorate. I thank you for framing the issues so magnificently.

Koch conducted himself as only a true VID district leader would. Doling out patronage and doing favors, the traditional functions of a district leader, were out. Constituents who called for help even with simple matters, such as getting excused from jury duty, were uniformly refused. And they were likely to be lectured sternly—first on the evils of using political influence and then on how important it is for all citizens to do their duty in the cause of justice. As for getting people jobs? Forget it. Costikyan, the county leader, received so many complaints that Koch was refusing to help people—voters—that he worked out an arrangement with Koch to send them to other district leaders who would do the favors for them.

But being a success in the club—a star even in the pages of the *Voice*—is a far cry from getting ahead in politics. Koch sized up his political situation with the utmost pragmatism and quickly became impatient with what Michael Harrington called "the almost suicidal devotion to principle of some of the people around the VID, people who were in love with defeat, glorious defeat." It was clear that, even to keep hold of the small bit of power he had, Koch would have to broaden his base of support. DeSapio had been a convenient villain, but now that he had been dispatched Koch needed a new political agenda. The otherworldly idealism that had toppled DeSapio had served its purpose, but was too remote from everyday concerns to sustain a political career. Liberal pieties, no matter how heartfelt, were not a recipe for lasting success.

So Koch had to find a way to serve his constituents without resorting to the traditional system of patronage politics. His political instincts took over, and he soon fell into a pattern that he would follow for as long as he pursued the mayoralty. Instead of nudging government from within to help people, he began to battle it from without, attempting to bully and bludgeon it into doing what his constituents wanted. He became the consummate nattering, nagging outsider. If the city wanted to widen some streets and the neighborhood didn't want the bulldozers coming in, Koch would be on the battle lines to stop them. If people were upset about vagrants and drug users in Washington Square Park, Koch would scream and yell for the police and the parks department to do something.

Yet he also realized that he would never be able to stay in office, let alone move up, if he only represented the VID segment of his district. After all, he'd only won by forty-one votes. He had to work with everyone, and that meant trying to win over the Italians in the South Village. Verrazano Street notwithstanding, the VID had paid little more than lip service to reaching out to the Italians. Many in the club looked patronizingly on them, as if they were simply incapable of understanding the VID's higher order of political thinking. Koch didn't see it that way. What he saw was votes. Regardless of whether the Italians were reformers, there were a lot of them and they always turned out at the polls. It marked the first time that he realized the need to court the middle class.

Reaching out for the South Village was all the more important, because regardless of the VID's jubilation, DeSapio was not done tangling with Koch. Within days of the election, he chal-

lenged the results in court. There had been some minor irregu-
larities in the voting—about thirty ineligible voters had cast ballots for Koch—and with a margin of victory down to a small
handful, the state's highest court ordered a new election. Koch
was forced to run against DeSapio again in 1964, a campaign that
is noteworthy because Koch adopted a tactic that he would use
throughout his career. While struggling to hold together what little
there was of his law practice, he showed up at subway stations
at morning and evening rush hours to greet constituents and
distribute flyers. In the afternoons he shook hands in supermarkets, and at night he attended small gatherings of potential voters in the apartments of friends. He also displayed, for the first
time, the extreme umbrage he takes when his integrity is im-
pugned even slightly.

Capitalizing on the court's finding that Koch's cause had been
helped by ineligible voters, DeSapio publicly accused Koch of
election fraud. That to Koch was an outrage since DeSapio had
not charged Koch with fraud in the suit that overturned the election. When the two men met in a hallway for the taping of a
television interview program, DeSapio greeted Koch and extended his hand.

"Hello," Koch answered, turning his back on his foe. "He has
committed libel," Koch charged. "He has now gone past the
bounds of propriety, even for a politician. I have no intention of
shaking hands with him again—ever."

Koch made a bridge to the voters in DeSapio's stronghold in
the predominately Italian South Village through a controversial
neighborhood issue—the cafés on MacDougal Street. The street
was part of a solid working-class neighborhood of five- and six-
story walk-up buildings, many of which had small stores and
shops on the ground floor. Many of the apartments had been occupied comfortably by the same families for decades. But all that
began to change in the early 1960s as Greenwich Village became
a mecca for the young hippies of that time. The Villagers had
always accepted and tolerated the odd lifestyles of the artists,
beatniks, and bohemians who had flocked to their community
because, for the most part, the newcomers had respected the na-
tives' way of life. But the new youth movement, with its emphasis on drugs and sexual freedom, changed all that. MacDougal
Street was suddenly swamped with cafés that drew crowds of

young people at all hours of the night, and the neighborhood was not such a nice place to live anymore. A politician looking for an issue to rally a conservative ethnic community couldn't ask for more. Even though Koch and the VID had won the battle to open Washington Square Park to folk singers, they now led the charge to limit the bohemian influence. Dapolito, the chairman of the community planning board, remembers that he was baking biscuits when he got a call from Koch. "He said, 'Tony, could I be placed on the agenda for next Thursday's meeting?' I said, 'Yeah, Ed, what's up?' He said, 'We just passed a resolution at the VID. It calls for a clean-up of MacDougal Street.' I said to him, 'Well, all right, Ed, you're on for the meeting.' " As he hung up Dapolito couldn't help thinking to himself, 'Oh, what a reversal.' The ultra-liberal VID, the outsiders, actually wanted to help.

Koch's pursuit of the South Village Italians was his first, very formative immersion in ethnic politics. Most in the Italian community looked upon him, quite rightly, with suspicion. After all, sodomy, abortion, and divorce—the SAD issues around which he had built his campaign against Passannante only two years earlier—were not exactly their issues. The cafés were a perfect opportunity to offset that, but Koch also knew that if he was going to win the community he would have to get the stamp of approval from at least some of its leaders. John LoCicero, who later became one of Koch's closest political advisors, saw Koch first in 1961, campaigning on the street in Wagner's race for mayor that year. He didn't like him or his shrill manner of street-corner oration. But several years later, in the midst of battling DeSapio, Koch met LoCicero and asked him to join the VID. "You want me to join because I'm Italian," LoCicero told him. "That's right," Koch answered.

Koch eventually found ambassadors to the community in a young lawyer named Emmanuel "Wally" Popolizio and a community activist named Dina Nolan. He won them over with the energy and drive he brought to the effort to close the cafés or to at least bring them in line. Together they wound up forming a new active civic organization, the MacDougal Area Neighborhood Association (MANA) which began to push to improve the quality of life in the community. Koch stopped by almost every night to help the group plan its battles, whether it was suing to force the city to crack down on the cafés by enforcing its own regulations or mounting a mass demonstration outside Gracie Mansion.

By dint of perseverance and hard work, Koch gradually became acceptable to the Italians despite his odd amalgam of crazy liberal ideas and community activism. The liberal causes, the great world issues that the VID debated at all hours of the day and night, were remote to the South Villagers. What they wanted in a politician was someone who could deliver for them on matters affecting their homes, streets, and schools, and they were willing to forgive a great many sins if someone could do it. They'd forgive almost anything to be rid of the coffee houses. At election time, Popolizio would walk door to door with Koch telling people in effect, "On most things he is crazy, but on our issue he is right." Their issue was the cafés.

When the votes were counted in the election rerun in June, 1964, Koch had beaten DeSapio, by 164 votes—5,904 to 5,740— thanks largely to the endorsement again by Mayor Wagner, who made a point a few days before the election of consulting with Koch on Village community problems.

The following year—1965—was a regular election year and brought the third and final Koch v. DeSapio bout. Koch, of course, won again, this time decisively. The Chief, The Bishop, was finally politically dead, and a lasting major change came to New York City politics. As Moynihan and his coauthor Nathan Glazer wrote in *Beyond the Melting Pot:* "Carmine DeSapio was far and away the most competent politician the New York Democrats produced in the postwar era. Significantly, the middle-class reformers, while able to destroy him, were quite incapable of replacing him. The immediate result was not a transfer of power but a vacuum."

And four years after his last defeat, on December 13, 1969, the authorities would finally prove that DeSapio was corrupt. He was convicted that day of a bribery conspiracy and in 1971 he entered a federal prison.

The final election fight between Koch and DeSapio showed the inroads Koch was making in the South Village. The election was complicated by the fact that the city was undergoing reapportionment and the legislature was redrawing district lines. Since Elbridge Gerry—the inventor of gerrymandering—redistricting has been a time-honored way of rewarding friends and punishing

enemies. The new lines proposed for Koch would have markedly changed his area—most importantly by lumping into it more
of the Italian South Village, a shift that would make it harder for
him to win reelection and easier for DeSapio to make a comeback. Koch and Micki Wolter took the bus up to Albany, the state
capital, to testify against the proposed changes, arguing that the
lines were drawn in such a way as to divide the Village in two.

That same day, J. Raymond Jones, an ally of DeSapio who took
over as county leader after Costikyan, told reporters that Koch
had expressed to him a much different reason for fighting the
new lines. He charged that, after looking at the new lines, Koch
had told him: "I can't win with all those Italians in there. I want
them out." Jones also said that Koch was seeking a redistricting
that "would get rid of the Italians in his district."

Koch denied making such statements, and realizing that the
dispute was going to be printed in the papers the next day, he
met with friends at the VID that night to plan how to respond.
They decided to call a press conference in the morning, but noting Koch's fury they counseled him to be temperate when
speaking to the reporters.

"You mean I can't call a spade a spade?" Koch asked with a
smile.

The white liberals gathered with him broke into laughter and
groans. J. Raymond Jones is black.

In the morning the battle heated up. Koch branded Jones's remarks as "utterly false" and Jones shot back that Koch was an
"unmitigated liar." He produced two witnesses from the county
Democratic organization who corroborated his version of events.
The allegations would have been a devastating blow to Koch were
it not for his tireless work in the South Village. As it was, the
impact was bad enough. "We had gone somewhere for dinner,"
remembers Wolter. "We were on Sixth Avenue. I said he should
be walking in the South Village. So we went down there, walked
around and talked to people. At first we got a lot of yelling from
people, but we really felt that facing the people defused the antagonism."

At MANA, the neighborhood association he helped found,
there was no antagonism at all. Popolizio, Nolan, and the group
either refused to believe that Koch had said such things or were
willing to forgive him. They welcomed him at a party the night
after Jones made his allegations. As he munched on baked clams

oregano, eggplant Siciliano, and *cuscinetti di prosciutto*, Koch said that it was "the best bar mitzvah I ever attended."

The year 1965 also brought another election that was crucial to Koch's career, although he wasn't a candidate. The race was that year's mayoral contest. Four Democrats—including two liberal reformers—competed in a primary election to be the party's standard-bearer. The winner was Abraham Beame, a bland, diminutive accountant who had risen through the Brooklyn clubhouse system to become the city comptroller. Democrats outnumber Republicans by such a lopsided margin in New York that the winner of the Democratic primary is usually assured of election. But not that year. The Republican and Liberal Party candidate for mayor was a tall, handsome, charismatic, well-to-do congressman from Manhattan's wealthy East Side "silk stocking district"—John V. Lindsay.

Lindsay was everything that Beame wasn't. In appearance, polish, and philosophy he seemed the walking embodiment of good government while Beame seemed a creature from the Dark Ages of politics. With the backing of the city's newspapers and the help of media wizard David Garth, it became clear that Lindsay was making a run of it. In the liberal, reform-minded Village, he was the overwhelming choice of the voters. "Everybody was going to vote for Lindsay," remembers Carol Greitzer, Koch's coleader.

As Democratic Party officials, Koch and Greitzer were seemingly bound by party loyalty to support Beame. But the day before the election, they went with the tide around them and publicly endorsed Lindsay. With Greitzer and Martin Berger, then president of the VID, at his side at a press conference in his law office, Koch declared that he couldn't stand by silently while the mayoralty was delivered to a candidate of the bosses. Later he met with Dan Wolf, the editor of the *Voice*. "He kind of looked sick," remembers Stephanie Harrington. "He looked worried, very worried about the political consequences of what he'd done." The next day as the voters were going to the polls, Koch's statements were played prominently in the papers—he even made page one of the *Daily News*.

Lindsay won. There were many reasons for his victory, but both Beame and Robert Price, who was then a key Lindsay aide, believe that the margin of victory was small enough—102,000 votes—that Koch's last-minute endorsement was at least partly responsible. "It may have meant the difference," Price says. "For a Democrat to vote Republican then was a sin. It was equivalent to leaving the church. Koch and Greitzer probably made it more palatable, something you didn't have to be ashamed of." To Beame, it was—and still is—an act of unpardonable disloyalty.

As Koch had feared, the leadership of the Democratic Party was furious. But it mounted only a limp and ultimately unsuccessful attempt to strip him and Greitzer of their posts as district leaders. Still, the endorsement did wonders for Koch's career by setting a chain of political dominoes falling. With his victory, Lindsay resigned his congressional seat. The city councilman from Koch's district, Theodore R. Kupferman, then gave up his seat to run successfully for the spot vacated by Lindsay. That in turn gave Koch the opportunity to run for the City Council in 1966.

On March 22, 1966 he announced his candidacy for the $10,000-a-year, part-time job and soon won the backing of the Liberal Party, which was grateful for the service he had performed for Lindsay. The endorsement was crucial to Koch because, running in a district that had been held by Republicans for nearly forty years, he needed all the help he could get. His slogan—"The City is for People"—was uninspired, but his street-corner campaign style was well-honed. And well aware of how valuable he had been to Lindsay, Koch hoped that the new mayor would endorse him or at least remain neutral in the race. To Koch's dismay Lindsay did neither, announcing that he was supporting Koch's lackluster Republican opponent. Nonetheless, Koch won and the votes that put him over the top came from his political stronghold—the South Village. "I got my job through *The Village Voice*," he quipped.

From the day Koch took office, on January 1, 1967, he wanted out and up.

"This is not where I'm ending up," he would tell David Brown, who later became his congressional chief of staff and deputy mayor.

Long viewed as a gaggle of clowns, the Council is dominated by the city's Democratic machines. Koch was accepted as an eccentric nobody who voted most often with the machine leadership even though he was distrusted by most of his regular organization colleagues. He was "docile," remembers Tom Cuite, who was a powerful committee chairman while Koch was a councilman. "No runs, no hits, no errors," says Stanley Friedman, who was counsel to the majority leader and is now the Bronx boss.

Still, two aspects of Koch's years on the council are worth noting. The first is that instead of pocketing the $5,000 bonus for "expenses" that every councilman received, Koch announced that he would pay $500 stipends to bright professional people who would provide him with ideas for being an effective councilman and pitch in to help him draft legislation. The announcement drew 130 applicants for ten spots and Koch began to develop a circle of bright advisors to whom he turned for information and advice throughout his legislative career.

The second is perhaps even more characteristic of Koch. He became a press hound, dropping repeatedly into Room 9, the City Hall press room, to distribute reams of releases. By dint of perseverance, he got coverage, but usually in just four- or five-paragraph stories buried toward the rear of the papers. He just bubbled with bright ideas. By now a reformed smoker, he urged that the Transit Authority be forced to supply advertising space in the subways for antismoking messages. He called for construction of a railroad line over the George Washington Bridge to New Jersey. He proposed a program under which city officials would be hauled in front of the Council every week to answer questions. He devised a plan under which construction workers would get bonuses if they completed their projects quickly. He introduced legislation much favored by South Village residents that would have shut down bars in residential areas at 1 A.M. and imposed mandatory fines on unlicensed coffee houses. None of that went anywhere. Koch's primary legislative success was enactment of a bill that renamed a street in the Village after his idol, Fiorello La Guardia.

Koch's ticket out of the council was the next big election that came along—a race in 1968 for Lindsay's old congressional seat. The district ran north from the Village and took in the largely Hispanic Lower East Side and the middle-class communities of Turtle Bay and Stuyvesant Town. But its political and economic heart was the wealthy and prestigious East Side of Manhattan. This was the neighborhood of Park Avenue, major corporate headquarters, and fabulously expensive apartments overlooking Central Park. The cream of New York society lived there, and for more than three decades the congressional seat had been held by Republicans. Once again Koch was the outsider, and he entered the race painfully aware of the differences in class and background between many in the district and himself. They were for the most part moneyed Protestants. He was a threadbare lawyer, the son of Polish immigrants, and Jewish.

"I think that being Jewish added to his sense of being an outsider," says Henry Stern, one of Koch's closest friends then and now. "This was an age in which Jews still couldn't get jobs in law firms and that Jews couldn't live in many of the apartments in the district. Koch was also a Polish Jew as opposed to a German Jew. Even within the Jews he was definitely not 'Our Crowd.' "

Lindsay had been preceded in office by Frederick R. Coudert of the Coudert banking family and was followed by Kupferman—Theodore Roosevelt Kupferman—a less dashing but still appropriate figure. When Kupferman announced in the second year of his term that he would not seek reelection, the field was wide open. The Republican candidate who emerged against Koch was Whitney North Seymour, Jr., a respected Republican state legislator and partner in a major Manhattan law firm who traced his American ancestry to the Revolutionary War. Seymour became the odds-on favorite in the race. The district, perhaps the most prestigious in the country, obviously wanted someone whom the voters could be proud of. Someone Ivy League. Someone with money. Someone familiar and distinguished. Like Seymour. Even Lindsay, who owed Koch, spurned him when Koch went to City Hall to ask for the mayor's support. The rejection is one Koch has never forgiven.

Koch fit the district only in that it had long had a reputation as liberal and progressive. Koch's reform credentials and his record on civil rights were plusses. So was his position on one other major issue—the war in Vietnam. By now the war was well on its way to tearing at the country's soul, and opposition to it was steadily growing. In the forward-thinking silk-stocking district, dissent was already in full flower. So much so that two years earlier, one of the country's first antiwar candidates—a Democrat—had given Kupferman a run for his money. Koch and Seymour both reflected the district's growing antipathy toward the war—though Koch much more strongly.

Koch campaigned as he always did, relentlessly appearing at subway stops and community meetings, shaking as many hands and handing out as much literature as he could. This was for the big time, but, as Mary Nichols remembers, Koch still had the aura of "a loser who desperately wanted to win."

"He certainly didn't have polish," she says. "I remember sitting in a room with a friend of mine and we were drilling him on how to behave on television. She was teaching him to sit straight and pin his ass to the back of a chair so he wouldn't slouch, and to stop pointing his finger like a schoolmarm when he talked. He was awkward, gauche, really terrible."

He also had little grasp of national and international issues. So on Monday evenings experts would be summoned to his apartment to hold seminars instructing Koch in everything from welfare reform to foreign policy. "We'd spend two or three hours tossing these issues around," remembers Phil Trimble, then a bright young lawyer who signed on as one of Koch's $500-a-year Council aides. "The object was to prepare him for the issues he'd face in the campaign and in Congress. That was when I realized he was a smart man. He never seemed to forget anything."

Koch also stepped up a number of politically popular activities in the Council. He continued a long battle against plans to construct an expressway across lower Manhattan. When tens of thousands of New Yorkers found that they were being hit with suddenly soaring rents, he joined a politically popular campaign to extend rent controls for them. That, even though just the following year he would privately tell Larry Mandelker, a young lawyer who was supporting him politically, that he believed that rent control "is eventually going to ruin the housing stock of this city." And he proposed a novel idea that, he predicted, would result in "real improvement in Negro living standards in a very few years." His proposal had two components. The first was the creation of an insurance program that would protect a white homeowner from a "real or fancied" drop in his property value if blacks moved into his neighborhood. The second was the establishment of a task force to recommend large-scale housing rehabilitation programs so that blacks would have better housing—in their own communities.

Like so many of his other proposals in those days, that idea went nowhere. But for Koch that meant little, because in the end, he fooled all the experts, pulling an upset by defeating Seymour handily. In January 1969—just two years after he entered the City Council—Ed Koch was on his way to Washington, a member of Congress.

Koch entered the House awed by the power and grandeur of

Washington and conscious of the fact that he was now a part of a club whose successful members are true insiders. If he was going to be accepted, he would have to change his style. This was not a place to be ranting and raving against those more powerful, as he had in New York. This was a place to get along by going along. Koch accommodated beautifully.

Legislatively, he was never a great success. Although he did win passage of bills creating federal commissions to study privacy laws and the decriminalization of marijuana, his causes for the most part were too liberal to win general acceptance. His reputation, in fact, was that of a liberal's liberal. He was staunchly antiwar and pro–civil rights. He consistently won 100-percent liberal ratings from Americans For Democratic Action and perfect or near perfect scores from the Leadership Conference on Civil Rights for his votes on such issues as busing and school desegregation. And he was described as the most radical member of Congress by a conservative group.

Still, Koch was determined to make as many friends as possible, even among those who would seem his natural enemies. He began courting the House leadership with great deference and did so for the nine years he remained in Congress. He also made a point of becoming a regular figure at a table in the private members dining room where a large group of congressmen gathered for lunch every day. His deference and friendliness slowly gained him acceptance, popularity even, without ever costing him the image that was so valuable to him at home of a liberal progressive reformer.

Nothing tells the story of the variety of Koch's friendships better than his relationship with Wayne Hays, the bullying, less-than-liberal chairman of the powerful House Administration Committee. On September 6, 1969, the day after Ho Chi Minh died in North Vietnam, Koch took the floor of the House declaring that to many Vietnamese, President Ho "is George Washington, Abraham Lincoln and John Kennedy."

"Whatever we may think of him and knowing that he was a tough and dedicated Communist," Koch continued, "we must recognize that he was, above all, a patriot in his own country."

The remarks provoked what Koch described as "vicious and venomous" attacks on him by some of his more conservative colleagues, including Hays, who said, "It makes me sick to hear anybody praise that cold-blooded murderer Ho Chi Minh."

Afterward, Hays, who regularly ate at the same table as Koch, was surprised to find that Koch shrugged the episode off. "The thing got pretty bitter, but he didn't seem to hold any resentment," Hays remembers. "I liked that and I think you could say we developed a friendship." So much so that when the House leadership moved to strip Hays of his cherished committee chairmanship in 1972, Koch was among those who rallied successfully to his defense.

"He made a speech to the effect that, 'I'm sure you people are wondering what a nice little sweet boy from New York is doing here speaking for a big bully like Wayne Hays, but the reason is that his word is good and he gets things done,' " says Hays, who never forgot that, nor the fact that when he married in 1976, Koch gave him and his new wife a gift: a porcelain picture frame complete with Koch's picture in it. "He obviously meant the frame to be the present," Hays remembers, "but there was a little letter with it that said that he thought it was such a nice frame it should have an equally nice picture." The picture, and the frame, still adorn Hays's den.

Koch remained loyal to Hays even after he was embroiled in scandal after being found in a Washington tidal pool with stripper Elizabeth Ray, whom he had placed on his House payroll.

"Koch had a hard time coming to the conclusion that Hays had to go," remembers Charles Flynn, one of Koch's congressional aides. "Initially his attitude was, 'I want to see the facts,' but when the facts came out, obviously Hays had to go. It wasn't easy for Koch."

If Koch was not a grand success at winning passage of his legislative ideas, he was still terrific at campaigning. And that, for all intents and purposes, is what he did nonstop for his entire nine years in Congress. He told his staff his aim was to be reelected every two years with a larger and larger majority. And he was, beginning in 1970. His liberal views on domestic and foreign policy issues matched those of many of his constituents. But equally important was the high-gear effort that Koch mounted to personally help each and every voter who called on him for service. His experiences in the South Village had taught him well the importance of having satisfied, grateful constituents and he became fond of telling his staff that he was a "heat and hot water guy."

Every morning he would walk among his staff of six or eight young aides with a long list of ideas and projects in hand, checking on the status of each and every assignment he'd given them and adding to their workload if possible. He had an iron rule that every letter from a constituent was to be answered, and if necessary, major battles were to be launched to get the bureaucracy, whether in New York City or Washington, to move as quickly as possible. The office became quite effective at it. David Rothenberg, a prison reform advocate, once turned to Koch for help when an inmate in a city jail needed some unusual assistance. "There was a case where an inmate had his wooden leg stolen and the Correction Department wasn't doing anything about it," Rothenberg remembers. "And so I called the congressman and he called the prison itself. Within twenty-four hours the man was helped."

Koch's emphasis on constituent service was even more pronounced in his New York City office. And within a few years his district operation became highly regarded among his colleagues. "He had probably the best district office at least by reputation among the members of the New York delegation," remembers Julian Spirer, who served as counsel to Benjamin Rosenthal, a liberal Queens Democrat, before going to work for Koch. "They were extremely effective at covering the political events in the district, at making Koch's views known at opportune moments and providing service. One of my responsibilities was overseeing Rosenthal's district office and one of the first things he told me was, 'You should use Koch's office as a model for whatever we do.' "

A good example of Koch's method of constituent service is the barrage of letters he dispatched following a meeting with Lower East Side residents who complained to him that construction of the Second Avenue subway was causing a variety of problems. Demanding a response, Koch forwarded the complaints to the heads of eight city agencies, including the Transit Authority and the transportation, sanitation, traffic, fire, and police departments. He then wrote to his constituents telling them about all the people he had written to on their behalf.

The standard third step in Koch's method would come when his correspondence file overflowed. At that point he would turn it over to a newspaper in an effort to milk his efforts for publicity.

When the members of Koch's Washington staff finished answering the mail and wrangling with the bureaucracy, they were free to move on to whatever more glamorous, substantive projects interested them. Koch's aides viewed that as part of the deal: they would do whatever he wanted in the way of nuts-and-bolts work and in return he would champion causes they brought him if he thought them worthwhile. Koch kept his part of that bargain, and out of it emerged some of his more distinguished congressional efforts, mostly dealing with human rights abuses around the world. Still, he kept the staff plenty busy. One item they all dreaded was the daily chore of the "record statements."

The Congressional Record publishes the daily proceedings of Congress, but it also permits each member to request the publication of as many as three added statements a day on any subject. "At noon every day Koch would religiously ask for three extensions to the record," remembers Sean McCarthy, another of his aides. "He would use them to put his views in on a variety of subjects. Say he got up and read in the *Times* something about Indira Gandhi's policy on birth control. He'd give us his thoughts about that and say, "Why don't you polish this up and see if the facts are right?' So we'd write it up for him and the next day it would appear in *The Congressional Record*, 'Mr. Speaker, I was concerned to read about Indira Gandhi . . .' "

If Koch thought the subject was really important he found a way not just to have his statement published but to have it displayed on the front page of *The Congressional Record*. "Ed has this sixth sense about news," remembers Ken Kay, another of Koch's aides. "He was in effect his own press secretary, and the thing that was so terrific was that he could read the papers in the morning and find out what the stories were. Then if he thought it was important he would leave the office at 11:30 or quarter to twelve and camp out on line so that his statement would be the first accepted and would be on the front page."

Koch's fascination with the press and its workings became legendary among his staff and colleagues. David Brown, his congressional chief of staff, saw the love affair first hand.

"I lived with him in Washington for about six weeks in 1970 or '71," Brown remembers. "The guy would watch the news before he went to bed, watch when he got up, and read the papers. The news was the first thing in the morning and the last thing at night for him. It was a kind of wonderful interest in what was going on, especially if he was going to be appearing. He would call me up and say, 'Hey, I'm going to be on this particular program at eleven.' We even used to send out notices to friends."

For all the effort he was putting into becoming a Capitol Hill insider, Koch hated life in Washington. How far out of synch he was with the capital is best illustrated by a small incident that happened in 1975, six years after he took office. On the night of his birthday that year, December 12, an aide was driving him home to his apartment, a basement unit so spartan that when it was once burglarized the police refused to believe a congress-man lived there.

"You know, Washington is really a beautiful place," Koch re-marked to his aide as the car passed a large edifice bathed in light. The aide agreed. Then, pointing out the window, Koch asked, "What's that?"

"That's the Jefferson Monument," the aide answered, amazed that Koch hadn't known.

Given Koch's work habits, perhaps that was understandable. At every chance he got, he raced back to the district, which he described as populated by "40,000 Puerto Ricans to the south and David Rockefeller to the north." Most weeks, he flew in on the Washington–New York shuttle on Thursday night, the unofficial end of the congressional work week. At 7 A.M. the next morn-ing—rain, snow, or shine—he and a team of aides would assem-ble at one of the subway stops in his district to greet his constit-uents and distribute between 2,000 and 3,000 copies of *The Congressional Record* statements that he'd had run off that week under the heading, CONGRESSMAN ED KOCH REPORTS FROM WASH-INGTON. The statements were usually distributed with verbal questions sparked by his craving for approval.

"Did you get my newsletter? Was it OK?" he would ask. "Did you get my questionnaire? Was it OK?"

One week he gave out a flyer that became known in his office as the "Cats and Argentina statement." The flyer initially con-tained only a very serious expression of outrage by Koch about human rights violations and anti-Semitism in Argentina. But as his aides were about to have it printed up, Koch stopped them.

"He said, 'Wait a minute. Let's do another statement on the other side, something that other people might be interested in,' " remembers Charles Flynn.

The choice was a statement by Koch expressing opposition to scientific experimentation on cats. The juxtaposition seemed absurd, but Koch assured his staff that issuing the cat statement was a wise political move.

"The people who like animals," he told them, "if you have them on your side, they will do anything for you."

He had given up his law practice, and so he could spend virtually every waking moment on politics. In his district office. At community meetings. Conducting meet-your-congressman sessions at which his constituents could sit down with him at various locations in the district. His constant presence kept him tuned in to hometown concerns. In Stuyvesant Town, a sprawling, family-oriented, middle-class apartment complex, he learned how important the fear of crime was to ordinary New Yorkers and helped push the development's owner, the Metropolitan Life Insurance Co., for better security. In his home base, the Village, he picked up on another middle-class problem and mounted a major campaign against it.

The issue was the Lindsay administration's growing use of seedy hotels as emergency housing for homeless welfare families. After Mary Nichols described in the *Voice* the abysmal conditions in one Village hotel, the Broadway Central, Koch became interested and learned that a four-year-old boy had slipped through a broken bannister in the hotel and plunged five floors to his death. He made the issue public in a big way, and touched several raw nerves at once. The public was appalled at the conditions in which the families were living. It was angered at the astronomical rates that the city seemed to be paying for the abysmal accommodations. And the middle-class communities in which some of the hotels were located resented the problems of crime and drug abuse that some of the welfare families brought with them. This was even true in the ultra-liberal Village.

"The Lindsay administration filled a lot of hotels with welfare people in the Village," Mary Nichols remembers. "The Village was liberal. If the administration had done the same thing in Queens the people would have revolted. We were hoist on our own liberal petard."

Koch ran with the issue for a number of years, persistently criticizing conditions in the hotels and the cost of housing families in them. He criticized City Hall for failing to find suitable and less expensive permanent housing for the families and for disrupting the middle-class residents of the Village. In retrospect, there is great irony in that. For as mayor, Koch has been plagued by the same problems on an even grander scale. New York now houses more homeless welfare families in more hotels that are just as abysmal at far greater cost than the Lindsay administration ever did. And his administration has proven just as unable to stem the torrent of poor families who are made homeless every year by the city's declining housing stock.

Koch's sixteen-hour-a-day work regimen—even on the weekends—became the envy of his congressional colleagues, most of whom were saddled with other responsibilities, such as wives and children. If Koch had any free time he'd go to the movies, often with others, but not always. "On weekends if he couldn't find anybody to go with him, he'd go by himself," remembers Mary Nichols. "I'd often run into him at the Waverly movie house just by himself."

On Saturday evenings and Sunday mornings, Koch would often host informal dinners and brunches at his cramped apartment at 14 Washington Place to which he invited intelligent, liberal people. The guests were as varied as Bess Myerson, the former Miss America with whom he'd become friendly when she served as Lindsay's consumer affairs commissioner, and Frank Serpico and David Durk, the two cops who exposed widespread police corruption in the city in the early '70s. Koch picked their brains for ideas and regaled them with his wide-eyed, almost naive stories of life on Capitol Hill. Many who attended those gatherings came away impressed that as politicians go Ed Koch seemed remarkably open and accessible. His home phone number was even listed in the directory.

On Monday mornings Koch would head back to Washington churning with pent-up energy and things to do. Sometimes he expressed irritation that his staff, trying to make normal lives of their own, had not worked the weekend through. Facing him coming through the door raring to go while they wanted to ease back into the grind became known as the "Monday morning problem."

"Weekends, he didn't rest very easily," remembers David Brown. "Since public service was at the center of his life, the private time when he had to tread water was not easy."

In the off hours, after the gavel closed House business, Koch had nothing to do. But he dreaded being alone, so in his early years in Congress he began to dragoon his staff into keeping him company at dinners, movies, whatever, just so that he didn't have to be alone. A frequent victim was Ronay Arlt, a tall, shy staff aide who was single.

"While Ronay ran the Washington office, she would go out to dinner with Ed every night as kind of a companion," Brown remembers. "He had nothing else to do. He didn't go out with other members of Congress very much and didn't like the Washington circuit. I finally had Ronay come up to the New York office. I said, 'I don't want you to have to go out with Ed the rest of your life.' I could see Ronay never having a life of her own."

She would certainly not have it with Ed Koch. His hunger was not for the warmth of a human being. He wanted to be mayor, and the two were not compatible in his mind. Less than two years after he entered Congress, he already had his timetable worked out. A mayoral election would be held in 1973, and Koch was planning to be in it. "Stick with me," he told Brown in 1970. "I'm going for the mayoralty."

His first stop was in Queens—Forest Hills, to be exact.

THE OPPORTUNIST

A predominantly middle-class Jewish community, Forest Hills was the site in 1971 of one of the most bitter racial confrontations New York City has ever had. The issue was a low-income housing project of three high-rise towers containing 840 apartments that the Lindsay administration proposed to build on a vacant eight-and-a-half-acre plot. "Low-income," of course, meant blacks, and the announcement stirred an immediate firestorm of resentment from residents.

A brainchild of 1960s liberalism, the project was part of the Lindsay administration's "scatter-site" housing program. On paper, it was a terrific idea. Instead of building high-rise monoliths in slum neighborhoods—buildings that became vertical slums in themselves—the program called for the city to shift its low-income housing construction to better neighborhoods. That way two noble ends would be achieved at once: The poor would get decent housing while integration would be fostered in predominantly white neighborhoods.

Putting the program into practice was something else. As soon as plans for the Forest Hills development were unveiled, the cry of "Not in our neighborhood!" rose from the streets where hundreds of protestors gathered day and night. Some opposed the project simply out of racism. Others were motivated by the fear that an influx of poor families would bring all the problems of the ghettos—crime, drugs, troubled schools—into a middle-class haven they'd worked long and hard to preserve. Whatever the reason, supporters of the plan viewed opposition as an effort to exclude blacks.

The project became a litmus test of New Yorkers' commitment to social progress. You were either for it or against it. No com-

promise or discussion was possible. It was in that atmosphere
that Congressman Koch from Manhattan journeyed to Forest Hills
on November 28, 1971 and addressed several hundred demonstrators. He urged them on in their battle and predicted the city
would scale down the project. "I wanted them to know they are
not racists because they oppose the project," he said later. "It's
wrong to try and lift the poor solely at the expense of pulling
down the middle class."

Koch had hinted at such feelings before, with his criticism of
the welfare hotels in Greenwich Village and his proposal for rebuilding the ghettos so that blacks would not have to move to
white areas to find decent housing. He had chosen his language
carefully in those cases, putting forth ideas that seemed designed to benefit blacks as well as whites. But Forest Hills was
different—he was taking a position that was clearly pro-white.
The incident was, he would say years later, his "Rubicon."

Koch's long-time liberal cohorts were shocked and angered, as
he had been warned they would be, not only by his opposition
to the plan but by his appearance beside Jerry Birbach, the Forest Hills resident who was leading the fight against the project.
Here was Koch, who had marched for civil rights in the South
and who had voted for every school busing amendment in Congress, supporting a cause they viewed as racist. The fact that he
had urged not that the project be scrapped, but only that it be
scaled down, made no difference. With the extreme polarization
surrounding the issue, Birbach, who was regarded as a racist by
many blacks and white liberals, took Koch's remarks as supporting his cause 100 percent. His liberal friends had warned Koch
that he would be viewed as antiblack, and he was.

Koch had gone to Forest Hills because he was genuinely opposed to the plan. But that alone would not be enough to get
him outside his district for such a heated battle. A more important reason was that he wanted to broaden his base of support.
Regardless of what his liberal supporters thought and feared, Koch
knew that he had no future in citywide politics unless he could
shed his ultra-liberal image. What better way to do that than to
support the middle class against a project for blacks? By now adept
at taking the public pulse, Koch had correctly understood that
times had changed since his days in the VID. Liberalism was
dying, or was at least very ill. It amazed him that Lindsay and
others didn't see what was happening and adjust their politics

accordingly. Quite simply, the white middle class was demanding that its concerns be addressed, and Ed Koch was ready to help.

The changes that Koch perceived were already unfolding when Lindsay took over City Hall in 1966. The great Southern-born civil rights movement had shifted its attention to the nation's northern cities. By legislative fiat, Washington had outlawed racial discrimination once and for all, but the abysmal conditions in which blacks and other minorities lived in America's urban ghettos made painfully clear the gulf between legislating equality and achieving it. For as jubilantly as the legal advances were celebrated, they also produced mounting frustration—at times rage—that meaningful changes were slow to come to the day-to-day lives of impoverished blacks. The horrifying and lawless urban rioting that resulted seemed to many an understandable response, a natural vent for pent-up anger. Those most liberal went as far as to accept the violence as an appropriate tactic of protest.

Because Lindsay's civil rights credentials were impeccable—in Congress he'd drafted and helped shepherd to passage important sections of the 1964 Civil Rights Act—he seemed the right man for City Hall. He would do more than pick up the garbage and police the streets; he would improve the lot of the city's poor blacks and Hispanics. Lindsay's concern paid off for New York in that the brunt of the urban rioting fell on other cities. When racial violence flared in the city, he walked the streets and seemed able to bring calm. But it would not have worked without what was going on behind the scenes. For in large measure, Lindsay was buying the peace—through massive new antipoverty programs, through summer jobs that were handed over to potential troublemakers, through a program as simple as dispatching buses to trouble spots to cart restive youths away on recreational day trips. A drive to reform the city's welfare system, which was seen by many as draconian and repressive to the poor, was begun. And a new plan for building housing for the poor, the scatter-site concept, was adopted wholeheartedly.

But the peace was fragile. The hastily assembled programs descended into a miasma of mismanagement and theft. The welfare rights drive became radicalized and resulted in an extraordinary relaxation in eligibility requirements. With the ranks of poor swelling, there was an explosion in the city's welfare caseload. The costs were enormous. During Lindsay's tenure the tab rose from $400 million a year to $1 billion, and a backlash from those whose taxes were paying that tab was inevitable. The *Daily News*, the voice of the city's blue-collar taxpayers, took to calling Lindsay's welfare commissioner Mitchell Ginsberg, "Come-and-Get-It Ginsberg."

At the same time, many blacks in the civil rights movement were growing more radical. Tired of white paternalism, blacks wanted true equality, not token excursions into white society. "Black Power" replaced "We Shall Overcome" as the most popular slogan and organizations such as the Black Panthers sprung up in urban areas. Soon it became clear that a black/white confrontation was brewing, with the only question being where it would occur. The answer was the public schools.

Efforts at integration in the classroom had failed, in part because middle-class whites had fled the public schools—and the city itself—in such large numbers that racial integration was no longer numerically possible. With their children making up a majority of the students, many blacks began advocating a new concept called "community control," a euphemism for blacks having complete authority over their own schools. The theory behind the idea was that the white-dominated school hierarchy was so steeped in racism that it was guilty of "educational genocide." The issue first surfaced in 1966 when the Board of Education moved to open IS 201, a new intermediate school in Harlem. The board had hand-picked the staff of the school based on their sensitivity to racial issues, but the teachers and principal for the new school were still greeted by strident picketing and boycotts that kept the school closed. The tone of the demonstrations was both antiwhite and—because many of the city's teachers were Jewish—anti-Semitic.

"We got too many teachers and principals named Ginzberg and Rosenberg in Harlem," one picketer was quoted as saying in the press. "This is a black community. We want black men in our schools."

The boycott of IS 201 was brief, but it was soon followed by a much more divisive confrontation along the same lines. The Board of Education set up three experimental districts in which community control concepts were to be put into practice. One of them was in Ocean Hill-Brownsville, a greatly impoverished black community in Brooklyn, where local leaders selected Rhody McCoy, a veteran black educator, to administer the project.

Problems quickly cropped up. When McCoy, in effect, began firing teachers and school administrators and replacing them with
personnel of his own, it became clear that militant community
leaders wanted far more power in running their own schools than
the Board of Education and the teachers union were willing to
cede them. The result was a bitter three-way power struggle that
culminated in three strikes by the United Federation of Teachers
that shut down the entire school system for weeks in the fall of
1968. Once again, the conflict quickly became a black/Jewish confrontation marked by accusations of racism and anti-Semitism.

By 1971, as Koch was readying himself to run for mayor, Forest Hills had become the scene of the third major dispute between blacks and Jews in five years. And Lindsay, who had come
to be seen as anti-middle class, was now perceived by some as
anti-Jewish as well. Among the protestors who picketed the site
selected for the development were some carrying signs calling him
Adolf Lindsay.

Eventually, Lindsay called in a Queens lawyer named Mario
Cuomo and asked him to forge a compromise. On July 6, 1972,
Koch and Cuomo met for the first time in Koch's downtown
Manhattan congressional office. By all accounts, the discussion
was congenial and both men were favorably impressed by each
other. As Cuomo recounts in his diary from the period, Koch informed him that he and a number of Queens officials had decided that the project should be scaled down. And in the end,
the compromise worked out by Cuomo was much the same as
proposed by Koch: the towers were built, but at about half the
size.

Still, many of Koch's liberal supporters remained unhappy
about his actions and viewed him as an opportunist who would
sacrifice his principles for power. Stephanie Harrington, for one,
remembers coming away from a meeting with Koch deeply disturbed that "he was trying to work out a position that would appeal to those people whose neighborhoods were being inte-
grated and didn't like it.

"He sort of tried out a position on us which was, 'Why should
blacks be forced to move out of their neighborhoods? Why don't
we just improve their neighborhoods so that they could stay in
them if they want and not have to move into a white neighborhood?' He also said there ought to be a sociological-impact statement before any public housing is put into a neighborhood. It

was that evening that I got the sense that he was really deliberately staking out a position that was different from what one would have expected four or five years prior to that."

But the dismay of Harrington and others who had long believed in Koch were only minor annoyances to him. He had but one goal—the mayoralty—and if he had to court conservative whites to reach it, well, that was OK with him. With each passing day, he was moving closer to becoming a formal candidate and away from the issues he had emphasized in his liberal past. His new focus became clear on February 12, 1973, the day he officially entered the mayoral campaign: Law and order, frequently used as an antiblack code phrase by rednecks, was his number-one campaign issue. "Overriding all is the paramount problem of crime—crime in our streets, crime in our schools, crime within our government," Koch declared at a news conference in the Hotel Biltmore—the same hotel, ironically, that long ago had served as the headquarters of Carmine DeSapio.

Koch's dreams were grand but his efforts were naive and amateurish. Despite his long political experience, he knew next to nothing about city government and so arranged to be tutored by Gene Bockman and Henry Stern. He also began hosting what seemed an endless series of wine-and-cheese gatherings in his apartment to organize a corps of supporters. And now that he needed their help, Koch also declared that the political bosses weren't so bad after all. He announced that he would "love" the support of the city's Democratic county leaders. "Times have changed," he said, adding that the bosses whom he'd made a career out of pillorying as devil figures weren't necessarily "evil."

His new attitudes got him nowhere. His get-tough-with-crime posture further angered his liberal supporters but his conversion was only scoffed at on the right. He was a man without a constituency. The bosses had the same reaction. Meade Esposito, the old-line Brooklyn machine leader, agreed to see him over a drink at the Rifle Club in Little Italy.

"I remember having a drink at the bar with Koch," Esposito remembers. "He asked, 'Can you support me?' I said, 'No' and that was that. He was a flaming liberal and a reformer."

Koch went to court the Bronx boss, Pat Cunningham, with equally miserable results. With Micki Wolter he bought a ticket to the machine's annual boat ride and while the two worked their way through the crowd, they bumped into Cunningham. A short

while before, Wolter had successfully managed the campaign of
a reform congressman who had defeated one of Cunningham's
candidates. Koch decided to boast about that to Cunningham.

"This is Micki Wolter, and I've got her," Koch said proudly,
as if that would impress Cunningham. It didn't. It only embarrassed Wolter. "I felt it naive in the extreme," she says.

Koch even dispatched an emissary to Cuomo in an effort to
persuade the architect of the Forest Hills compromise to run for
City Council president on a Koch ticket. Cuomo, who was contemplating a mayoral run of his own, refused.

Koch was unable to shake his image as an insular Manhattan-
ite and with good reason. While traveling in a car one day, he
told Mary Nichols he got "nosebleeds" anytime he left urbane
Manhattan for backwater Queens. On another occasion, he ate
with a group of Queens residents and could not go beyond the
quality of the spaghetti in dinner conversation. In a fair turn-
about, they found *him* boring. If his new schtick didn't sell in
Queens, he was done. And before long, it was obvious that his
campaign, which consisted primarily of shaking hands and passing out 80,000 lapel pins bearing the New York City flag, was
not working. Discussions began among his supporters over who
should be the one to tell him to drop out.

"I got a call from Victor Kovner," remembers Allen Schwartz,
who with Kovner had been law partners with Koch until he went
to Congress. "He said, 'Allen, tell Ed he has no chance. Tell him
to withdraw.' I said, 'How can I give Ed advice on something he
is expert in and I don't know anything about?' "

Finally, on March 28, seven weeks after he announced, Koch
abandoned the race, saying he could not raise enough money to
mount a successful media campaign. The mayoralty was won by
Abe Beame, and dispirited that he'd failed to attain the goal of
his life, Koch returned to Washington and resigned himself to a
career there.

"That was the last mayoral race I'm ever going to make," he
told Martin Tolchin, a *Times* Washington reporter. "That's it. I'm
going to devote myself to Congress. This is where I'm going to
make my mark. I love this place."

He plunged back into congressional life with an emphasis on
constituent service and a buckshot approach to the issues that
caught his fancy. He became embroiled in disputes over aid to
foreign governments as well as to local subways. Some of his

causes appealed to liberals. Others to conservatives. It became hard to detect patterns, other than that he was involved in so many causes his aides felt he was stretched too thin to be effective on any of them. He became known as a strong supporter of Israel, a loud critic of communist Russia, and an advocate of human rights just about everywhere. Lithuanians, Rumanians, and Ukrainians all got proclamations honoring their struggles for freedom. To be sure, Koch's efforts on behalf of such groups were not entirely altruistic. Consider a memo sent to him from a translator at the Library of Congress, who had complied with a Koch request that he translate a Hungarian document:

For: Representative Edward Koch

Translator's Note: As specified, only those parts of the pamphlet . . . were to be translated where the Congressman's name was mentioned.

Koch sometimes battled dictators, and in one case he almost singlehandedly forced the government to cut off military aid to Uruguay, an act for which he became convinced that the Uruguayan generals were going to have him killed. He just barely lost an attempt to force a similar cutoff to the Nicaraguan regime of Anastasio Somoza, but not before Somoza summoned him to a meeting in a suite in the Waldorf Towers where the strongman attempted to convince Koch his ideas about Somoza's government were wrong.

"We went to see Somoza in the penthouse suite," remembers Charles Flynn, a staff aide who was instrumental in focusing Koch on human rights issues. "We walked through eight or ten bodyguards, but it seemed more like forty. Koch said, 'This is great. I'm meeting with kings and tyrants.' We went in there and Somoza goes into this long, detailed thing about how Nicaragua is not part of the western judicial system but is part of the Napoleonic system. He was really blowing a lot of smoke. He also says it is not a dynasty, it is a Democratic republic. It just so happened that his family had long controlled the government. Ed is nodding the whole time and finally Somoza's son walks through the door. Koch points to him and says, 'Is this the next president of Nicaragua?' It caught Somoza totally off guard."

At home, Koch advocated more protection for the environment, more money for the subways, and guarantees that the truly needy would not suffer while changes were being made in the food stamp program. At the same time, he continued to distance himself from his liberal friends, as well as his own past, on some social issues. In 1976, for example, he introduced a bill in Congress calling for a study on whether integration through busing had helped or hurt education. Koch's own feelings were clear.

"As I review the situation, I am increasingly concerned that some of the racial balancing now imposed on schools is not helping achieve quality education, and that it may in fact be effecting a more regressive re-segregation because of middle-class 'flight' (both black and white) from the public schools and affected communities," he wrote in one of his regular constituent newsletters.

The bill alienated even more of his liberal backers, among them Nat Hentoff, a writer for *The Village Voice*. He remembers that Koch sounded him out on the idea and that they ended up in a shouting match because Hentoff believed that busing was too new for proper evaluation.

"It struck me that he was looking for a way to show that busing or anything else like it didn't work," Hentoff says. "I told him, 'It's a lousy thing you're doing.' "

Koch's staff was concerned that the bill would be seen as anti-black and told him so. One young staff member in particular approached Koch and suggested that Koch should get behind some issues that were viewed as problack.

"If you can find something I ought to do, I'll be glad to do it," Koch answered. As the aide began walking away, Koch had an afterthought. "Face it," he said. "Blacks don't vote."

Koch went ahead with his busing bill, even taking the unusual step of alerting the three television networks that he was holding an important press conference. However, he refused to tell them what the subject was, and so the networks didn't come. The bill went nowhere.

It was about this time that he, and just about everybody else in government, became interested in what was happening with New York's fiscal situation. By 1975, the city's short-term debt had climbed to nearly $6 billion, a sum so large that paying it would have consumed half the city budget for the entire year. Even the big banks that had been funding the city's hand-to-mouth existence became alarmed about its ability to repay. In the spring of that year, for the first time, they refused to lend the city more money.

With the likelihood that a city collapse would take the state with it, Governor Hugh L. Carey enlisted some of the best minds on Wall Street, union leaders, and politicians of both parties in an emergency rescue effort. The first step was the creation of the state Municipal Assistance Corporation with the plan that it would refinance city bonds, which were overdue, and issue new ones so the city could continue to function. Next came the Emergency Financial Control Board, another state agency, which was given the task of looking over the collective shoulder of Mayor Abe Beame and the rest of municipal government to make sure the books were balanced honestly. More than 20,000 city employees—from street sweepers to cops—were given pink slips in an effort to trim expenses. But even that was not enough, and so in November, the Federal Government reluctantly pitched in to loan the city $2.3 billion.

Ed Koch watched with growing interest, and began to think that the cloud over New York might contain a silver lining for him. Beame, elected in 1973, had clearly lost control of the government, which was now being run by Albany, the banks, the unions, and Washington. Near the end of 1975, Koch gathered his congressional staff and told them, "Get ready," because he was going to try again to become mayor in 1977. The reaction was hardly enthusiastic, with some suggesting that the best he could hope for would be a replay of 1973.

Nevertheless, he ordered them to start searching out issues that would give him citywide attention, and told them all it was crucial for him to win his congressional election in 1976 by the largest margin ever. For his part, Koch began focusing on local issues as never before. He wangled himself an appointment as an observer to the Emergency Financial Control Board. He began looking for waste and inefficiency in city programs on his own. And he even arranged for the police to give him a guided tour of midtown Manhattan. With wide-eyed astonishment, he reported to his constituents that "the seamy side of life was on exhibit with porno flicks, massage parlors, and porno book stores, for the most part legal, all competing for attention—along with some 300 prostitutes confronting passersby." Most of the people in his congressional district knew that already, but Ed Koch was out to make a name for himself. And quickly.

PACKAGING ED KOCH

On March 4, 1977, Ed Koch, for the second time, formally declared himself a candidate for mayor. This time, he believed he had the right issues to build a campaign around: "The continued threat of bankruptcy, the loss of more and more jobs and the steadily increasing crime rate." Abe Beame was "incompetent" but he, Ed Koch, was ready to captain the city of New York through its "darkest hour."

New Yorkers could not have cared less. A collective "Ed Who?" would have been heard if anybody had noticed him. Just how insignificant the body politic considered Ed Koch's announcement was made painfully clear to him that very night. He had thrown himself a party at a Manhattan restaurant called Charlie O's with some supporters—many from his young congressional staff—who had pledged to help him pursue his dream. In the midst of the festivities, someone went out for the early editions of the morning papers. The first to come back was the *Daily News*. It had a fourteen-paragraph story on political developments, with the top of the story devoted to Bella Abzug, a long-time Koch nemesis, saying she was a potential candidate for mayor. Koch's press conference to announce his candidacy was not mentioned until the twelfth paragraph.

Next came the *Times*. It led its political story of the day with Koch's announcement, and ran a picture of him. Not bad. But the second paragraph said that one of Koch's first tasks would be to "scotch skepticism over the seriousness of his candidacy." There was a thinly veiled suggestion in both papers that the real candidates had not yet announced and that early entries like Koch—he was the second man to announce—would fall by the wayside as soon as things got serious. Like bleached cattle bones in the desert, the remains of the campaign riffraff would soon dot the landscape.

Being considered a throwaway candidate was something that Koch had feared and he did not need the *Times* to remind him how important it was that he overcome the image of a loser. Otherwise, the perception that he could be ignored would take on a life of its own and his campaign would be over before it started. He had seen it happen so often to good candidates—people who, for one reason or another, never really got to talk about the issues because they were always having to explain why they were running. It had happened to him his last time out of the gate in 1973.

But Koch, of course, had more than a professional reason for wanting to be taken seriously. Politics was his whole life. A result of his one-dimensional existence was that he was still an outsider in any setting that was not strictly political. Of course, the glare of success that comes with being a highly regarded congressman often prevented people from seeing how isolated he was, especially strangers and political groupies. But he knew all too well who and what he really was.

"Ed Koch has always been the guy with his face pressed against the glass," says David Garth, who would help him overcome that image. "He's the uncle you don't invite to the wedding because he's too Jewish."

It had been that way ever since high school in Newark, and Koch needed to get on the inside. He had devoted himself to his career in an effort to make it happen, and now his career was on the line. It is not an exaggeration to say his whole life was also on the line. Years later, he would tell an aide that he would have killed himself if he had not won in 1977. For now, he had simply said there would never be another chance. He had told his congressional staff that, after his aborted attempt in 1973, the '77 mayoral race would be his last chance to go for the brass ring. Another loss would mark him as a hopeless loser, the Harold Stassen of New York City. A two-time loser in New York politics is looked upon with as much expectation as yesterday's garbage and has about as much chance being elected Mayor. No, Koch said, if he did not make it in 1977, there would not be a third campaign. If he lost this time, he could look forward to spending the rest of his days as a maverick congressman, standing outside City Hall, the State House, and the White House shouting at those who had the real power. Sure, he was a congressman, but New York had seventeen congressmen and their number made them all relatively anonymous outside their districts. And as long as he stayed where he was, the issues would always be the same—neighborhoods, transit, housing, and crime. Worse, the people would always bring the problems to him, and he would have to go hammering at those who had the power to solve them. Could anyone blame him for being tired of that?

And all the traveling back and forth between Washington and New York was getting to him as well. Like a laboratory rat on a treadmill, he often felt doomed to riding the airline shuttle every week, shaking hands here, attending endless committee and House meetings there. A continuation of that life was the best he could hope for if he lost this time. The worst was getting kicked out of the business altogether. He had seen that happen too. Politicians who seemed unbeatable in their districts, who had waited in the wings for years to get seniority on congressional committees, then watched helplessly as everything went down the drain in an instant because young turks cut the legs out from under them in their districts. Hadn't the VID done just that to Carmine DeSapio? The district is always the weakest chink in the armor of any politician. Koch knew that. That's why he worked his district so hard. But he couldn't keep it up forever. Someday, someone would come along, maybe in a year, maybe in ten years, and simply persuade the voters that it was time for a change. If that happened to him, Koch would have to go back to practicing law. He knew he couldn't do that—he had gotten too used to eating regularly.

Despite the stakes and the long odds, Koch exuded confidence and impressed his small campaign staff with a single-minded sense of purpose. His street-corner oratorical skills, tirelessness, and uncanny ability to sense the mood and beliefs of his audience would now come into play. The absence of a family or any other deep personal attachments would assure Koch's total commitment to the pursuit of his dream. But Koch's 1973 debacle had convinced him it was impossible to succeed with the doorbell-and-handshake approach to campaigning that had served him so well in more modest races. To reach the voters of a city as vast and complex as New York, Koch would need an extensive and effective media campaign and the money to finance it.

The new approach became apparent the moment he announced his candidacy. For he did not go alone to the podium at his news conference in the New York Hilton. He was surrounded by three people: Jack McGregor, David Garth, and Bess Myerson. McGregor, the executive vice president of the New England Petroleum Corporation, was invited in the hope that the press would view him as a big contributor, the kind who, along with a few well-heeled friends, could buy Koch respectability. McGregor, however, would eventually prove insignificant. Quite the opposite must be said about Garth and Myerson. Over the course of the next nine months, they would do more than anybody else to make Ed Koch Mayor. Indeed, they probably did more for him than he did for himself. Without them, he would have failed miserably. Garth, the media wizard, would package the ugly duckling, the flaky congressman, in such a skillful manner that Koch would steadily become the most attractive candidate. His virtues blazing, his weaknesses concealed behind Garth's glossy commercials, Koch would soon become, if not a household word, at least a familiar face. There was no sense in trying to give Koch a Kennedy-like image, the rugged outdoorsman walking the beach with a jacket jauntily thrown over his shoulder. Talking is what Koch does best, so Garth would have him on television, talking to voters about their city and what he wanted to do for it. Never mind that Koch didn't know much about many of the problems—he would learn and, when necessary, he would claim as his own the ideas of others.

If glamour was to be part of the Koch campaign, it would have to come from Myerson, a homegrown Miss America and the only Jewish woman to win the title. As she had during his opening announcement, she would stand by Koch's side throughout the campaign so that it was virtually impossible to get a picture of him without having her in the lens as well. The strategy was to have her beauty and popularity translate into credibility for Koch. In an odd sort of way, the funny-looking outsider who could never get a girl now had *the* girl. That there was nothing romantic between them, that they were merely packaged together to humanize Ed Koch, did not prevent them from encouraging suggestions that Koch's bachelorhood would end in a dramatic marriage to Miss America. So much the better to deflect inevitable speculation about whether Koch was a homosexual.

The backdrop of the campaign would be Beame and his handling of the city's mounting fiscal woes. The layoffs of thousands of workers, combined with a general demoralization of the remaining work force, was taking its toll on services in the city. New York was slipping, and the question was not when will things improve, but rather, will they improve. But there would be others factors in the campaign as well, some of them fateful, such as a massive power failure that would spawn a night of looting and lawlessness in the ghettos. Then would come the conclusion of the Son of Sam drama, as New Yorkers ignored the candidates to focus their attention on the gory exploits and capture of the maniacal .44-caliber killer who shot thirteen young men and women. Even the federal government would play a role in the mayoral contest. A Securities and Exchange Commission staff report would accuse Beame and others in government of misleading investors regarding the shaky condition of city finances. The campaign would be the most expensive in city history, with the candidates spending more than $6 million, some of it in questionable payments of thousands of dollars to political leaders to line up voters. Finally, in its stretch run, the 1977 campaign for Mayor would degenerate into a gutter fight, with an exchange of smears ugly even for New York. Koch was labeled a homosexual; his chief opponent, Mario Cuomo, was rumored to have Mafia ties. Some saw the election as pitting Catholics against Jews. Koch would be accused of using racial code words and of pitting blacks against whites.

Koch would need money as well as support from many people to survive such turbulence in a grueling marathon that would eventually require him to win three elections before claiming City Hall. He would get what he needed, but help in politics always carries a price tag. The coin of the realm is patronage—jobs—in exchange for support, and Koch would make his promises to black and Hispanic leaders and party bosses. He would bow to pressure from Rupert Murdoch, the publisher of the *New York Post*, and promise to appoint a Murdoch favorite to a high position in his administration in order to get the *Post*'s endorsement. But all that would come later, much later. In the beginning, the heavyweights were Garth and Myerson. Koch, the candidate, was an extra in his own drama.

David Garth is a smallish, plump man with close-cropped silvery hair and a penchant for small cigars. Forty-seven years old when Koch hired him, he had made his name in New York politics handling the two successful mayoral campaigns of John V. Lindsay, in 1965 and 1969. The second victory was especially sweet because Lindsay was widely unpopular after his first term and the Republican Party, to which Lindsay belonged, had even denied him its nomination. Garth confronted the unpopularity issue head on, and ordered up a batch of commercials in which Lindsay said "I made mistakes." In 1974, Garth scored an even more impressive electoral victory by helping to make Hugh L. Carey Governor of New York. New Jersey Governor Brendan Byrne had come to Garth when he faced the Lindsay dilemma as he ran for a second term. He won and so did Tom Bradley as Mayor of Los Angeles, another Garth client.

Garth lost a few, too, such as John V. Tunney's bid to be reelected as a California senator, but his successes were so well publicized that candidates were in bidding wars to get his services as though his name alone guaranteed them at least respectability if not victory. Soon after he agreed to work for Koch, Koch called him a "genius" and used his name as a calling card with potential campaign contributors. He dispatched a fund-raising letter that hailed Garth as the miracle man who had taken Carey from obscurity and made him governor.

"He can do the same for me," Koch wrote in a pitch for money. "But to accomplish this, we must raise at least $800,000—if we do, David Garth believes I have a real chance to win." With such a reputation, Garth's fees rose astronomically, and by the time Koch hired him, Garth was getting up to $15,000 a month plus commissions of 15 percent of the cost of putting commercials on television. Even when his candidates lost, Garth won, pulling in over $250,000 a year for himself. Though he says he never works for a candidate he doesn't like, he knows that a politician is, well, a politician first and last. Above his desk hangs a quotation attributed to an earlier political advisor, one by the name of Machiavelli. It is Garth's warning to himself: "Whoever causes another to become powerful is ruined," Machiavelli said, "because he creates such power either with skill or with force; both these factors are viewed with suspicion by the one who has become powerful."

He showed the sign to Koch one day, saying, "This has never been proven untrue."

"In my case, it won't be true," Koch responded.

Garth tells the story, waves his hand with a laugh, and says,

"Bullshit. Read his book." Koch's book, *Mayor*, reduces Garth to a bit player in the 1977 campaign and disparages him later. Myerson's name would not be mentioned except in a picture caption.

As the campaign got under way, Garth was busy trying to package Ed Koch. They had been introduced in the middle of 1976, when Myerson, who knew both, had them to a dinner party at her house. It was no accidental meeting. Koch had asked Myerson to arrange it so he could feel Garth out before deciding whether to try to hire him. Soon afterward, Koch called Garth and asked him to lunch. There he talked about his plans to run for mayor the following year and asked Garth whether he was interested. Garth said he was committed to Mario Cuomo, then Secretary of State, and that he had been trying to persuade Cuomo to run against Beame. Koch said he understood, and asked Garth to keep him in mind if things did not work out with Cuomo.

"Mario Cuomo was a friend and he is the only guy I have asked to run for office," Garth says. "We talked about it for three or four months. Koch approached me about the same time. He said, 'I know that if Mario runs you will do him but if not, would you do me?' I said fine. I thought he was a good congressman, but I didn't think he had a chance to be Mayor."

While Koch worked at tempering his liberal image by getting involved in issues outside his congressional district, Cuomo agonized over whether to run against Beame. After what seemed an eternity, Garth gave Cuomo an ultimatum: yes or no. Cuomo said no.

"I called Koch and said, 'OK, you're a twenty-to-one shot but we'll make the best shot we can,'" Garth said.

With Maureen Connelly, his Tab-drinking young assistant, Garth began mapping an advertising campaign to help Koch shed his nebbish image and make him a household name. As he always does, Garth began by polling to gather information about the voters. Who are they? What are they concerned about? What do they like, and dislike, in politicians? What newspapers do different racial, ethnic, and income groups read? What are their television and radio habits? What did they think of Ed Koch? More importantly, had they ever heard of Ed Koch? The answers would be crucial to determine what kind of package Garth would wrap his client in for delivery to the voters. Garth also dispatched Connelly to research Koch's record. Everything positive and negative had to be compiled so that Koch's strengths could be superimposed on the wishes of the voters and his weaknesses concealed.

On November 11, 1976, Connelly reported back to Garth. The news was mixed. Koch's congressional record was considered good, but it presented problems in terms of what the polls showed the majority of voters in New York wanted. The polls had reflected widespread resentment in the so-called outer boroughs—Brooklyn, Queens, the Bronx, and Staten Island—toward Manhattan, the rich, glamorous core of New York. By a margin of more than 2 to 1, those polled said they agreed with the statement that "Manhattan officials don't understand the problems faced by most New Yorkers." Koch, who had once joked that he got nosebleeds by going to Queens, was typecast as a Manhattan politician—liberal, single, and a lawyer. Connelly correctly saw that as a trouble spot, and her research on Koch had turned up little in his record to smooth it over.

"At this point," she wrote to Garth, "it appears that most of Koch's major initiatives—privacy, equal credit, congressional reform, etc—will not appeal to voters outside of Manhattan. The fiscal crisis and crime are the two most important issues, according to our poll. Koch has done virtually nothing in the area of crime control and *The Almanac of American Politics* pointed out that his sudden conversion to "law and order" in 1973 cost him support among the liberals in Manhattan and non-Manhattanites didn't believe him." Connelly might have added, but didn't, that Koch had done little about the fiscal crisis because he was not then, nor ever would be, good on the intricate numbers of budget making. In short, Garth had a client whose strengths were shortcomings to most voters and who was lacking in the two areas the voters cared about most. Moreover, only 6 percent of the voters outside his district had even heard of Koch—hardly a figure to inspire the notion of electability.

There was another problem, too. The question that had dogged Koch since his Village days was almost certain to come up again: Was he a homosexual? Garth is not one to mince words. He asked Koch for the truth. "If you've got a problem—personal, sexual, or criminal—I want to know now," Garth said to him. Koch said there was nothing. Garth had heard rumors about "boyfriends" and that sort of thing, and says he checked out "five or six stories." He will not say how he checked them out, except that he had "sources" run down every rumor until he was sure it was just that. Garth says he believes that Koch was hiding nothing, if only because the stakes and visibility were too high. "If he was, I'll give him a 10 on consummate acting," Garth says. "And a 10 on balls." Still, innuendo and appearance can be as damaging as fact in politics, and Koch was, after all, an unattached bachelor from Greenwich Village. Not only was the city not ready for a gay mayor, Garth believed, but a nasty campaign full of innuendo would be enough to do his candidate in. An antidote had to be found. Its name was Bess.

Born and raised in the Bronx, Bess Myerson was named Miss America in 1945—while Ed Koch was still in the Army. She was 21, very beautiful, and smart. That was the first year the judges in Atlantic City added talent to the swimsuit and other "looks" aspect of the contest. Myerson, who had attended the High School of Music and Art and Hunter College, played the Grieg piano concerto and some Gershwin on the flute. Jewish New Yorkers exulted when the crown was placed on her head, the victory yet another confirmation that they were Americans, too. Myerson used the scholarship she won for postgraduate studies at Columbia University. Over the years, she married twice and divorced twice and had a daughter. In 1969, she went to work as part of the best-and-brightest crew Lindsay took to City Hall, becoming his Commissioner of Consumer Affairs. She and Koch, who were about as unlike as any two people can get, were thus traveling in similar circles, and it was then they met.

She left the government in 1972 to take a number of consultant jobs, working for banks, Bristol-Myers, and *Redbook* magazine. She also found time to write a column for the *Daily News* and dispensed consumer advice on television. Her beauty had remained pretty much intact and her name was often floated as a political possibility. After seeing what she could do for Koch, she would later run for office herself, making an unsuccessful run for the United States Senate. But in 1976, she decided she wanted to help Ed Koch. She invited Koch and Garth over for dinner, and leaned on Garth to take Koch on as a client. She promised she would do whatever was needed to help. What that would mean became obvious when Koch announced his candidacy. Reporters on hand made jokes about how she strained to be in all the camera angles at the same time. It would go on like that for months—Bess and Ed, Ed and Bess. Beautiful, Jewish, and popular, she would have been an asset to any candidate. For Koch, she was a lifesaver: she was a woman, and a maturely sexy one at that. Garth quickly saw to it that she was seen with his bachelor candidate as much as possible. He made her chairman of the campaign and even put them together on Koch's campaign posters. "It may be the only campaign poster in history that has the candidate and a woman who wasn't the candidate with him," Garth says now with a knowing smile.

As the campaign wore on, Koch and Bess were seen holding hands, whispering, smiling, giving long, languid looks at each other. It was all playacting, but the public fell for it. Instead of "Is Koch gay?" the questions became "Are they lovers?" and "Will they marry?" Often they were asked about their relationship, and their answers were full of suggestive tones, smiles and vague descriptions. "We're good friends," they would say. Sometimes they declared coquettishly that they never discussed their private lives in public. Once Koch told a reporter, "You will be the first to know after I tell my father." Another time, he said marriage could not be ruled out.

"It is always a possibility, but I don't want to talk about it," the candidate said. "She's an incredible person—a warm human being that I really adore."

In a narrow sense, Koch and Myerson gave truthful answers. They were friends, and anything is possible. But, at the same time, their answers and the flirting were false, for there was nothing romantic between them. The suggestions to the contrary were designed to mislead the public, to put to rest the notion that Koch was gay.

"She was an ambitious woman and I don't think they had a personal relationship," says Edward Costikyan, who later became, with Myerson, cochairman of Koch's campaign after briefly running himself. "It was a David Garth creation. David saw that one of Koch's liabilities was his bachelorhood so he created a mate. It was part of an effort to humanize Koch. I never saw the slightest exhibition of emotional attraction between them."

Bernard Rome was the Koch campaign treasurer. "There was no romantic linkage, none," he says, adding that the strategy was simple. "From Koch's point of view, the one thing that could undo him was an allegation of homosexuality." Rome, who subsequently broke with Koch, is the only member of the campaign inner circle who is known to have asked Koch about his relationship with Myerson. The impetus was a remark by Rome's mother-in-law, who after hosting a fund raiser for Koch attended by Myerson, asked Rome why Koch didn't marry Myerson. Rome replied, "Oh, mother, there's nothing serious between them." His mother chipped in with, "I understand that, but it would be very good for his career."

The remark stuck in Rome's head until, several days later, he and Koch were having dinner together.

"By the way," Rome said, "everybody is talking about you marrying Bess."

Koch did not respond.

"They say it would be good for your career," Rome offered.

This time Koch's silence was accompanied by an icy stare across the table. Rome never mentioned the subject again.

Myerson still refuses to discuss her feelings for Koch, but she did offer an unflattering assessment of him soon after he was elected. "Just remember," she warned Peter Solomon, who was going to work for Koch. "He's a man always alone. He's so alone he never even walks a dog."

Because he is a devotee of television, Garth was perfectly content to let Koch take charge of what he regarded as a secondary operation—day-to-day campaigning. It was something Koch knew well and he waded in with enthusiasm. He campaigned on the streets from early morning to late at night with a handful of young staff members. Leon Roday, a young man from Long Island, became the candidate's driver, advance man and all-purpose, six-teen-hour-a-day aide.

Roday showed up as a volunteer at Koch's campaign headquarters in early June. He had never met Koch and knew very little about him. Roday was quickly pressed into full-time service because there were so few volunteers. His desirability was enhanced by his twelve-year-old Chevy Malibu—a car that Koch quickly commandeered.

"It was in good running condition but it didn't look too pretty," Roday says. "All the upholstery was sort of coming out. We had no car in the damn campaign. This is pretty bad—this is the guy running for the Mayor of the City of New York."

Roday chauffeured Koch in the Malibu to a campaign appearance in Queens. Driver, car, and candidate made it, but it was clear the old car with frayed upholstery would not take Ed Koch to City Hall. The next day, the campaign rented a car and Roday became the driver. Eventually, the campaign would move up to a rented Winnebago.

"I always felt my Malibu was responsible for the campaign moving into the modern age," Roday laughs.

Over a three-month period from June to September, Roday spent almost every day with Koch. By his own description, Roday was unschooled politically, even naive, but it quickly became evident even to him that Koch was a long shot. And everyone seemed to know—except Koch.

"Koch always seemed confident," Roday remembers. "He always seemed to know where he was going and how he was going to get there."

Koch's drive was not lost on others. Joyce Purnick, then a political reporter for the *Post*, covered Koch on the campaign trail early in the race, before Garth's television commercials began to give him widespread public exposure. She was amazed—and impressed—by his refusal to waste even a few moments of free time. On one occasion, a campaign event in lower Manhattan was cancelled and Koch found himself with thirty minutes to kill before his next scheduled appearance.

"He turns to his staff and says, 'Come on, we're going to the World Trade Center,' " Purnick recalled. "They got over to the Trade Center concourse and Koch spends his time shaking hands. He was driven, determined. Most other candidates would have gone out for coffee, but not him. And that was before anyone was taking him seriously. It made me think about what he was doing."

On a typical campaign day, Koch would ride with Roday in the Winnebago, which the campaign had dubbed the "Kochmobile." It was plastered with posters and a tape deck blared a song called "N.Y.C." from the Broadway show *Annie*.

The composer, Charles Strouse, had given the Koch campaign permission to use the song. Strouse was introduced to Koch after the campaign as the composer. Ever grateful, Koch told him: "If I have to hear that song one more time, I'm going to kill myself."

The song was heard all over the city as Koch went from neighborhood to neighborhood, from subway stop to senior citizen center, shaking hands and talking, always talking. More often than not, people saw an Ed Koch quite different from the one Garth would project on television. Koch was sometimes a clown, sometimes a bully, sometimes a cheerleader. Those who encountered him in the streets got a glimpse of the brassy style that would become a trademark. Many got it via bullhorn.

"I would always be the one carrying the bullhorn," Roday said. "He would say, 'Hello, I'm Ed Koch. Nice to see you.' "

The difficulty was that Koch did his talking through the bullhorn while the citizen who stumbled into conversation with him had only a voice to rely on. Mickey Carroll of the *Times* recalls one such encounter at a campaign stop near Penn Station.

"Leon had the bullhorn and Koch was saying, 'I'm Congressman Koch, how'm I doin'?' Well, some poor guy comes by and says, 'You're doing pretty good except on . . . ' and then he mentions some issue. That was it. 'What!' Koch lights into him with the bullhorn. The guy repeats himself. Koch challenges him through the bullhorn 'What do you mean!' The guy says, 'I like you except on' whatever the issue was. Koch kept blaring at him through the bullhorn and sent him scurrying away. That was the first time I realized how belligerent the bugger was."

Microphones were a boon to Koch and he knew there were more around than most people imagine. All you need is to walk into a supermarket to find one and have enough nerve to ask to use it.

"He would do things I'm sure many candidates would feel uncomfortable doing," recalls campaign volunteer Kenneth Halpern. "If there was a neighborhood shopping center, he'd go to the supermarket, he'd find the manager and say, 'I'm Ed Koch. I'm running for mayor. Would you mind if I used the microphone?' Then he'd go to the mike and say, 'Hi, shoppers, I'm Ed Koch. I'm running for mayor. I just want to say hello. Let me take a minute to tell you something about myself.' Then he'd do a two- or three-minute spiel with some humor, and I think it left a good impression."

All of this suited Garth. The long daily schedule kept Koch busy in his element and gave the newspapers and television crews something to cover. Just so Myerson stayed close to Koch.

The day Koch declared his candidacy there was officially only one other hat in the Democratic ring. It belonged to Percy Sutton, the Manhattan borough president and a long-time leader of the city's growing black community. Over the next few months, nearly a dozen Democrats would test the waters, with some, like Ed Costikyan, never getting much beyond the trial-balloon stage. By the September primary, the field would shake out to seven candidates: Beame entered after being urged not to run by many of the powers that be; Abzug took the plunge and immediately became the favorite; Herman Badillo, a liberal Hispanic congressman from the Bronx; Joel Harnett, a largely unknown civic activist; and finally, Cuomo, who, after changing his mind, announced on May 10. Cuomo was immediately dubbed the puppet candidate of Governor Carey. For months, Cuomo had resisted the governor's entreaties that he run, and eventually agreed to do so as much from exhaustion as desire for the job. For his part, Carey had come to believe that Beame, a quiet 71-year-old accountant, was no longer capable of dealing with the city's massive problems.

Carey had reached his conclusions about Beame by 1975, when the extent of the city's fiscal crisis was evident. As comptroller, Beame should have known about the bookkeeping gimmicks that obscured the fact that the city was spending more money than it was taking in and that borrowing to cover the difference was getting out of hand. But Beame didn't know, or at least had said he didn't. He had also said that it was the Mayor's job to know such things. By 1975, he was saying the Mayor couldn't know every detail of the budget. Either of those statements might be true, but taken together, it was clear Beame accepted no responsibility for the problem. That was unacceptable to many New Yorkers, Carey among them, and he began an effort to replace Beame. He tabbed Cuomo, even going so far as asking Koch to drop out and Garth to work for him. Both, of course, declined.

The minute Cuomo announced his candidacy, politicians and editorial writers placed him at or near the top of the pack. Since the days when he mediated the Forest Hills housing dispute, Cuomo had cultivated the press. He was obviously intelligent and thoughtful, often discussing social issues in moral rather than political terms. Never mind that he'd never won elective office. His candidacy was viewed as the second coming and Garth was forced to revise his estimates of the odds against Koch. Instead of 20 to 1, Garth told his client, he was now a 40-to-1 shot.

"The day Abzug announced was the first real low day in the

Koch campaign," said one volunteer. "The day Cuomo announced was the second. It seemed that one of them would win."

The seven candidates were generally divided into three groups in terms of their chances of winning. Cuomo, Abzug and Beame were regarded as having fairly equal chances, while Koch was lumped with Sutton and Badillo as having little or no chance. Harnett was in it just for the thrill, but the others didn't seem to mind. As long as he stayed in, it meant that none of the others would suffer the humiliation of coming in last.

For Koch, the problem was obvious. Being lumped as an also-ran made it difficult for him to get press attention, and without press attention, getting himself known throughout the city was virtually impossible. There was even some question of whether Koch could collect the required 10,000 signatures of registered Democrats to qualify for the primary. Of the seven candidates, Koch collected the fewest signatures—23,048—1,200 fewer than Harnett and 80,000 fewer than Beame. Abzug, Cuomo, Sutton and Badillo all turned in at least 48,000 signatures. Koch's total was so low the party bosses did not bother to exercise the time-honored rite of challenging the signatures. The challenges, ostensibly designed to make sure those who sign petitions are qualified, are in reality the organization's chief weapon of preventing upstart opponents from getting on the ballot without regular party support. Thus, the regulars look for misspellings, wrong addresses, and other minor errors that could make a signature invalid. But they did not do that with Koch because they believed his only contribution would be to take votes away from Cuomo and Abzug. Stanley Friedman, now the Bronx party boss, was Beame's top political operative in 1977 and was part of the decision not to challenge Koch's petitions. Somewhat ruefully, he says now, the party was convinced that the challenges could have blocked Koch from getting on the primary ballot.

The only way for Koch to counteract the forces against him was through television, which cuts across all income, racial, and ethnic groups. But buying air time is expensive—up to $5,000 for 30 seconds. On top of that were production costs and Garth's cut. Fund raising was neither fun nor his forte. In part he considered it begging, not unlike the days he was hustling for tips in Krueger's Auditorium. And getting a yes from contributors is generally possible only when the big spenders believe the candidate has a chance to win. In short, Koch was trapped in a vicious circle. And his personality wasn't helping. Despite a penchant for street speaking and shaking hands, he had a habit of getting into arguments with people if they did not agree with him. That can be devastating to a candidate who is known to only 6 percent of the voters to begin with. The point was driven home to the Koch campaign in April at the Ninth Avenue Food Festival, a mile-long gastronomic bazaar that draws hundreds of thousands of people to a street feast. The event, with block after block of booths set up to sell ready-to-eat foods of virtually every ethnic group in the city, is a street campaigner's dream. Or it should be, but Koch struck out there in 1977. He worked his way through food and crowds from 59th Street to 39th Street, having no trouble with the food, but the people were something else.

"I would say that one or two people recognized him," remembers campaign volunteer Kenneth Halpern. One of those who recognized Koch was a woman who lived in his congressional district.

"He picked a fight with her," Halpern said. "She said something innocuous, complaining about one of those things that it would have been very easy to say, 'Look, I'll look into it.' He didn't believe what she was saying was true, and said, 'That's ridiculous.' She was just disgusted and walked away."

Koch was doing the same sort of things as he made his rounds at the political clubs throughout the city. In the beginning, he was doing a lot of commuting from Washington, coming to New York as often as possible to go to the clubs at night. There, he would speak to meetings that averaged only about twenty people, telling them he wanted their support and answering questions. As often as not, according to aides who accompanied him, Koch got into arguments with the people whose support he had come to ask for. Then he would head out the door, on his way to another club, and, often, another argument.

At the same time, there was a positive side to being part of such a large field seeking the nomination. With so many candidates, the vote was guaranteed to be split and any candidate need only build on the base of support he or she supposedly started with to be a contender. Moreover, election laws stipulate that if no candidate receives at least 40 percent of the vote in the party primary, a runoff of the top two finishers must be held. That a runoff would be necessary was viewed as a foregone conclusion early in the 1977 campaign not only because of the size of the field but because it was an ethnic potpourri. Beame, the city's first Jewish mayor, got most of his support from middle-class Jews in Brooklyn and Queens. Cuomo, as the only Italian in the race, could count on his ethnic brethren in Queens and Staten Island. Badillo, a Puerto Rican, had a largely Hispanic Bronx constituency, while Sutton's supporters were mostly black. Abzug, the only woman, had liberal Jews, women, and much of affluent Manhattan in her camp. The division along racial and religious lines led editorial writers at the *Times* to predict, accurately, that 175,000 votes would be enough to qualify for a mayoral runoff in a city with more than 7 million people. The paper warned that the campaign was spawning a dangerous and growing sense of "tribalism."

All of that suited Koch just fine. Despite a perception that he needed to show how he was different from the other candidates, he knew that all he had to do was skim a few votes from each of the front runners in each borough while doing well in his own district. As a Jew from Manhattan with a liberal image, he aimed especially to get some of Abzug's voters and some of Beame's. In addition, he went for some of Cuomo's by making numerous trips to the outer boroughs, where he espoused the law-and-order philosophy he had suddenly adopted in 1973.

Garth saw the opposition this way: "You had Bella, who was a flamer. You had Mario, the finagler. You had Badillo, passion." Polls showed that those three, plus Beame, all were well known by the voters, but were not necessarily well liked. To Garth, that meant there was an opening for an unknown candidate to slip in if the voters would trust him. He sized up his client this way: "Koch didn't look like John Lindsay. He was never the flashy guy who went out for the long pass. He was the Bronco Nagurski of politics, three yards and a cloud of dust." The strategy was to package Koch as the "issues" candidate, a no-nonsense, down-to-earth New Yorker who was angry about what had happened to his city. He would fight to protect every nickel coughed up by the abused middle-class taxpayers, and would not shrink from taking on the special interests, especially the municipal unions backing Beame. In short, he would do everything he could to become the candidate the polls said the voters wanted. Especially the white, middle-class voters in the outer boroughs. There were a few accessories to the strategy. First, Koch had to lose 25 pounds—he weighed over 205—so Garth put him on a diet and exercise regimen. Second, Koch had to think before talking. Garth did not want any wiseass comments damaging the image. And, of course, Bess had to always be there for the pictures.

All the candidates shared Garth's view that television was essential, that nobody was going to handshake his or her way into City Hall in 1977. It just couldn't be done in a city as large as New York, especially in the age of television. So the scramble was on for money to buy air time. The big money from the fatcat insiders was going to Beame, who as an incumbent, still had the power to reward and punish, and to Cuomo, whose relationship with Carey made fund raising all the easier. Except for a few people, such as David Margolis, head of Colt Industries, the firearms maker, Koch knew very few rich, powerful people to whom he could turn for contributions. Raising money was like pulling teeth, and the campaign took on a Sad Sack quality. Early on, Allen Schwartz, Koch's old law partner, visited Koch's congressional office in lower Manhattan and listened to how poorly things were going.

"I left and started walking to the elevator and went back with a check for $500," Schwartz remembers. "I felt sorry for him. That's why I did it."

When Koch began wooing Garth in 1976, he had $50,000 in campaign funds in the bank, a surplus from his last congressional race, but a pitiful sum in high-stakes New York City politics. By January 1977, he'd upped that by only $13,120, and by May had increased his bankroll to $311,944. Still not much, considering the fact that the opening ante to retain Garth was a quarter million dollars. With a few aides, Koch turned to hustling money at small fund-raising parties or pleading for even small donations over the telephone.

"The first meeting I went to was with fifty-nine of his quote-unquote friends in Bess Myerson's apartment. Only a handful of his friends gave any money, maybe nine of the fifty-nine, and Margolis and I gave him $4,000, most of what he got," remembers Rome, the campaign treasurer. "Let's say that someone would give us a fund raiser. They would invite all their friends to their apartment and we could come. Maybe thirty people would be there. Ed would talk to them and afterwards he would get a list and call and say, 'Would you help me?' It was very difficult to raise money that way. Koch also wasn't a particularly good speaker at the affairs. He was the congressman from the silk-stocking district, yet he was terribly uncomfortable in fine homes in his own district. He was not a wealthy guy, and he would make this speech about what a wonderful home it was. Every once in a while he would see these businessmen sitting there and would seem to feel that they were thinking that he, Ed Koch, was not able to run this city. He used to say, 'There may be many people more able than I, but they aren't running.' I think this reflected what he felt, that he felt somewhat inadequate."

New York *Daily News* columnist Ken Auletta witnessed Koch the fund raiser in action, and reported on a call Koch placed to Marcel Lindenbaum, owner of a New Jersey propane gas company. As Auletta described it, ". . . the phone rang. A total stranger was calling. 'Mr. Lindenbaum,' Ed Koch introduced himself, 'I'm running for mayor and need your help . . . Would you donate $1,000 to my campaign?' Lindenbaum was stunned. Koch persisted, refusing to let his victim go. Back and forth they went, until Lindenbaum surrendered, agreeing to donate $200.

"An aide whispered something and suddenly Koch exclaimed, 'Now I know who you are. You're the stepson of Max Stern, and you should give more than $200. Would you give us $500? I'm going to be the next mayor. Will you do that?' With no escape, Lindenbaum promised to send $500."

Occasionally, after one of Koch's pitches, someone would promise a substantial contribution and offer to send a check through the mail. But that is an old dodge, and Koch took no chances. "We'd tell them, 'No, don't mail the checks,' and then we'd send someone right out to pick them up," remembers one aide. Things got so desperate once that Koch sent an aide to the bank to withdraw money from his own account—$10,000—and Koch was scared he was wasting his meager life savings. But he declared the money a loan and got it back later. Winners always have a surplus of cash. Losers have debts."

Sometimes, according to Rome, Koch would get very, very lucky in his quest for money.

"We went to a fund raiser in the Village. There were nine or ten people there. One was a very nice, quiet elderly lady. She sat there and didn't say a word. Afterwards, I left with some of the people who were there. They weren't impressed by Ed. I didn't think anything more about the evening. The next thing I know Ed calls up the woman and asks for money. She was very

wealthy. She says, 'I'll send you $10,000.' This was fantastic and
we did, in fact, get $10,000 from her. A month goes by and Koch
calls a lot of people back. He calls the woman again. She says to
him, 'Did I contribute before?' He said, 'Yes, and we hate to have
to come back.' She asked, 'How much did I contribute?' He told
her ten. She sent another ten and a third ten. He had never met
her before and this woman gave all that money. It was the kind
of dumb luck that he had."

By the middle of September, Koch had raised nearly $900,000,
an impressive amount, but still less than some of his rivals, including Cuomo, who was then bankrolled for $1.4 million. Most
of Koch's money came in relatively small donations from people
who didn't belong to the circle of wealthy real estate, construction, financial and business executives who make the city's heaviest political contributions. Not that Koch hadn't tried to get help
from these people, but their rejection allowed him to paint himself as a consummate outsider. Not only could he crow that he
was disdained by the bosses—the clubhouse—but he could also
declare that he was beholden to none of the big-money boys. "You
turn your weaknesses into strengths," Maureen Connelly says.
The money Koch raised did not sit around in cookie jars. More
than anyone, Rome, the treasurer, knew why. Garth was pouring most of it into television. "He'd call up and say, 'How much
money is in the bank?' " Rome remembers. "When I'd tell him,
he'd say, 'Send it over.' " Eventually, Rome began asking Garth
how much he needed, to which Garth inevitably responded,
"How much do you have?" Concerned that all the campaign's
money was being taken by Garth, Rome one day refused to send
any more. Koch, trailing a few key aides, soon stalked into Rome's
office and demanded to know what the problem was. Rome told
him his concerns, and Koch responded by asking how much
money was in the bank.

"We've got $29,000," Rome answered.

"So why can't we give Garth $27,000 or $28,000?" Koch and
the others asked.

"Ed, you want to have a responsible campaign," Rome said.
"All these guys are running up bills. And you're giving Garth all
the money. We owe the printer $50,000."

Koch's response stunned Rome.

"Look, I want to be on television," Koch said. "I don't care
what, I don't care how much debt. I don't care."

So Garth got the money, and Rome learned a lesson. The campaign would soon begin borrowing to meet its expenses.

Apart from winning fights over money, Garth was busy sticking ribbons and bows on the packaged Ed Koch he'd soon be delivering to the television stations. The blitz had three basic phases, all revolving around the theme of "giving competency a chance." That Koch had never run anything larger than a congressional staff seemed forgotten as he hammered away at Abe Beame. One wave consisted of Bess the Beauty looking the camera in the eye to talk up her man. Next came a host of regular New Yorkers who testified that as a congressman, Koch helped them with whatever problems they brought to him. The third and final phase had Koch himself tick off the problems and people he would tackle as Mayor:

The city's $885 million Police Department had 25,000 cops but only 1,500 were on the street at any one time. He would change that.

About 40 percent of the cops, and many other city workers, didn't even live in the city. Koch would press for a residency requirement for city employees.

Every cop who donated a pint of blood got "blood days" in return—two days off with pay—while ordinary citizens like Koch only got a Lorna Doone and a cup of coffee. He, not the police union, would run the Police Department.

The Board of Education was spending $3 billion a year and still graduating students who were functionally illiterate. Unionized teachers were getting an average of $26,000 in salary and benefits for 161 days work. Koch would take over the Board of Education and clean up the mess.

These "issue"-oriented ads were accompanied by a snowstorm of "position papers," legal-like documents researched largely by Connelly. She drew them together from the mountains of studies that were conducted in the wake of the fiscal crisis, all detailing what was wrong with the city and offering ways to solve the problems. Koch picked up Connelly's position papers and ran with them. "We published more of those than could fit in the public library," Garth says. "They were never, ever used. You could have had a binding on both ends and blank paper in between and no one would have ever known. If a reporter asked something, Koch would say, 'Didn't you read the position paper? I answered that on page twelve.' "

The result of this seriousness was the perception that Koch was bland, dull, colorless, boring. So Garth, after Koch begged to be allowed to be himself, removed the muzzle for a moment, but only for a moment. His fear was that what he calls Koch's schtick—the biting, aggressive lip—would obscure the image of a man serious about the issues that Garth had so painstakingly created. He allowed Koch to do one commercial the way he wanted.

"Most political campaigns lack humor," Koch says into the camera as he stands outside City Hall, "but it's obvious this one is going to be different. Four years ago, Abe Beame told us he knew the buck. When he was mayor we didn't have any bucks. . . . Now Mayor Beame is asking for four more years to finish the job. Finish the job. Hasn't he done enough?"

(Koch did not return the favor on commercials. Garth wanted to do more on Koch's military service—"merchandise it," he says—but Koch would not let him say more than "combat infantry." "I was no damn hero and I'm not going to play the game that I was," Koch told Garth.)

The images in the commercials took hold, right down to the kind of clothing Koch was wearing. One spot on crime was taped outside City Hall on a blustery day. Koch was wearing a nondescript raincoat that campaign aide Leon Roday remembers as "a piece of white, thin rag," hardly the attire of a crime fighter. The coat was so flimsy that Koch was obviously chilled by the wind. Between takes, Roday, a blond, golf-playing Long Islander recently graduated from college in California, offered Koch his own, more substantial coat. It was a newly purchased, second-grade trench coat with epaulets galore and pretenses at imitating a Burberry.

"Koch used to call it my James Bond raincoat," Roday remembers. "He used to tell people, 'I make all my advance men wear them.' "

Koch put the coat on as a temporary buffer against the wind, but its tough-guy styling quickly caught Garth's eye.

"He comes running out of the production trailer and tells Koch, 'You've got to wear that raincoat.' So he did, and he kept it," Roday recalls. "Then the commercial is broadcast and after a while people start coming up to Koch and saying, 'You really wear that raincoat!' My raincoat became a big hit. We didn't exchange raincoats again until after the campaign was over."

In retrospect, there are two main reasons why Garth's packaging was able to sell Koch so successfully. One is that it displayed Koch as he was—plain-speaking, combative, angry. More importantly, the commercials caught the tenor of the times. The public was ready for a change from Abe Beame.

The empty city treasury resulted in fewer cops to patrol the streets, fewer sanitation workers to keep them clean, fewer fire fighters to put out the fires, and fewer teachers to instruct the children. Every city service suffered badly. Crime soared. The streets, never the model of cleanliness, became filthier. Arson and fires spread like cancer. The classrooms became overcrowded. And the parks, streets, and subways began to deteriorate because the city stopped maintaining them.

The public, of course, had grown increasingly demoralized since the crisis began in 1975, and its frustration was beginning to generate a great untapped fury. The City of New York had been forced to go hat in hand to Washington like a profligate ne'er-do-well. And all across the country in all the small towns—such as Los Angeles, Chicago, and Washington, D.C.—that had long been jealous of New York, the city was being written off as a has-been on the ropes. *The Washington Post,* for example, had the chutzpah in 1976 to write that "New York no longer has any real or symbolic role to play in the life of the country." And at the height of the campaign, Ellen Goodman, the syndicated columnist, wrote that the city had simply lost its ability to intimidate. "New York without intimidation," she wrote, "is like Rome without force and South Africa without fear."

The pain and humiliation caused by the fiscal crisis were palpable. The most obvious target of the public's fury was Abe Beame. The fiscal crisis wasn't entirely his fault, by any means, but he was the Mayor and before that he had been the comptroller and before that, the city's budget director. He had participated in the fiscal follies that led to the disaster. For all his protestations to the contrary, the public knew that it was true.

All the old ways of doing business—with which Beame and the Democratic machine were so closely identified—were suddenly no longer tolerable. When the city seemed fat with money, nobody but a few picky editorial writers and good government groups got overly excited about the bloated municipal payroll. Nor was there any great outcry about all the political hacks the Democratic clubhouses funneled into high-paying city jobs and onto the bench as judges. Nor did anyone seemed overly worked up over the fact that the municipal labor unions often seemed as powerful in running the city as the Mayor himself. But now the money had run out, and the public was looking for someone who would vent the city's collective spleen. Garth delivered Ed Koch.

Koch began taping his commercials in early June, and the first one aired on Channel 2, the flagship CBS network station, on a Friday evening one minute before the start of Walter Cronkite's evening news broadcast. A group of Koch's campaign aides, knowing how crucial television was going to be, gathered to watch it.

"We were sitting there with our tongues hanging out to watch this thirty-second Garth commercial," one remembers. "We were wide-eyed. We got the schedule of the commercials over the weekend and watched them all."

Garth's broadcast strategy depended on the amount of money the campaign was able to raise. At the least, he wanted to be able to blitz the airwaves with Koch's face and message during the first few weeks of July, the last week or so of August, and the eight days of September that led directly to the primary. Money permitting, he would keep the commercials on the air in lesser concentrations the rest of the time. That's exactly how it worked out—heavy in July, lighter for much of August, and heavy again as the election drew near.

Garth followed the initial barrage of commercials in July with polling to measure how the electorate was responding to the ads. To his delight, the polls showed that the commercials were beginning to work and Koch was inching up in the field. He had started out as sixth, and maybe he was only fourth or fifth now, but it was movement in the right direction. On the streets and in the neighborhoods, he was no longer a nonperson.

When he asked a crowd on a subway platform in Brooklyn whether they'd ever heard of him before, the response soon came back, "Who hasn't heard of Ed Koch?" Some people could even recite parts of the dialogue from his commercials, with almost the same familiarity as the public knows that Wisk is supposed to attack ring around the collar and Bounty is the quicker picker-upper. Leon Roday remembers one incident in particular that happened as Koch campaigned at a Brooklyn shopping center. As Koch shook hands with passersby a neighborhood woman saw him and stopped.

"She's got the curlers on, what I would call a typical housewife from Sheepshead Bay going shopping," Roday remembers. "She walks past Ed, turns around, does a double take and says, 'You're Ed Koch, right?' He said yes. She said, 'Why is it that I believe you? In the TV commercials you're the one who told us Abe Beame told us four years ago he knew where the buck was . . .' And Ed says, 'Two years later we had none.' And she goes, 'That's right, you're him. I'm sitting there watching you on TV and listening carefully to what you say and my husband looks at me and sees that my mouth is open and says, 'Are you interested in him?' and I say, 'No, no, no, I just believe him.' "

There was no denying that the commercials were cleverly done and the packaged Ed Koch was attractive. What remained unclear for much of the campaign was whether the public believed that the candidate inside the package was real. Even Koch was concerned. When another Brooklyn woman told him she liked his commercials, Koch pursued her, bullhorn in hand. "That's me," he crackled over the loudspeaker. "The commercials, they're me."

Because of the success of the commercials, Koch's opponents and many commentators soon began characterizing him as a Garth-created product. It drove him crazy.

"I think the reason he got so upset about saying, 'I'm not a creature of David Garth,' was because, in fact he was," Rome recalls. "I used to say, 'Ed, stop calling Garth a genius. It is not reflecting well on you. Say he is good. Say he has won a lot of campaigns. Don't say he is a genius.' Koch kept saying it and at the end of the campaign he's all pissed off because everybody is saying he is a creature of David Garth."

Before long, television would invade the homes of New Yorkers with images of a different sort. These images, while not political, appeared so suddenly and dramatically that they had as much to do with the outcome of the campaign as anything Garth had wrought.

Once a decade, or perhaps once a generation, an event happens that is so monumental that it becomes part of the individual and collective histories of all who survived it. Years later, people will remember exactly where they were and what they were doing when their event took place. The assassination of President Kennedy is a good example. On July 13, 1977, such an event took place in New York City.

At about 8:30 P.M., the lights went out. *All* the lights.

Six bolts of lightning struck an upstate transformer owned by Consolidated Edison, and the resulting massive short circuit threw an eerie black veil over every inch of the city. Street lights, traffic lights, house lights—everything went dark. There was massive, and sometimes tragic, confusion in hospitals as nurses and technicians struggled to make emergency generators work to keep respirators, dialysis machines, and other life-support equipment running. Some succeeded, some did not. All over town, people were trapped in elevators. People on the street looked up and around as they were suddenly plunged into darkness. Apartment dwellers went out into the hall or looked out the window. All they saw was darkness. Not knowing what had happened, most were frightened.

But not all New Yorkers reacted the same way. In ghetto neighborhoods, bands of young men began roving the streets, looking for action. The darkness, conveying a sense of lawlessness, emboldened them. Then it started. The sound of breaking glass as a stone flew through a store window. Then a bottle was shattered, then another window. Suddenly, men and women were climbing through windows, taking from the blackened stores whatever they could find. A business protected by metal gates was suddenly vulnerable as a car backed up to the gates, a chain was attached and the gates ripped off as the car leaped away from the curb. Now hundreds of people were on the streets. More breaking glass, shouting, running, gun shots. Fires were set. Sirens wailed, more shots, shouting, crying.

When the lights went out, Abe Beame was in Co-op City, a giant, moderate-income apartment complex in the Bronx, making a campaign pitch to several hundred people in a basement meeting room. There was a moment of confusion when the room suddenly went dark, then calm as people began to feel their way out. A reporter who had with him a police-band radio learned the magnitude of the problem and asked Beame what he intended to do. Beame looked quizzically at the reporter, who was carrying a flashlight, and said he would leave the situation to the repair crews. Astounded at Beame's casual response, the reporter hunted down Sid Frigand, Beame's press secretary.

"Sid, this is a major blackout, the lights are out all over the city and the Mayor says only that the repair crews will take care of everything," the reporter said. Frigand hurried away, conferred with Beame and came back shortly. "The Mayor is going to City Hall to take command of the situation," he announced.

When daylight came the next morning, and as the electricity began to flicker back on, first in one neighborhood, then another, the extent of the damage became clear. Whole blocks had been vandalized, damaged, or even burned to the ground. Harlem, Bedford-Stuyvesant, the South Bronx, Bushwick—the largest ghettos in each borough had all been hit. The pictures were carried by newspapers, but most vividly by television. Crews from all six commercial channels captured the scene. Some of the action was still going on as the contents of a few stores were being carted away. The police were doing their best—they had made 4,000 arrests, but the cops had merely let many go free because they had all they could handle.

Politicians in search of an office look for a chance to get their names into the big stories, but most of the seven mayoral candidates did not know what to do with this one. Beame, operating out of a "command room" at police headquarters, tried gamely to project the image of an executive in charge. His rivals, while picking at some of his decisions, offered few alternatives. Except Ed Koch. Koch, who had been meeting with a group of politically active homosexuals when the lights went out, tracked Garth and Connelly down the next morning in Westchester County, where they'd gone to escape the shut-down city. He told them he was going to jump on the issue and began publicly criticizing Beame for failing to call in the National Guard to stop the looting and burning—a move that many felt would have caused great bloodshed.

The city was grateful when quiet returned, but over the next few days, many people became angry. Virtually all of those arrested were black and Hispanic. The situation was so fraught with racial overtones that both Herman Badillo, the Hispanic candidate, and Percy Sutton, the black candidate, denounced the lawlessness, in part because they feared a backlash against their candidacies by white voters. They said that what the city needed was a mayor who could walk the streets in such situations, as John Lindsay had done in the 1960s, to calm things down. Their comments led reporters to begin assessing what effect the incident would have on the mayoral race. There was disagreement on whether Abzug or Cuomo would lose votes because they were considered liberal, or whether Beame had shown himself too calm under fire. But one thing that was widely agreed on was that Ed Koch had taken the most conservative position with his call for the National Guard. He had made it absolutely clear that, if he were mayor, he would not tolerate that kind of behavior. He would get tough with criminals, and- he would take back the streets from the hoodlums. When someone noted that the Guard was not prepared for that sort of duty, Koch shot back, "Then you should abolish the Guard."

Koch was not alone in his sentiments. While it was not clear whether most New Yorkers agreed with the notion of calling in the Guard, polls showed that about 60 percent of those questioned had no sympathy for the actions of the looters. They saw them as ordinary criminals who had to be dealt with swiftly and harshly. Significantly, whites, as a group, were angrier than nonwhites. They agreed most strongly with Koch that law and order had to be maintained.

On the night of July 31, terror struck again when the "Son of Sam" claimed his twelfth and thirteenth victims. Stacy Moskowitz and Robert Violante, twenty-year-olds from Brooklyn, were attacked as they sat in Violante's car in Bath Beach. It was their first date. Moskowitz was shot and killed, the sixth to die in a thirteen-month reign of terror. Violante lost an eye, the seventh person to be wounded. Television carried the grisly scene, the car windows shattered by bullets, the bloodstains, the grieving families. The largest manhunt in city history grew again as more detectives were assigned to the case that had gripped an entire city with fear. Young people stopped going out at night, and women began cutting or hiding their hair as police speculated that the killer stalked women with brown hair or shoulder-length hair or women in Queens or women in Brooklyn. In short, despite notes left by the killer at some murder scenes, they were not sure what his motive was. Or where he would strike next. Abe Beame's New York was partially paralyzed by a lone gunman. Not for nearly two weeks, until a chubby postal clerk from Yonkers named David Berkowitz was arrested and confessed to the murders, did the city breathe a sigh of relief and stop looking over its shoulder. As the story unfolded, it became clear how deranged Berkowitz was. He claimed that he killed when his neighbor, a kindly man named Sam Carr, gave the command. The command was always, Berkowitz said, delivered by Sam Carr's dog. The night he was arrested, thanks to detectives who traced his car through a parking ticket he was given near one of the killings, he had with him a machine gun. He was, he said, "going hunting."

The summer of 1977 was the summer of crime. The looting and the Son of Sam, conspiring with the usual litany of robberies, murders, and rapes, had galvanized the feeling that something had to be done to make the streets safe for decent people. It was a sentiment shared by all New Yorkers, regardless of education, race, religion, or ideological persuasion. Not surprisingly, the subject of crime and punishment came up often in the mayoral primary. And when it did, the discussion often turned to the ultimate punishment—the death penalty. Were the candidates for it or against it? Two were for it—Beame and Koch. The rest were opposed. Sutton said it was a code word for whites killing blacks. Many whites saw it that way, too, some happily. But it is also true that many people were simply fed up with crime and with a decade of talk about the rights of the accused. What about the rights of the victim? Seeing what the public wanted, Beame, who had opposed the death penalty, made an about-face and espoused it. His move was viewed as that of a desperate man, even pathetic.

But Koch's position was different. He had voted for the death penalty for hijackers while in Congress, though his liberal colleagues were surprised to learn that he was for capital punishment. More importantly, coming on top of his call for the National Guard, his image as tough on crime was enhanced.

He was rapidly becoming the candidate who would put the city's house in order. He would handle the fiscal crisis by taking on the unions and holding down spending. He would cut waste and corruption in the poverty programs by expelling his favorite villains—"poverty pimps and poverticians." He would clean up the mess in the education system. He would call in the National Guard to quell riots. He would execute criminals. Or would he? There's the rub, for despite his strong advocacy of the death penalty, Koch knew that, as Mayor, the subject was outside his jurisdiction. Passage by the state legislature and approval by the governor are required for a death penalty measure, and Gov. Carey had made it clear, with vetoes of such a measure virtually every year, that no executions would take place while he was in office. And even if the bills passed by the legislature had been signed into law, they would have applied only to crimes such as killing police officers in the line of duty. The Son of Sam would not have qualified.

Yet Koch pressed the issue, discussing it in countless forums, especially in nursing homes and senior-citizen centers in the outer boroughs. He almost never raised the issue in liberal Manhattan. And literature prepared and distributed by his campaign committee mentioned that Koch was for the death penalty only if the literature was destined for one of the other boroughs. Separate literature, never mentioning the death penalty, was distributed in Manhattan. Nor were there any commercials on the subject. "I gave a firm order on that," Garth says, adding his belief that it was a "bullshit" issue. Yet time and again, Koch discussed the issue with the elderly, who are the most frightened of crime. Sometimes, he was asked about the death penalty, but often he raised the subject. In nursing homes and senior centers, all the residents would gather in a room and Koch, standing in the front, would ask those who agreed with him to raise their hands. They were overwhelmingly on his side. When the other candidates criticized him for his tactics, he responded that he was only discussing an issue of concern to the voters. But his minireferendums—Koch's plebiscites on death—became the focus of controversy and criticism, even from within his own campaign. The strongest criticism came from Cuomo, who was opposed to the death penalty and viewed Koch's persistent use of the issue as pandering to the fears of the elderly.

In one televised debate, he crystallized his contempt after Koch acknowledged raising the issue without prompting from his audience. Cuomo tore into Koch with perhaps his best performance of an otherwise dismal campaign: "What you have said now is that there were occasions when you went out to elderly people and inserted this as an issue knowing by your own description that the death penalty couldn't make them safe from anybody but a terrorist or a kidnapper and that what they were afraid of was mugging and getting hit over the head. You make yourself a big, tough hero at their expense."

A similar, unflattering assessment of Koch's conduct was offered by Ben Rosenthal, Koch's old congressional friend. Rosenthal, who died several years ago, had told the following story to Nat Hentoff of *The Village Voice*: "I'm a good friend of Ed's, and I campaigned with him in the mayoralty race. But I was a little troubled one day at an old people's center in Queens when Ed was doing his death plebiscite. You know, 'How many here are for the death penalty?' he says as he raises his own arm. Something must have shown on my face because Ed leaned toward me and whispered through his teeth, 'Listen, this is the only way I can get in.' "

Koch denied making the comment, but Rosenthal, though he apologized for causing a fuss, did not retract the story. The friendship ended there.

By August, Koch's movement in the polls had intensified. Beame was fading fast, with the final nail being the federal report criticizing his actions on city bonds. Abzug was fading, too, with voters expressing a weariness with her style, and it was clear that Badillo and Sutton were far behind, their tottering candidacies killed by the looting. Despite persistent attacks that he was the governor's puppet, Cuomo was still strong, thanks in part to an endorsement by the *Times* on July 31. Though Koch was in third place at best, virtually every poll had him within striking distance of the top. Moreover, the polls showed that a large proportion of voters—20 percent in some cases—were still undecided. Koch was not a nonperson anymore and, increasingly, he became the focus of attack from the other candidates at their many debates, an indication that their polls showed him strong. He was still a dark horse, but he looked like a comer. A break or two and Koch could win it all.

On August 19, he got one. The *New York Post* endorsed him for Mayor. In an extraordinary front-page editorial—not labeled as such for several editions—the paper said he was the man to get New York moving again. The editorial had been ordered and shepherded into the paper by Rupert Murdoch, who had only recently purchased the *Post*.

Once a respectable afternoon paper favored by Jewish readers in the outer boroughs—its nickname was "Mama Post"—the paper had gone into a decline, losing readership, advertising, and vitality. Its owner, Dorothy Schiff, finally decided to sell. Murdoch, who owned scores of glitzy newspapers and magazines in his native Australia, promised he would not change the paper's style. But before long, red banner headlines began appearing on the outside and scantily clad women on the inside. Murder was a favorite topic, along with cats stuck in trees, political deals and gossip. By the summer of '77, with the Son of Sam and the blackout under his belt, Murdoch was itching to get into his first mayoral race. He was welcomed to the game, for in every election, candidates strive to win the endorsements of the city's three major daily papers—the *Times*, the *News*, and the *Post*. The mayoral contenders in 1977 were no different, going through the traditional ritual of meeting with the papers' editorial boards to present themselves and their positions. The supplicant's hope is that the winner of the endorsement sweepstakes reaps both contributions and votes from the papers' readers. Cuomo was viewed as the odds-on favorite to win the nod from all three papers, especially after the *Times* had come out first for him. Political reporters at the *Post* were certain that Murdoch was about to follow when the paper's gossip column and barometer of Murdoch's thinking, "Page Six," suddenly had an influx of favorable references to Cuomo. Even the *News* was lining up in Cuomo's camp, and a sweep of the endorsements would have almost certainly guaranteed him victory.

But Cuomo, the reluctant candidate, blew it. His interviews with the editors at both the *News* and the *Post* went badly. Mike O'Neill, then the editor of the *News*, was unhappy with Cuomo's performance, as were others at the interview. The *News* was looking for specific proposals to cut the budget and deal with municipal unions. Cuomo responded with meaningless generalizations about the need for unity and conciliation. O'Neill, who had been well disposed toward Cuomo, would find another candidate to endorse. The *Post* had a similar reaction to Cuomo: "He was up to lunch and the word after that was that Murdoch was very unimpressed," says Joyce Purnick. "He didn't feel that Cuomo was focused enough, strong enough, conservative enough." In addition, there was widespread belief that Murdoch viewed Cuomo as belonging to the *Times* and that he had nothing to gain by endorsing him. He was accustomed to playing the role of kingmaker, and he wanted his own candidate, one who would owe his election to the *Post*.

So Murdoch began casting about for someone to back, looking especially closely at Badillo and Koch in private meetings with both. In the meantime, Steven Berger, who was director of the Emergency Financial Control Board, had a conversation with Murdoch about whom the paper would endorse. They had talked earlier, when Ed Costikyan was still in the race, and Murdoch wanted to know why Berger thought so highly of Costikyan. Berger told him that he believed Costikyan knew city government well, was committed to reform and restructuring it, and, had he been electable, would have made a good mayor. Murdoch, noting that Costikyan had become cochairman of Koch's campaign after dropping out of the race, raised the possibility that Costikyan might go to work in a Koch administration, perhaps as first deputy mayor. In effect, Murdoch was not sure that Koch was tough enough or had any administrative abilities. He was looking for someone to be in day-to-day charge of the massive bureaucracy in the event Koch won.

"I said I thought it would be terrific and important because Costikyan knows more about the city than Koch does," Berger recalls. "As I remember it, Murdoch wanted some confirmation, some assurance that Costikyan would be in the administration with Ed. I came away believing that if Costikyan was in the administration, Murdoch was going to endorse Koch."

Costikyan's stock was high in government circles because of his long involvement in politics, culminating in his work on the Scott Commission several years earlier. The Commission had proposed numerous reforms designed to streamline government, make it more efficient and more accountable to the public. More importantly, Costikyan knew the political game and the players. His brief run for the mayoralty drew respect, but he dropped out when he realized that he and Koch were going after the same voters. The only difference was that Koch had a political base, David Garth, and $300,000 in the bank. Indeed, Koch and Garth had been able to persuade Costikyan to drop out and join forces with them in part by saying that some of the position papers they had issued were nothing more than retouched versions of Costikyan's ideas. "Listen," Garth told him, "we're going to steal every plank in your platform, and to prove our good faith we've already stolen two of them." Part of the deal was that, if Koch did not win in '77, he would not run in '81 so Costikyan could. After dropping out in May, Costikyan found contentment once again in his law firm. Then, one day in court, a call from his secretary was put through to him. The Koch campaign needed him urgently.

"They wanted me to go with Koch to meet Murdoch," Costikyan remembers. "I was told to get to Garth's office by 5 o'clock. When I got there, Ed was getting into his station wagon. He grabbed me, and said, 'Come on, we're going down to see Murdoch.' " In the ride to Murdoch's office in the *Post* building on

South Street, not far from City Hall, Costikyan asked what was going on. "We're going to talk about an endorsement," Koch said. "There are two things I want to ask you. I want you to listen and then I'll tell you what I want you to say. First, I want you to be deputy mayor. Second, I want to ask you to be in charge of the transition team. You've got to say yes on the transition, and on the other, tell him that at least you'll think about it."

Costikyan was taken aback by Koch's willingness to go along with Murdoch in exchange for the endorsement, but he agreed to do as Koch asked. He thought to himself that Koch obviously had not given any thought to who would be in his administration, let alone who would be first deputy mayor, the most important appointment a mayor can make. "Koch didn't even know what the job was," Costikyan says now. "It was Murdoch's endorsement, not whether I was the right guy. He didn't really have a sense of what it was to run the government." Garth recalls the scene somewhat differently, saying Koch had already decided that he wanted Costikyan as a deputy mayor if he won. But Murdoch had specifically suggested that Costikyan as first deputy mayor at the meeting.

"You need Ed Costikyan as first deputy mayor," Garth remembers Murdoch saying.

"That's a good idea," Koch said.

"My feeling is that he made a commitment to Costikyan because he was pressured by Murdoch," Garth says. The meeting with Murdoch went smoothly, Costikyan following the script Koch laid out for him.

"Murdoch called me a day or two later," Costikyan says. "He asked was I really thinking about being first deputy mayor, and by then, I was. I told him that I would really like to do it but that I couldn't make a long-term commitment."

"Could you go for six months?" Murdoch asked.

"I was thinking more in terms of a year," Costikyan answered.

"Great," Murdoch said. "OK, we're going ahead."

The endorsement appeared several days later, its display startling not only the political establishment but the paper's reporters and editors as well. "It was a totally big shocker for the *Post*, which had been a very staid newspaper," said Michael Rosenbaum, a political reporter there at the time. "All of a sudden, one morning there is an endorsement of Ed Koch, who at this point was still very much a dark horse. And it is on the front page and they had, of course, forgotten to write editorial above it."

With Murdoch now behind him, Koch began to benefit from the *Post*'s newly slanted coverage, as Cuomo briefly had. Over the next two weeks, *Daily News* columnist Ken Auletta counted fifteen flattering stories and pictures of Koch, four items mentioning him on "Page Six," and no negative articles. During the same period, Beame, still a top candidate, suffered twenty-four negative stories. Purnick and Rosenbaum, the paper's leading political reporters, were disgusted. "What happened was that what I wrote and what other serious reporters wrote was almost an afterthought," says Purnick, who now covers Koch for the *Times*. "Our work was surrounded by propaganda, surrounded by pictures of Koch and Bess Myerson, or by an article by someone who knew nothing about the campaign." Rosenbaum, now a producer for WCBS-TV, agrees. "If it was a story that made Cuomo look bad, it would wind up being played prominently," he says. "If Koch did something that made him look good that would be played prominently, too. Otherwise, it would be on page 97." Finally, fifty of the paper's reporters and editors signed a petition complaining that the coverage had been biased. By coincidence, the petition reached Murdoch on a day he had invited Koch to lunch. In the presence of Purnick, Rosenbaum and others, Murdoch asked Koch what he thought of the coverage. "I had no problems with it," Koch said. Afterward, Koch called Purnick to say how "awful" he felt over the situation. Murdoch's reaction was that those who did not like the way he ran his paper could resign. Many did.

Murdoch later slipped even more comfortably into a role normally reserved for back-room political deal makers, attempting to convince Congressman Mario Biaggi, one of the city's most popular Italian-American elected officials, to endorse Koch over Cuomo. Murdoch, Koch, Garth, Costikyan, Biaggi, and several others met in Murdoch's office and discussed the question. The meeting was important enough to Murdoch and Koch that Costikyan was summoned in by seaplane from an eastern Long Island summer colony. But it was all to no avail. Biaggi came out for Cuomo.

Five days after the *Post* endorsed Koch, the *News* did, too. Now his campaign was in high gear, and the primary was just weeks away. He had peaked at the right time. "The money coming in went from about $1,000 a day to $7,000 to $8,000 a day on the basis of the *Post* endorsement," Rome, the treasurer, remembers. "When we got the *News*, the money went to $14,000 a day." His coffers overflowing, Garth was able to keep the ads running right up to September 8, Primary Day. When the votes were counted, Koch had come in first, but just barely. His 180,000 votes, or 20 percent of the total, were only 10,000 more than Cuomo and meant that the top two had to go head-to-head in a runoff. Beame finished third, 7,000 votes behind Cuomo, the first incumbent mayor to lose an election in twenty-five years. He wept when he conceded, his career finished. Abzug finished fourth, with 150,000 votes, Sutton was fifth with 131,000, Badillo was sixth with 100,000, and Harnett . . . well, he did get 14,000 votes.

With the runoff set for eleven days later, September 19, Koch and Cuomo embarked on a furious effort to win over the hundreds of thousands of voters who had opposed them. They did so through marathon debating sessions, arguing and shouting and trading accusations in fourteen different debates over ten days. Their television blitzes continued apace, and between them they were spending $50,000 a day. Cuomo, whose own media campaign was masterminded by Gerald Rafshoon and Pat Caddell, who had both worked for Jimmy Carter, aired two new commercials. One showed Koch's face dissolving into that of the much-scorned John Lindsay. Another pictured a weather vane and suggested that Koch went whatever way the wind blowed. Both infuriated Garth and Koch. They retaliated with a yet another spot, starring Bess. "What happened to character, Mr. Cuomo?" she asked. "We thought your campaign would be better than that."

Both candidates reserved their most crucial pitches, however, for the political brokers, starting with the defeated candidates. Koch quickly lined up Beame, who was not about to support Carey's candidate, but Cuomo was able to counter that by getting Abzug. So the focus switched to Sutton and Badillo and their organizations. Badillo was the first to make a deal, accepting Koch's offer to become the campaign's third cochairman and the promise that he would be consulted on Hispanic patronage. Sutton balked at making a deal with Koch, saying he did not trust him because Koch had used what he considered racial code words, such as his call for the death penalty and the phrase "poverty pimp." So Koch turned to other black leaders, among them City

Clerk David Dinkins, Basil Paterson, and Harlem Congressman Charles Rangel. While on a self-declared campaign moratorium to observe Rosh Hashanah, Koch convened a secret meeting in Garth's Fifth Avenue offices. In front of about twenty black leaders, Koch promised to be more careful about what he said. "Poverty pimp? OK. If the rhetoric is bothering you, let me know, I'll change it," Koch told them. "I don't know the code words." He also promised them jobs, saying, "I will have more minorities in my administration than my three predecessors combined." The deal was made, and Koch received the support of most black leaders the next day.

The focus then turned to the Democratic Party bosses, the machine leaders. With Beame out of the running, they were up for grabs. Up to now, both Koch and Cuomo had disdained the bosses, making a virtue of the fact that they were in Beame's camp. But that was before, at least as far as Koch was concerned. When Steve Berger sought out Koch to offer his congratulations, he was enlisted to make a call to Meade Esposito, the Brooklyn county leader and head of the largest clubhouse in the city. He made the call on a Saturday.

"Would you take a call from Ed Koch?" Berger asked.

"Sure, send him down tomorrow," Esposito answered in his raspy, gruff voice.

The next day, Koch, Garth, and John LoCicero, a Koch associate from the Village, descended into the basement of Esposito's mother's home in Canarsie, a middle-class Italian community in southern Brooklyn. Esposito, with Tony Genovese, one of his lieutenants, was waiting. A small, burly man, Esposito had hoped that Cuomo, his ethnic brother and fellow non-Manhattanite, would come calling, but the supplicant in front of him was Koch. Esposito had seen him before, as a nobody in 1973. How things had changed. He looked at Koch and remembered how he had toppled his old friend Carmine DeSapio. How he had sneered at the bosses until he found them useful. He had run against the regular party organization in this very race. He had seen the sort before, knew the self-righteousness all too well. Yet Esposito is a patient man, who once described his political philosophy in terms of a parable in which two bulls, a papa bull and his eager young son, gaze down from the top of a hill at an alluring herd of cows grazing in a meadow below. "Daddy, daddy, daddy, let's run down there and screw a cow," the young bull says in Esposito's tale. "No, son," the wise old bull answers patiently, "Let's *walk* down and screw 'em all."

Esposito clearly shared the papa bull's long-range view of life, and he put his hurt aside now that Koch had shown his true colors. He was here now, in Esposito's mother's basement, surrounded by the memories and mementos of the many candidates who had come in past campaigns seeking support. George McGovern and Henry "Scoop" Jackson had come when they were running for President. Of course, every local candidate had come. Like Koch and Garth now, they had all eaten his mother's meatballs, the best in Brooklyn, many people said. Nobody had ever turned down the meatballs. After a few bites and pleasantries, Esposito rose, motioned Koch aside, and said with a grunt, "Look, I'm supporting you. Make a good mayor and be honest with me."

Garth, watching and listening, was so surprised he dropped his meatball on the table. "I don't believe what I'm hearing," he said. The meeting was over. Esposito had committed the Brooklyn machine to Koch. He had asked, explicitly, for nothing in return. He didn't have to. This was not a legal contract. It was a political deal, a contract of a higher order. It would require loyalty on both parts. Esposito would support Koch, though Koch preferred that the support be kept secret, and Koch would be filling some jobs with the Brooklyn regulars. To name a few, Tony Ameruso would become the Commissioner of Transportation and Tony Gliedman would become the Commissioner of Ports and Terminals. But that would come later. For now, Esposito looked Koch in the face and laughed at the striking resemblance to Frank Perdue. Turning to Genovese, he motioned to Koch and said, "Take this guy out and help him sell some chicken."

On the night of September 19, Koch was celebrating at a midtown hotel and Cuomo was mourning his loss in a gloomy Queens ballroom. Koch captured 55 percent of the vote in the runoff, or 432,000 votes, to Cuomo's 45 percent, or 355,000 votes. In eleven days, Koch had beaten Cuomo twice, but he still had one more race to go. Although it is traditional for the loser in party primaries to support the winner, Cuomo had promised the Liberal Party that he would be their candidate in the general election even if he lost the Democratic line. So Koch and Cuomo would have to go at it one more time. Yet Koch was delighted. Surrounded by his father Louis, and his stepmother, Rose, Koch beamed as a band played "Happy Days Are Here Again" and the crush of supporters chanted "Eddie, Eddie, Eddie." His father walked around the room, saying how he had advised his son not to run, that the job was too hard, but now he was glad his son had not listened. "How wrong I was," said Louis Koch, nearly seventy years after he had arrived at Ellis Island.

The victory had been grueling and expensive. Included in the $1.2 million Koch spent—Cuomo spent $1.5 million—were more than $200,000 to Garth for his services. The campaign spent $310,000 on television commercials in the last twenty days alone. Other payments were only vaguely reported. On runoff day, for example, Koch gave the Brooklyn and Bronx organizations thousands of dollars for payments to "captains." Attempts were made to disguise them on reporting forms by calling them "delivery expenses," but Bernie Rome conceded they were nothing more than payments to party workers. The biggest sum went to Esposito's aide, Genovese, who officially received $11,000. In short, the payments are the modern legal method of getting out the vote. It is just called something else these days—"delivery expenses"—and it is even reported on government-required documents. Ed Koch, the outsider, the reformer who pretended not to be beholden to anyone, had learned to play the game. On his own, he had gotten nowhere. Now, with the party machine behind him, he was one step from his dream.

That final step would prove difficult, even excruciating. Koch, as the Democratic nominee, started off as a thirty-point favorite in the polls. But then something began to happen. Cuomo, after self-destructing for the last six months, suddenly seemed to come alive. He effectively painted Koch as the insider, and charged him with cutting deals with the bosses and taking money from the big real estate boys, who had begun pouring money into Koch's campaign the minute he seemed a sure winner. In addition, the thing that Garth dreaded most—the issue of homosexuality—emerged. Koch workers reported seeing signs on Queens lampposts saying, "Vote for Cuomo, not the homo." Cuomo workers hired a private detective to try to find out who Koch's "boyfriend" was and attempted to plant stories with the press that Koch was gay. Cuomo lieutenants approached Joe O'Connor, who knew Koch from the Village, and offered to pay an organization he headed, United Catholic Parents, to publish a newsletter suggesting Koch was gay.

At the same time, although there is no evidence that Cuomo

was personally involved in the dirty tricks, he began raising the issue in a clever way. Both he and Koch supported a bill before the City Council that would outlaw discrimination against homosexuals in hiring and housing, but now Cuomo suggested that Koch also supported the right of homosexuals to "proselytize."

The pressure was driving Koch crazy, in part because of anxiety that the issue was about to explode and because there was no way he could undo any damage that might be done. It was a sort of "when did you stop beating your wife" question that could only hurt. Koch considered holding a press conference to deny the rumors, but Garth advised against it, saying there was nothing to say after that. Moreover, nothing had been written about the subject during most of the campaign. The first time the subject appeared in print was on October 30, when John Corry, writing in *The New York Times Sunday Magazine*, mentioned the "Vote for Cuomo, not the homo" signs as proof that the rumors about Koch's past had finally surfaced despite the use of Bess Myerson and the failure of Koch literature to mention his support for the gay rights bill. The same day the *Times* article ran, Koch was asked on a television show whether Bess had been used in the campaign solely to deflect suspicion that he was a homosexual. Koch said no, denied that he was a homosexual, and added that he hoped he would have the courage to admit it if he were. Though he did not say so publicly then, Koch believed that Cuomo had broken what few rules of their game that had not been previously violated. And he was furious, so much so that he has not forgiven Cuomo to this day. Garth, meanwhile, concerned that Koch was slipping into a depressed, angry state of mind, feared that Koch would explode in public. He searched for what he calls a "body man" to stay with Koch and keep him cool. The man they selected was Dan Wolf, the *Voice* founder and former editor, who was assigned to ride in Koch's car and keep him company between stops.

"There was a tremendous amount of pressure at that time on Ed," Garth says. "I did not want him to blow his cool. I just wanted somebody to be with him who I thought had very good political judgment, who was a close personal friend, and who could say to Ed, 'Relax, kid, don't let this get to you.' "

Once again, Garth's strategy was on target. Koch kept his cool, despite a steady decline in the polls during the seven weeks between the September runoff and the general election in Novem-

ber, a decline that saw his lead shrink to four points just before
the election. Not everyone else held up as well under the pressure.

Searching for reasons to explain why Koch's popularity was
dropping, many in the campaign began to believe that the homosexuality issue was doing him in. Because of the sensitivity of
the subject most of the press had shied away from it. Except for
the *Times* article and that single question on television, the issue
had gotten limited coverage. Still, it seemed to many—Myerson
included—that it was dragging Koch down and might even cost
him the election.

With just a few days to go, Purnick of the *Post* interviewed
Myerson, who was furious. She knew Koch and knew how much
of his personal life—love, friendship, sexual relationships—he had
sacrificed to get this far. Now it seemed as if he was about to
lose everything he struggled for. Myerson made what could have
been the worst blunder of the campaign.

"She went public with the whole thing," Purnick remembers.
"She said, 'I don't care anymore,' and she denounced Cuomo.
She denounced Koch's enemies. She said, 'What a terrible thing.
This man has worked all his life.' She was really opening up an
issue that so far at least had been mostly *sub rosa*. You could
imagine the headlines. You know: MAYOR'S CHIEF SUPPORTER SAYS
. . . You fill in the rest."

Purnick and Myerson were riding in Myerson's car when a call
came in over the radio phone. Purnick listened as Myerson appeared to be talking with Garth. She could only hear one half of
the conversation, but it was enough. Whoever was on the other
end clearly understood the damage that Myerson could be causing Koch by raising the issue publicly.

"I don't care. It just had to be said," Myerson nearly shouted
into the phone. "I don't care what impact it has. It's about time
we raised this, talked about it."

Purnick raced back to the *Post*, deeply troubled. Publishing the
story with so little time left before the election would clearly have
a devastating impact on the results. There'd be no time for Koch
to really discuss the question fairly, nor for Cuomo to mount a
defense to the charge that his people attempted to smear Koch.
Purnick talked the issues over with fellow political reporter Mike
Rosenbaum and then took the question to her top editor. Jointly
they decided to hold the story until right after the election, when

they published a lengthy account of the entire homosexuality issue. In that, Koch was extremely lucky, but he was still far from
certain himself that he was going to win. According to the polls,
the election seemed to be slipping inexorably from his grasp.

On the Sunday just two days before the election, Purnick, who
was unaware of the polls, met Koch in his apartment in the Village to interview him about what plans he was making for taking over the government once he won. To her surprise, he was
distracted.

"You might be wasting your time," he said. "I might not be
Mayor after all."

"Are you serious?" Purnick asked, astounded.

"I'm not sanguine," Koch replied.

The polls, of course, were wrong, and Koch prevailed. On
November 8, 1977, his life's dream came true. Koch got 713,000
votes, or 50 percent, to Cuomo's 587,000, or 42 percent. Republican Roy Goodman got 60,000 votes and Conservative Barry Far-
ber got 58,000.

The new Mayor was elated and he celebrated long into the
night. But there was one thing he wanted to get off his chest,
one pent-up emotion he wanted to let out of its bag. Mario
Cuomo, he told an interviewer a few days later, was surrounded
by "lowlifes." Having said that, he felt very happy.

Just how happy was made clear to Allen Schwartz, his old law
partner, who had played virtually no role in the campaign. Koch
wanted to meet him for dinner, so they met in a little Italian restaurant on Thompson Street in the Village the night after he was
elected. While the evening was still young, Koch offered Schwartz
the post of Corporation Counsel, the job of heading the city's huge
law department, and said the Department of Investigation would
be folded into it. "It'll be just you and me, forget the deputy
mayors," Koch said, promising Schwartz wide authority. As the
evening wore on, dinner was finished and the two old friends
began walking through the Village, through the area where the
new Mayor had started in this "filthy business." All the while,
Koch kept up a nonstop chatter about what kind of government
he was going to have, how his was going to be the best ever.
Schwartz remembers thinking about how improbable it all seemed.
This funny-looking outsider who had no real political base, no
real connections to the establishment, was now going to be on

top and have a chance to do it his way. Still they walked, and still Schwartz listened.

"Ed Koch wanted to bring New York City back," is what he heard. "He wanted to make it like it was. Like one person was going to make it all different. He was not going to follow the paths of his predecessors. His perception was that they took the easy way out, the shortcuts. He would not. He was going to take on everyone who had to be dealt with, from the labor leaders to the financial community to the real estate community. His appointments were going to be the best. He was going to deal with the problems, all the problems."

That was a long time ago, but Schwartz remembers it like yesterday because of Koch's exuberance. "It was like magic, like a dream, like something out of a fantasy," he says. "Ed Koch was going to be Mayor."

WHOOPEE, HOW'M
I DOIN'?

The line of people snaked its way across the front of the large meeting room, up the aisle toward the back, nearly reaching the wall. Some were tired of standing, but most were patient, these middle-class people from Queens. They had waited years, in some cases, to tell City Hall their problems, and they could wait another ten or twenty or thirty minutes until their turns came. Still, they craned their necks to the front of the room, to get a look at the long, narrow table. Seated behind the table, and facing the people, were a half dozen or so top government officials who were responsible for all kinds of city services—schools, planning, roads, police, garbage. As their turns came, the people in line sat down, one at a time, in the empty chair on the side of the table opposite the officials. Most introduced themselves briefly, then got right to the point of what was bothering them enough to come out on this wintry Saturday afternoon. Potholes, many said. Muggers, the schools, welfare cheats, dirty parks, the subways. The problems and questions were stated loudly enough so that all the officials could hear, but the comments were directed to the tall, bald, chubby man seated in the middle of the officials. He listened briefly to the statement of each person who sat down, sometimes repeating what had just been said to make sure he understood correctly. Then he gave an answer—we will try to do something, or there is nothing we can do. Some of the people then got up to leave, while others tried to protest that they were not satisfied with the answer, or that they had another question. But they didn't have a chance to do any of that. It was his turn now. Leaning forward in his chair, his eyes suddenly brighter, he posed the question on his mind: "How'm I doin'?"

Some were startled by having the tables turned on them, but most had a ready answer, for savvy New Yorkers in early 1978 had come to expect a bit of zaniness each and every day from Edward I. Koch. Since his inauguration on New Year's Day, he had come barrelling out of the chute, quips and one-liners blazing like six-shooters. Asking you for your approval—negative answers to "How'm I Doin'?" were not appreciated—was the least of it. Why, just a few days before that Queens meeting, Koch had publicly branded the 1974 city-owned Chrysler he had inherited from Abe Beame a "deathmobile" and accused the car of trying to kill him by spinning out of control and hitting a snowbank. But it was not an idle complaint—there was a huge Cadillac limousine sitting in a garage the Mayor wanted to use instead. After all, the city owned it and there was no sense having the car locked up in a garage, where it had rested and rusted since the Queen of England was given a ride in it during a 1972 visit to New York. "Should I continue to use that same deathtrap that tried to kill me while a limousine sits in a garage and is used only to schlep the Queen of England from the airport?" the Mayor wanted to know. Then there was the fuss when, after living for less than a week in Gracie Mansion, Koch abandoned the sprawling official mayoral residence on the East River and moved back into his $250-a-month apartment in the Village for the weekend. "Gracie Mansion is nice, but it's like a hotel," he explained. "I rattle around in there. Maintaining contact with my life and reality is essential, and that means living in my apartment." And there was that incident with Fiorello La Guardia's desk. Koch was shocked when he found it being used by a secretary, and immediately claimed it for himself. Then he had trouble getting it through the narrow doorway into his office, then found that when he sat down to it, his knees bumped underneath. When a by-the-book maintenance man observed that the desk was too short, Koch promptly issued one of his first commands as Mayor: "So lower the chair."

But New Yorkers had learned that their new Mayor's flamboyance was not confined to where he lived, how he traveled, or what desk he used. His plain-speaking, let's-cut-out-the-crap style was the way he carried out important city business as well. One of his first big acts was an impromptu announcement that he was going to issue an executive order that would ban discrimination against the hiring of homosexuals by all city agencies, including the police and fire departments. Asked for details, top aides said they didn't have any because the Mayor's announcement had caught them by surprise. A few days later, Koch repeated his campaign charges that many of the local programs that grew out of Lyndon Johnson's Great Society legislation were run by "jackals and poverty pimps" who were "ripping us off" and started cutting off funds to private groups if they did not remove from their payrolls people he found unqualified or unsavory. He cited a man named David Billings, a Brooklynite who had been convicted of using $15,000 of government money for a down payment on one of his houses. Billings, who owned five cars, including a Rolls-Royce, had resisted being ousted for two years—until Ed Koch got wind of him. Billings resigned before Koch had been in City Hall for a month. When workers in one group that had its funds cut off staged a sit-in, Koch told them they better clear out or he would have them all arrested. "The city is not going to bow to lawlessness," he said. "Those tactics are not going to work with me."

That was not all. On a day when the City Council was expecting to hear how the Mayor planned to upgrade the Commission on the Status of Women, Koch sent an aide to announce that he was abolishing it. Koch said he would like to do away with the Board of Education, too, calling it incompetent to run the city's schools. He asked the state legislature to let him take over so he could straighten out the teachers as well as the students. As he had promised he also asked for a new law to force all municipal employees to live in the city and not in the suburbs, where many resided. And when the good folks of Forest Hills complained that their streets were filled with potholes, Koch agreed, saying there were too many to fill them all. Instead, the city would just repave entire blocks, which was news to some highway officials.

As for city employees, they had better watch themselves. "Hacks" were to be fired immediately, Koch said, referring directly to the 186 workers in the Office of Service Coordination, whose jobs were being abolished. "Just because you're a municipal employee doesn't mean you have a lifetime job," Koch said as he mailed the pink slips. The same was true of associates and supporters of the former Mayor. They would have to go because political connections didn't count anymore. "Those days are over," the new Mayor declared, urging his commissioners to fire anybody who was incompetent. "If you want to fire them, don't call me. Fire them," he said. As for the 200,000 city workers who were permitted to keep their jobs, Koch had some advice: Work hard, and don't break the law. Anybody violating the public trust by taking a bribe will be shown no mercy. And by the way, he added, forget about the time-honored perk of getting paid even if you didn't show up on a snow day and keep the calls on city phones to no more than five minutes. The phone bill is already $45 million and we've got to cut back. Executives weren't immune either. Those who were accustomed to their cushy perks better get used to the new boy on the block. Nobody could have a chauffeured city car unless the Mayor received a written request with reasons he found acceptable. And, he warned, be careful what you say in those letters because I'm going to make them public. Many of those who wrote got rejection notices, such as Jay Turoff, the head of the agency that regulates city taxicabs. "You could always use a taxi," the Mayor wrote cheerfully.

One thing New Yorkers learned about their new Mayor was that he had a way with words. Not that he was erudite or eloquent. Far from it. "Library," for example, always came out "lie-berry." And "treasure" became "trez-ya." Yet he had real verbal skills that, in an earthy, salty way, enabled him to make his meaning perfectly clear. There was no doubt about what he meant when he said, with deadpan delivery, that maybe the job of mayor was "too big'" for the diminutive Abe Beame. Sometimes he summoned a Yiddish word for help, like the time he said that "Billy Budd was a *schmuck.*" Maybe that remark will never be as famous as Leo Durocher's "Nice guys finish last," but it is every bit as clear. These sort of comments inspired many New Yorkers to try to take a closer look at their new Mayor, but they were having trouble finding out just exactly what made him tick. In part that's because Koch never told them what he was, only what he was not. He had told them he was neither "a *schmuck*" nor a "kangaroo." Through succeeding events New Yorkers learned he was not a "coward," a "punching bag," a "pillow," a "nut," or a "genius."

What is he, then? "I am the Mayor," he was fond of saying, sometimes jokingly, but usually to pull rank when he wasn't getting his way. Later he went even further: I am, he declared, "Mayatollah."

In the beginning, New Yorkers were surprised with the exuberance their new Mayor displayed. Like the time he was invited to the American Stock Exchange and was asked to ring the opening bell. Grabbing the rawhide mallet, the Mayor swung mightily to deliver the customary single bong to open trading on the floor. Then he swung again. And again. And again. Not until he had whomped the gong six times with great gusto did he stop, an impish grin spread across his face. Such behavior was a far cry from Abe Beame, who, by any reckoning, seemed tired and out of date.

But the new Mayor's style was not only a contrast to Beame's, it was also a contrast to the personality Koch himself had displayed in the campaign. He had been mostly businesslike then, straight ahead, his eye on the goal. He didn't delight the reporters covering him with anecdotes or quips the way he did now, nor did he even seem particularly happy. Most thought of him as bland and colorless, a kind of lonely character bucking odds he could never overcome. Concealing most of the verve Koch had, of course, was part of Garth's strategy of making him the "issues" candidate. He had spent much time in private with Koch and found him to be a very funny man, especially with the biting one-liners. Such a personality can be a lot of fun over dinner with a bottle of wine, but Garth did not believe New Yorkers wanted a comedian in City Hall.

"He was unknown and I didn't want humor to be the opening picture they got of him, to get the idea the guy was a joker," Garth says. "When you're talking about running New York, with all its troubles, people don't want Henny Youngman." Garth laughs when he compares candidate Koch with Mayor Koch. The latter he describes as the "Whoopee, How'm I Doin'?" version.

So with victory firmly tucked under his belt, Koch could be Koch. Moreover, he was having the time of his life. He had waited and worked a long time for this, and he was going to enjoy it. It was nice being the center of attention, the one whose every utterance and action was considered important enough to be transmitted via newspapers, television and radio to everyone from the South Bronx to the White House. After scrambling for years to get some attention by the media, he could hardly turn around now without a reporter being there, scribbling notes and asking him what he thought about this or that or what was he going to do about this person or that person. Suddenly Ed Koch was *numero uno*. The ugly duckling was a swan.

There were some suggestions from some in his inner circle that he should tone it down a bit, and act more like a mayor than a showman. One such discussion concerned whether the Mayor should, as is his wont, leave his suit coat in the closet and appear at news conferences and other official events in shirt-sleeves. Some in City Hall felt it wasn't "mayoral" not to wear a coat. "Bullshit," said Koch, and Dan Wolf backed him up. "Be yourself," Wolf would say over and over. Create your own style, the public loves it. Most of the time, the public did love it, though they weren't crazy about the idea of Koch getting that limo out of the garage. The *Daily News* conducted a poll and, by a vote of 451 to 365, the people's choice was that Koch ride in the Chrysler. He agreed, saying, "The Caddy awaits the return of the Queen of England." But even that episode bore some fruit—the folks at Chrysler, chagrined that he had called one of their products a "deathmobile," offered to inspect and repair Beame's hand-me-down. So Koch just kept doing what he wanted, saying what he wanted and loving every minute of it. As he himself put it, being mayor "was like going to the moon."

Wake-up call for Ed Koch's lunar liftoff was scheduled for 6:30 A.M., January 1, 1978, but Commander Koch overslept. There had been some celebrating the night before when he had officially taken the oath of office before 120 supporters at the home of David Margolis, of Colt Industries. The oath, administered by Judge Len Sandler at 11:30 P.M., is a city tradition carried out so that when midnight arrives and the term of the incumbent expires, the new mayor has already been installed. That way, the city has two mayors for thirty minutes, but is not, for even a second, without one. Koch had enjoyed the moment and told all of his new "friends" that he was doubly happy to be their Mayor because he had been elected without the help of the establishment. He had no "entanglements," he proclaimed, and could run government without fear or favor.

It was not until 7:15 A.M., 45 minutes behind schedule, when Koch finally climbed out of the sack on the biggest day of his life—the day he was to be inaugurated on the steps of City Hall. He barely had time for a quick shave and shower before the doorbell rang. It was Mark Marchese, a pleasant young man who worked in the City Hall press office under Beame. Maureen Connelly, whom Koch had named as his press secretary, had asked Marchese to stay on for a while and his first task was to escort the new Mayor from his apartment at 14 Washington Place to City Hall for the inauguration ceremony. Marchese, who had eschewed New Year's Eve celebrating and had set not one but two alarm clocks so he would be sure to wake up on time, was carrying two cups of coffee in cardboard containers he had picked up at a nearby coffee shop. Koch let him in to the twelfth-floor apartment, but said he would pass on the coffee. He wanted to make his own. Besides, reporters had asked to come over and go with him to City Hall for feature stories, and so he was expecting a house full of people any minute. They, like him, would no doubt be wanting mass quantities of caffeine.

While Koch continued dressing, Marchese let himself out onto the narrow terrace that wraps around the northern and eastern sides of the three-room, rent-controlled apartment. The sky was overcast, with a hint of snow, and the temperature was in the mid-20s. He looked out over an uneven plain of rooftops, many of them topped by water towers and the remains of gardens. Manhattan's building-block skyline loomed to the north, dominated by the Empire State Building. New York early in the morning, especially on New Year's, has an eerie calm about it, almost as though all the people have just packed up and moved out. Even the new Mayor seemed a little detached.

"Koch was being inaugurated in a few hours, but you never would have known it," Marchese said. "He was very casual; we could have just been going out for breakfast."

Beth Fallon, then of the *Daily News,* and Mickey Carroll of the *Times* arrived a few minutes later. They wandered the small apartment freely as Koch continued packing and dressing. The living room, which measured eleven by eighteen feet, was painted stark white and furnished with two straight-backed chairs, a brown leather couch and glass and chrome coffee table. A pile of laundry was in one corner of Koch's bedroom. That room was dominated by a large brass bed, which Koch's sister had bought for him at a country auction for nine dollars. It was covered by a rumpled, hastily pulled-up blanket. The simple, functional furnishings were only slightly less spartan than those in the apartment he had lived in in Washington while in Congress.

Koch offered Fallon and Carroll some cookies out of a small box, and told them coffee was on the way. "I make the best coffee in New York," he said, and began reciting his recipe as though nobody else knew how to make coffee, right down to his brand (Martinson's). Fallon noticed the frayed wiring on his coffee pot, and Koch could not restrain a laugh as he said, "the Fire Department is insisting on getting me a new one." Fallon looked around her with amazement. Could it be true that this bald, paunchy guy who was trying to tell her how to make coffee really was getting ready to be inaugurated as Mayor? There he was, saying that he still wanted everybody to call him Ed. He intended to keep taking his own shirts to the laundry, to do at least some of his own shopping in the neighborhood so he would not become the "imperial mayor." His plan was to keep in touch with himself and from whence he came, not to "go uptown." That meant he would ride the subways and buses as much as possible, too. There was no reason to doubt him, if only because of some of his fuddy-duddy habits. He ate only an apple for breakfast, foregoing his usual grapefruit lest he squirt juice on his clean shirt. And the blue pin-striped suit was the first one he'd had made to order in his life.

Koch left the apartment—"bye bye," he said to it as he locked the door—and led his growing band of reporters into the elevator, through the lobby, and out onto the street. Passing the doorman, he said good-bye, but added, "I'm going to be back." The first person he met on the sidewalk was a derelict wrapped in a scruffy blue blanket and assorted rags. There weren't many homeless people in New York in 1978, certainly not enough for anyone to foresee that, under the combined policies of Ronald Reagan and Ed Koch, the number would grow to an estimated 40,000 by 1984. The one in front of Koch now was a solitary figure asking for a handout. Koch reached into his new suit, pulled out a dollar bill and handed it to the man. As Koch and the others stood there for a few minutes, waiting for a television crew that was late, he began reminiscing happily about his first run against DeSapio in 1963 and how, just before the polls closed, he had gone from door to door to escort people to vote.

"Young man, it's late at night and my vote doesn't count," one woman told him.

"I'm the candidate," he told her. "Would I be here if I didn't need you?"

He smiled, adding to his listeners: "I won by forty-one votes." He did not recall how DeSapio had challenged the results in court and that about thirty of those who voted for Koch had voted illegally. But nobody was of a mind to quibble with the new Mayor, and when the TV people arrived, the group ambled off to Broadway to wait for the public bus. Yep, the new Mayor, who could have traveled to City Hall in any style or manner he chose, went by bus.

"I saw this big crowd four or five stops ahead," remembers Robert Allison, the bus driver. "My first instinct when I see a crowd is, 'tourists.' I wondered what they were doing out here at this time of year. Then I saw the television cameras and I recognized him."

Plopping his twenty-five cents into the fare box, Koch joked that it was a wonderful idea having the inauguration on a holiday when the fifty-cent fare was halved. He took a seat by the rear exit door and was photographed, filmed, and interviewed. Over and over, his answers evoked those of the common New Yorker. He was trying hard to convey that he was just another guy going to work, and he was doin' pretty well. The laughs were coming quicker now, and his obvious delight in what was happening was making everybody on the bus feel good for him. Fallon called his mood "infectious."

Even Allison, the driver, was enjoying it. "He said he was going to use mass transit," Allison remembers. "That was good. I've always maintained that if the people who run this city had to ride those trains and buses, they would do something about them. They wouldn't be such a disgrace." As the bus passed Chambers Street, Koch reached up, pulling the bell cord to signal for a stop and let go with a shout of "Next stop, City Hall." As he got off, Allison called out, "Do a good job for us, Mr. Mayor."

His twelve-minute inauguration speech, delivered to 2,500 chilled people assembled before a stage in front of City Hall, revealed his main weakness as a speaker: he can't read a speech. "Wooden" was the most common description of his manner, and he was interrupted by applause only twice. Koch's delivery notwithstanding, his speech contained an important theme, one that would distinctly set his administration apart from Beame's. At a time when the city was clearly not yet out of the doldrums brought on by the fiscal crisis and the resulting talk of bankruptcy and layoffs, Koch issued a call for "urban pioneers" to come to New York and "grow up with the City of New York." It was unmistakably the speech of a man for whom the world was born anew that morning, and he saw no reason why the rest of the city should not share in his belief that, from now on, everything would be different.

"These have been hard times," Koch said. "We have been tested by fire. We have been drawn across the knife edge of poverty. We have been inundated by problems. We have been shaken by troubles that would have destroyed any other city. But we are not any other city. We are the City of New York, and New York in adversity towers above any other city in the world."

This defiance, this determination that anything was possible now was in stark contrast to the days when the city seemed out of luck as well as bucks. Fittingly, Beame stayed for a reception afterward, then slipped out the back door and down the granite steps to a waiting car. He wasn't even a lame duck anymore. "He was a sad, sorry figure," remembers Victor Botnick, one of Koch's young turks, who watched Beame leave. "I remember saying to myself, 'It's over. It's cold out. Bye bye.' " Koch soon left too, in a motorcade of twelve limousines, two police cars, and a press bus for a swing through each of the other four boroughs. Receptions had been planned in each and Koch was scheduled to spend an hour or so shaking hands and showing the flag in the outer boroughs. No, his administration was not going to serve only Manhattan, as so many before had. He was going to be mayor of all the people. The press bus lagged behind, but the reporters on board need not have feared. When they got to the tunnel that would take them to Queens, the caravan pulled over, and Koch jumped out of his limo and onto the press bus. "I am unaccustomed to limousines," he said.

Koch's choice of transport may have been only another attempt at symbolism, but it was fitting. For the men and women on that bus, and others like them, would soon help turn the new Mayor into the most popular and recognizable character ever to inhabit City Hall. And there have been some beauts, from Jimmy Walker, who liked the ladies, to La Guardia, Koch's idol. With David Garth's help, and with his own instincts now unleashed, Koch quickly came to master the art of media manipulation. Not that there is anything wrong with it. After all, it is axiomatic in politics nowadays that the way to get in office and stay there is to get your name in the papers, your face on camera. And don't forget radio. Modern politicians are so hungry for "exposure" and "name recognition" that they almost don't care what you say about them. For God's sake, just don't ignore them.

Ed Koch was the best. Starting that day, the adventures of the battling, unconventional new mayor unfolded like installments in an adventure serial. One could almost hear a carny barker shout out the headlines:

KOCH TO PROHIBIT BIAS AGAINST GAYS! MAYOR'S VOX POPMOBILE: A BEAME HAND-ME-DOWN! KOCH TELLS HIS TAXI BOSS TO GO TO HAIL! KOCH BLASTS JACKALS WHO LOOT AGED FUNDS! KOCH SCRAPS 186 MUNICIPAL JOBS! KOCH DISBANDS WOMEN'S ADVISORY PANEL! KOCH SAYS THE CITY WILL REPAVE WHOLE BLOCKS! KOCH WILL OUST DAY-CENTER SIT-INS! KOCH LEAVES GRACIE MANSION TO LIVE IN HIS VILLAGE APARTMENT! KOCH TELLS TOP AIDES TO DROP INCOMPETENTS! POVERTY PROGRAM FACING REORGANIZATION BY KOCH!

Day and night, the airwaves and newsstands were filled with Ed Koch. Sometimes he was funny, sometimes earthy, sometimes gracious, sometimes silly, sometimes angry. Always he was talking. What he was saying didn't matter so much as how he said it. Everything about him was New York. He was the most arrogant, wiseass, know-it-all, odd duck to come down the pike in a long time. He had a mouth like ten opinionated cabbies rolled into one. But his mouth had a bunch of microphones to talk into. Koch's image quickly became that of a man in New York's corner, a man who loved the city, would fight for the city, indeed, was the city. He cared enough to fix it up, bring it back, maybe even make it like it was. He wasn't going to take no for an answer, and he wasn't going to let anyone dump on his town. New York was Number One, and Ed Koch became its number-one booster. This new persona, something else reporters hadn't seen before, was transmitted most dramatically over television. Under Garth's tutelage, Koch made it work for him like no politician the city has ever seen. This Greenwich Village reformer who used to practically beg to get a mention anywhere showed veteran reporters a new thing or two. One was eye contact with the camera. If a reporter was interviewing Koch on camera, the Mayor would appear to be having a sort of casual, one-on-one discussion, totally unconcerned that he was being filmed or even beamed live. Or so it seemed. Suddenly the Mayor would wheel to look the camera right in the eye and deliver his punch line or concluding comment. Bingo. Right past the reporter, straight to the audience. He got better and better at it, much to the chagrin of the TV reporters who felt themselves little more than straight men or stage props for his antics.

One reason Koch did so well with the press was that most reporters liked him. They found him relatively honest, plain-speaking, and accessible—not to mention good copy, with all his antics and one-line zingers. After Beame, Koch was as refreshing as a cold beer at Suerken's, the favored saloon among City Hall regulars. While one hoped to catch a glimpse of Beame every now and then, and perhaps ask him a question, Koch came to the reporters. His announcement about an order on banning discrimination against gays, for example, was made in a casual visit to Room 9, the cavernous, filthy press room at City Hall. At the end of his first day of work as mayor, Koch walked in the door—a rarity for a mayor—and started chatting in a "let-me-tell-you-what-I-did-today" manner. When Lee Dembart of the *Times* asked him what he was going to do about the gay rights bill before the Council, the one that Cuomo had attacked him on, Koch told of his plans for the executive order. It was the big city story in all the papers the next day. Any more questions?

Lunch with reporters was fairly common, and one fine day Dick Oliver, the Metropolitan Editor of the *News*, and Don Singleton, a *News* reporter, took Koch and Connelly to a picnic lunch on Governor's Island, a bucolic Coast Guard installation in New York harbor. Sitting on the lawn, drinking wine and eating chicken and cheese, they gazed across the water at lower Manhattan.

"It was lovely," Singleton says. "I remember talking about the city bureaucracy and telling Koch I didn't think he'd really be able to move or change the great creeping meatball. He was sure that he could."

Another reporter remembers crossing paths with Koch in the hallway one morning, and the next thing he knows Koch is inviting him into his office to chat.

"I've got a half hour, forty-five minutes to my next meeting," the Mayor said, looking at his watch. "Come on in." The young man followed and he and the new Mayor spent the better part of an hour in a spirited discussion of politics. That sort of thing was not unusual. About that time a reporter who had worked late was walking through the City Hall parking lot when a big car pulled up beside him and stopped. The rear window was rolled down; Koch stuck his head out and said, "Can I give you a ride anywhere?"

Such close association with reporters became a hallmark of the fledgling Koch administration, but it was not a one-way arrangement. It was a symbiotic relationship—reporters got good stories fairly easily, and Koch got food for his ego. A man without a wife, kids, a lover, or even a dog turned to the media to find out how the world felt about him.

"He defined himself by whether he had press approval," Ken Auletta says. "He really believed that he would snooker us all. He would be so open, so much more accessible, so much more honest that, damn it, we would just drop our note pads and applaud."

Koch avidly read everything that was written about him, often going out at night to pick up the early editions of the next day's papers, sometimes sending his bodyguards or other aides out. Koch the next day would often chat with reporters about their stories, saying he liked this one, that one was wrong. Sometimes, he was amazed that everything he said was considered news.

Mickey Carroll remembers a day when Koch expressed surprise that something he had said the day before had turned out to be a big story in all the papers. "I used to say that stuff all the time in Congress and nobody ever put it into the paper," Koch said. Carroll remembers thinking that, "He's the Mayor, but he doesn't really know it yet." That's not to say Koch wasn't enjoying the attention. After a lifetime of being Mr. Outsider, he was now Mr. Insider. And he was going to milk it for all it was worth.

"Koch was on such a high," Beth Fallon says. "He had a lot of sheer, childlike glee at being the Mayor."

For reporters, covering him was blood sport one day, comic relief the next. Part of the thrill was watching him learn how to become Mayor. Every task of city government—from cleaning the streets to running the largest municipal hospital system in the world—was now his. He attacked them all with gusto, even if he didn't always know what he was doing. Everything was to be open, collegial. Although past comptrollers and Council presidents often feuded with mayors over matters of turf, Koch, Comptroller Harrison Goldin, and City Council President Carol Bellamy announced that the rules were being changed. They decided that it was a waste of time for all of them to attend the same ribbon cuttings and ground breakings, so only one of them would go to each ceremony, representing all three. They would take turns. Moreover, Koch and Goldin agreed that Goldin's audits of city agencies, which the charter mandates him to carry out, would be joint ventures. Koch would support Goldin's findings and would order commissioners to fix whatever faults Goldin found. If a commissioner hesitated, Koch would call him in and with Goldin present, read him the riot act.

Even Koch's palace guard reflected his concern that government be open to all the people, that every New Yorker feel he had at least an ear, if not a friend, at City Hall. He appointed the unheard-of number of seven deputy mayors—three was normal—and gave them all fancy titles, such as Deputy Mayor for Intergovernmental Relations, Deputy Mayor for Criminal Justice, Deputy Mayor for Management. Like Noah packing his ark, he even sought to get one each from the various ethnic and racial "tribes" that make up New York. Meetings to discuss important issues—the budget, the South Bronx—were open to just about everybody. They were unstructured free-for-alls where all ideas were welcome.

"There were very large meetings in those days," remembers Robert Wagner, Jr., who was named to head the planning commission and later became a deputy mayor and one of Koch's closest confidants. "There was never a meeting with fewer than twenty people and usually closer to thirty. Everybody was sort of watching everybody else and wanting to be part of the action, the excitement."

Yet, behind all the hoopla there was another side to Ed Koch, another dimension to the man and his mayoralty. For despite his accessibility—despite his frequent refrain that "what you see is what you get"—there was about him a constant guardedness that concealed some of the more telling aspects of his administration. He knew what he was doing, but few others caught on right away. Dembart, the *Times* bureau chief, was one who did. He recalls having dinner with Koch several times, at Koch's invitation. "I'll pick you up at your apartment," Koch would say, and on the appointed night, would pull up in front of Dembart's apartment—more and more he was using his city car and driver—and would go up to the doorman and say, "I'm here to pick up Lee Dembart."

Once they drove to a restaurant on Columbus Avenue on the Upper West Side, and over the meal Koch began boasting how he must be the most open mayor a reporter ever met.

"Don't I tell you everything?" Koch said, proud of himself and not really expecting an answer.

Dembart, who had observed him carefully in City Hall answered, "No, all you have really done is move the wall further back. We don't really get to see you. You give the impression that we are seeing all of you."

Koch, looking up from his food, answered, "What do you think I am, crazy?"

What the public was not seeing, at least clearly, were some of the darker impulses of Koch and his administration. For example, his charge after being elected that "poverty pimps" were ripping off government money broke a promise he made to black leaders that he would not use such "code words" if they supported him against Cuomo. They kept their end of the bargain, but he did not. And despite what he told Murdoch, Costikyan never made it to City Hall as first deputy mayor. Koch decided soon after the election that he did not want a first deputy mayor, having seen how John Zuccotti, who filled that job for Beame, upstaged the Mayor. Koch wanted to be the leader in his government. So he got the *Post* endorsement, but Murdoch did not get Costikyan.

That might have been Koch's loss, however, for the staff he appointed was in disarray. All the fancy titles Koch had given his deputy mayors only served to disguise the fact that none of them knew what they were supposed to be doing. There were so many of them and their responsibilities so blurred that the administration became, in effect, government by committee. And it was a committee that bickered and battled as people climbed all over one another to get close to Ed Koch. That was especially true regarding anything to do with the South Bronx, the symbol of urban decay that the city was trying to rebuild. Jimmy Carter had gone there in 1977 and promised to help and now the city was trying to figure out just what the Feds were willing to do, how much money should be involved, that sort of thing. In other words, the details. One aide says South Bronx meetings were like slogging through mud in the dark. Wagner remembers one that swelled to particularly gargantuan proportions. The centerpiece was a set of impressive color-coded maps pinpointing both the most devastated areas as well as sections that were on the verge of tipping but could be saved, perhaps.

"There had to be sixty people in the room," Wagner says, "and David Brown and I were sitting in the back. Herman Badillo would say, 'Why is this part still white on the map?', and Ed would say, 'Why shouldn't we do something over here on the Concourse?' And then somebody else would say something else. David Brown turned to me and said, 'Now I know how the war in Vietnam came about. They put up a lot of maps and put sixty people in the room.' "

Part of the staff problem was that Koch didn't really know most of the people working for him, and indeed, had trouble filling some jobs. He tried to solve that problem, and pay off some political debts, by hiring people sent to him by the party bosses and others. Badillo, for example, had been rewarded for his support by being named Deputy Mayor for Management, while Basil Paterson was rewarded for lining up black support by being named Deputy Mayor for Labor Relations. And they were not alone, for despite Koch's claim that he had no entanglements, patronage played a major role in filling out his administration. Those who had helped him defeat Cuomo generally got something in return, and most of the time, that something was a job. Old friends and campaign workers such as Ronay Menschel, Jerry Skurnick, John LoCicero, Allen Schwartz, James Capalino, Miriam Bockman, Bess Myerson, Henry Stern, Leon Roday, Kenneth Halpern, Mary Nichols, Wally Popolizio, Bobby Wagner, Maureen Connelly, Bernie Rome, and David Brown all eventually found their way onto the city payroll. Dan Wolf brought numerous people over from *The Village Voice*, and Koch gave them jobs at City Hall. Koch's speechwriter, Clark Whelton, had once been a *Voice* reporter. Abe Beame, who had borne the stigma of being a party hack for so long, sized up the situation with the quip, "When I hired someone it was patronage, when he puts his law partner into a job it's good government."

The bosses, such as Meade Esposito and Stanley Friedman, didn't need jobs for themselves, but they were able to put some of their people into city jobs. Sometimes Koch would directly be involved in these appointments, sometimes he would insulate himself and have the bosses deal directly with the commissioners, some of whom owed their allegiance to the bosses.

"After he was elected, he called us to City Hall," Esposito says. "He called us in and gave us some donuts. The powder came off on my pants and he said he wanted to work with us. He catered to us, in patronage, whatever." Esposito had some particular concerns, one of them being Tony Ameruso, an ally. Esposito had shoehorned him into the job of Highways Commissioner under Beame, and there were some rumors that Koch would give him the boot as a political hack.

"There were rumblings that Tony was going to be dumped," Esposito says. "I saved him by telling Koch that he's my guy, he's a good man, don't drop him." When a citizens search panel that Koch had set up passed over Ameruso for the post of Transportation Commissioner, Koch fired the panel and named Ameruso. Meade's guy not only got saved, he got a promotion.

Another Esposito contract was Tony Gliedman, a political faithful who had worked in Beame's administration. "I recommended him for a job," Esposito says. "I spoke to LoCicero, told him to take care of this guy because he's good." Gliedman was named first Commissioner of Ports and Terminals and later Housing Commissioner.

Friedman, the Bronx boss, got most of his jobs directly through the commissioners. "They do their own hiring," says Friedman, whose long cigars and purple ties and purple breast-pocket handkerchiefs make him look like a boss. "If Sanitation or the Department of Environmental Protection have vacancies and they solicit from us, we send them names. Some get jobs, some don't. To me that is patronage. It is the bread and butter of an organization."

The harmony among Koch, Goldin, and Bellamy soon turned to bickering about who would go where and there were charges that the scheduling secretary of each was being less than forthcoming. Goldin had a similar experience with cooperation over the audits. After a while, Koch lost interest in beating up on his agencies and commissioners. Goldin wondered why, and finally Koch told him: "It's not Abe Beame we're talking about any more." Goldin got the point—Koch was getting defensive. The responsibility was now his, not Beame's.

But perhaps the most vivid example of the two Ed Koches at work took place while Koch and Goldin were talking about what kind of city car they were going to get for themselves.

"How about you, Ed?" Goldin asked Koch.

"I want one that looks like a Chevy on the outside," Koch said, "and a Rolls-Royce on the inside."

DR. NO

As ego-boosting as all the hoopla and media attention were, there was more to being the mayor than having your face on TV and in the newspapers—although at times it was hard to tell. Ed Koch also had to govern a city deeply mired in problems. New York was again on the brink of bankruptcy, crime was rising, the court system was in chaos, the subways were horrors, the streets were rutted and filthy, and the school system was failing. There was no shortage of work for a mayor.

"I want to get things done," Koch said at the end of his first hundred days in office. "I know that I have an opportunity given to very few people. I want to make the most of it." The opportunity, as far as Koch saw it, was to earn a place in history—to become the Mayor, as he had told Allen Schwartz, who brought the city back, who made it like it was when you could leave your doors unlocked, when you could walk the streets without fear, and there was no graffiti on the subways. La Guardia had been the mayor in those days, and his desk offered Koch inspiration. "It has a little plaque on it," Koch told a television interviewer. "It says 'Used by Mayor Fiorello La Guardia,' and I say jocularly to some of the people who come into my office, 'Someday, I hope there'll be a piece of furniture in this office that will say "Used by Mayor Ed Koch." ' "

Koch paused ever so slightly before finishing, "And I hope it won't be the television set."

For the moment, Koch plunged into the job of governing with a headily optimistic, take-no-prisoners attitude. Up seemingly at the crack of dawn, he was often the first person in City Hall in the morning and one of the last to leave at night—ever eager to attack that great creeping meatball, as Don Singleton, of the New York *Daily News*, had called the bureaucracy. The world was full of promise and Koch and his troops took to the task brimming with faith that with enough right thinking and energy they could move mountains. Mountains maybe, but bureaucracies never. Day by day, Koch and his young administration choked on big spoonfuls of reality.

The State Legislature quickly chewed up and spat back at him his proposal to take personal command of the schools. The unions twitched their muscles and the Legislature killed his plan to make municipal workers live in the city. After all the subsections of the civil service regulations were taken into account, he was able to fire only six of the 186 workers whose jobs he had sought to abolish. He was required to keep the other 180 on the payroll in other positions. He'd described Westway, a multibillion-dollar highway proposed for construction along the Hudson River waterfront, as a disaster and vowed, pledged, promised, swore that it would never be built. But four months into his administration, bowing to political pressure and what he said was reality, he flipflopped and announced that he was all for the megabucks project.

The public's response was minimal, in part because every newly elected public official has a honeymoon as he settles into office—the time before it's fair game to criticize his failings. Koch enjoyed his own grace period—and much more. For this was New York vintage 1978—a city of drastically lowered expectations. For three years, two words—fiscal crisis—had become the reflexive answer for everything that went wrong. The streets were dirty? Blame the fiscal crisis. The swings were broken in your neighborhood park? The fiscal crisis. Children were dropping out of the schools in increasing numbers? What else? The fiscal crisis. If the city got a day's work for a day's pay out of its mayor, well, maybe that was all it could reasonably hope for.

The public's sights were perhaps lowered even further by the fact that as Koch took office New York appeared to be inching toward the precipice of bankruptcy again. Even rational, intelligent, well-informed people were discussing municipal insolvency as a realistic possibility. The government response was, of course, a crisis-atmosphere effort to keep the city from slipping over the edge. The battle dominated Koch's first six months in office, but its impact extended far beyond that. To a large extent, the crisis in which his administration was born set the agenda of the Koch mayoralty for at least the next six years. And the way he handled that agenda was perhaps the single most important accomplishment of Koch's tenure. Fiscal management, first and foremost, became the watchword of his City Hall. After years of profligate spending, Koch emerged as the mayor who would say no. No to new programs. No to agencies pleading for more money. No to officials asking for more police or better roads, whatever. And God help the commissioner whose agency ran over budget. The tough-guy mayor really enjoyed sticking it to them. And the public actually seemed to like taking Dr. No's bitter medicine.

The threat of bankruptcy also gave Koch the perfect opportunity to introduce himself to the city as New York's tireless, most optimistic cheerleader. No matter what the problem, the city was wonderful. No matter how dire the situation, the cavalry would get there in time and he'd be blowing the bugle. Bankruptcy? Ridiculous! Banish the word from the dictionary! Never mind that the big fat city budget with its mind-numbing columns of numbers and arcane supporting schedules read like Greek to him. Never mind that he had no idea what the city financial gnomes were talking about when they started sprinkling the conversation with RANs, TANs, OTPS, MIG, GAAP and other eye-glazing budgetary acronyms. Blissfully ignorant, Koch just wouldn't hear of the city going under. What, *him* worry?

Koch's out-of-synch optimism and ebullience—part genuine, part calculated—was summed up in the response he offered time and again to his many skeptics: He would do whatever had to be done. Trust me. Case closed. And there was a lot he had to do—including just figuring out what all those numbers meant.

The immediate task confronting Koch the day he took office was that he had only three weeks to submit a detailed report to the federal government assessing the city's financial picture over the next four years. It was a difficult but not impossible job for any new administration, and Koch and his staff plunged into what many of them now remember as one long sixteen-hour-a-day meeting. Slowly Koch mastered the numbers and when the plan was presented publicly at a press conference he was able to discuss it coherently. That in itself was an accomplishment, but in the larger scheme of things, just a minor one.

The real problem, of course, was how to pull New York back

from the brink. The city had stayed afloat since the 1975 federal bailout the same way it always had—through massive short-term loans. The only difference was that instead of borrowing from the banks, the city was picking up its cash from the federal treasury. The government, however, had signed on as the city's financier of last resort for only three years until June 30, 1978. Without a new source of cash, the city would be tapped out again.

Hugh Carey, Felix Rohatyn, an investment banker, and other key players on the team that had engineered the 1975 effort reassembled, joined by a rookie: Koch. The strategy this time was to return to the federal government to ask Congress and President Carter to permit the Treasury to guarantee repayment of long-term bonds. That way, the city could use the bonds to refinance and stretch out its short-term debt—in other words, ease the immediate burden by paying it off over a longer period of time.

In retrospect, it sounds simple, but given the bristling anti–New York sentiment in Washington, it was anything but easy. "We will never need a bailout again, and we won't come back for help," Carey had assured the federal government in 1975. "We are going to make it." Only the city obviously hadn't. Even worse, obtaining the loan guarantees was just one piece of a difficult political and financial puzzle that had to be assembled. While the federal government was being wooed, Koch would have to manage the city's current budget and negotiate a labor contract with the city's work force. A large settlement would not only throw Koch's budget out of balance but it would also confirm the city's profligacy to Washington. At the same time, the municipal unions with whom Koch was negotiating would have to be convinced to allow their pension funds to help refinance the city's debt by investing even more heavily in MAC bonds—something they wouldn't do without the federal guarantees.

In the end, the jigsaw pieces came together and were assembled. Koch's two-year labor settlement wound up awarding the city's workers 4 percent pay hikes annually plus added fringe benefits. Not bad as far as city labor settlements go, but not terrific for the city considering the fiscal hole that it was in. The agreement was even further off the mark in comparison to Koch's own stated goals. He'd pledged that he would bring the contract in at no cost to the city. It ended up costing hundreds of millions of dollars. He'd announced that he was demanding 61 money-saving givebacks from the unions. He got none. More spoonfuls of reality. His oft-repeated roar that "The municipal unions will no longer run this city" had remained a promise.

Still, the contract was reasonable enough that the rescue team could take it to Washington, where Koch played one of his most important roles. He walked the hallways of Congress, dropping in on his former colleagues in their offices, in the cloakrooms and in the dining areas, drawing on the good will and trust he had cultivated over his nine years in the House. "He was very popular. Everyone wanted to see Ed Koch make good," remembers Julian Spirer, then counsel to Congressman Ben Rosenthal of Queens. And by June, when Koch testified before the reluctant Senate Banking Committee headed by William Proxmire, he was able to put on a winning performance. Thoroughly schooled in the numbers now, Koch projected absolute confidence that he knew where he was leading the city and the determination to do whatever had to be done.

When the loan guarantees finally fell into place, they provided the city with the cornerstone on which to build its fiscal recovery. It was up to Koch to see that through, and over the next five years he said no time and again—the ever-vigilant watchdog over the city treasury. During those years, the city rode an economic roller coaster—from one yawning budget gap to another—but was always able to make ends meet. Along the way it passed several milestones. In March 1981, the city's credit was again good enough that its bonds received an investment-grade rating and it was able to market $75 million worth of them, the first sign that New York was again going to be able to raise money on its own for capital projects. At the end of that fiscal year, the city closed its books completely balanced for the first time according to the strictest accounting standards. By 1983 the picture had brightened to the point that the city ended the fiscal year with a surplus of approximately $500 million. The fiscal crisis was becoming little more than a haunting memory.

Koch has often credited himself with being *the* person who saved the city from bankruptcy. If New York had gone belly up, he has said, there is no doubt that he would have gotten the lion's share of the blame. That may be true, but his claims of credit are exaggerated. Many other people played crucial roles in devising the loan guarantee package and shepherding it through Congress—Carey and Rohatyn, to name just two. The municipal unions pitched in, too, by settling for raises below the rate of inflation, and by purchasing massive amounts of city securities.

Moreover, major reforms in how the city handled its money were already in place before Koch took office. The days when Abe Beame and his old school cronies would draw up budget numbers on the back of an envelope were long since gone, replaced by an emphasis on management that began when men such as John Zuccotti and Donald Kummerfeld took control in the second half of Beame's term. At the same time, the city's quill-pen method of keeping its ledgers had been brought into the twentieth century with the start of what is perhaps government's most sophisticated computerized accounting system in the country.

Even more importantly, Koch was legally required to have a balanced budget. All the old tricks had been outlawed, and the city's finances were subjected to extraordinary outside scrutiny and control. The Municipal Assistance Corporation and the Financial Control Board—the "Emergency" was dropped from its title—were constantly looking over the city's shoulder, ever ready to rap Koch's knuckles at the slightest fiscal misstep. So were the newspapers, good government and budget groups, and the special state deputy comptroller who was appointed solely to monitor the city's finances.

The controls were so tight that some have likened what Koch did to being given a new car—all gassed, tuned, and ready to go. All he had to do is get in and drive it without going off the road or through any red lights. That, too, is an overstatement. In truth, Ed Koch was an important player in a game that had many important players. All of them contributed, but none was irreplaceable.

No mayor has complete control over his budget. Too many outside forces, such as the levels of state and federal aid and national economic conditions, come to bear on it. Some drain the city of funds. Some fill its coffers. Koch was no exception to this. He suffered sharp cuts in federal aid, particularly under President Reagan, but the soaring inflation of the late '70s and early '80s was a boon because it pushed up tax receipts dramatically. So did a sudden boom in business and construction in much of Manhattan below 96th Street. So did generous increases in state aid to the city, including a state assumption of some Medicaid costs and a state takeover of the expenses of both the city court system and the City University of New York. All of those came to bear on the city, for the most part pushing its recovery along. Koch did his part by controlling spending, pushing for greater productivity, and—with exceptions such as persistently excessive overtime costs—generally keeping his agencies pretty much in check.

Measured in dollars and cents, Koch's efforts were but one of the factors that brought the city back to fiscal health. Another, which cannot be computed in a ledger book, is the impact of his personality, optimism, and hometown boosterism. They helped convince the federal government to come through with the crucial loan guarantees. They made it all the easier for rural upstate legislators to vote increasing aid for the city, such as the takeover of City University costs—a step that relieved the city of a $58 million annual expense. And in reviving the city's morale, they contributed intangibly to the economic growth that has resulted in a healthy spurt of new jobs during Koch's tenure.

"History will record Koch as having given back New York City its morale," says Senator Daniel Patrick Moynihan. "Hugh Carey saved the city, but at the cost of taking away its independence. With the exception of three years under Lord North, the City of New York has been an independent and self-governing place since the seventeenth century. That independence was taken away. The City of New York does not make its decisions, MAC and the FCB do, but people don't feel that. And it's because Ed Koch has made them feel we are running ourselves again, and we are on our own and we are the way we have always been. And that is a massive achievement."

Would it have been so bad had it been otherwise?

"Yes," says Moynihan. "It could have been faltering, fumbling, recriminatory, and the wound wouldn't have healed. Seizing the soul of the city, holding on to it, asserting it and marching up Fifth Avenue with thumbs up, it is a huge, intensely personal achievement."

There's much more to being mayor, of course, than cheerleading and guarding the public checkbook. In fact, a mayor's primary responsibilities actually lie elsewhere—in protecting the public against crime, in picking up the garbage, in cleaning the streets, in putting out the fires, in providing services to the poor.

In other words, in improving the quality of life in the city. Ed Koch was no exception. Indeed, this was the traditional mayor's job that Koch had sought for so long.

So much that what Koch saw outraged him—and rightly so— because for the average citizen the city just didn't seem to work. The examples were rife, but nothing symbolized the problem more than what happened a few months into his administration when Koch dropped in on residents of the Bushwick section of Brooklyn—one of the most blighted neighborhoods in the city—to listen to their problems. There were many, including arson, crime, and poverty, but one needed immediate attention. The residents told Koch that, despite repeated complaints to the police, the fire department, and the city's Environmental Protection Administration, a broken fire hydrant had been gushing water into a street nonstop for a month. No problem, Koch told them. As the neighbors looked on he picked up the phone in his car and called his environmental commissioner. The secretary who answered the phone informed Koch that the commissioner was on vacation and his deputy was "not available"—even for the Mayor.

"I am the Mayor. What does it take to get something done?" Koch fumed to the neighbors. Back in his office he promptly demanded accountings from all the agencies involved and when he gathered all their bumbling explanations he made sure the whole affair was published in the *Daily News,* thoroughly humiliating a raft of his own commissioners.

The common man's sense of anger with which Koch approached being Mayor played well with the public. He was as mad as everyone else at how government worked. He seemed to act as if he thought the only way to run his own bureaucracy was at arm's length and holding his nose—an attitude that created an extraordinary perception of separation that has served him well throughout his mayoralty: There was the government, and then there was Ed Koch, its Mayor.

Koch also impressed the public with another aspect of his personality—that he was honest. Almost obsessively fearful of scandal, he created a program of inspectors general who were going to root out those three tried-and-true evils of corruption, waste, and mismanagement. And when the Department of Investigation was tipped that many years earlier Peter Smith, Koch's Commissioner of General Services, had bilked law clients and his firm, Koch summoned Smith and cashiered him. In just a matter of months the commissioner was packed off to prison.

Koch's dealing with others often had more humorous endings, such as a late-night run-in with Donny Manes, the Queens borough president, over additions Manes and other officials wanted to make to the Mayor's budget.

"Koch and I were in the Blue Room at City Hall," Manes remembers. "It was about two or three in the morning and we were both tired. We had asked the Mayor to make additions of about $60 million in the budget. He was being stubborn, looked across the table at me and said, 'You can have $15 million, and that's it.'

"I said, 'Come on, be reasonable. You can probably get a settlement if you agree to $50 million.' He said, '$15 million, that's it. And don't be a *burvan*.' " (Translation from the Yiddish: a bull in a china shop.)

" '*Burvan*,' I said, 'You call me a *burvan*? The only person who would say that is a *prusta Yid*." (Translation from the Yiddish: A crude, vulgar Jew.)

"He jumps up from his chair," Manes continues, "and runs into his office. I storm out of the Blue Room. Meanwhile, John LoCicero had seen us both come flying out the door. I told him what happened, so he talks to Koch. In a few minutes, he comes back and says Koch has agreed to stand in the doorway of his office and wait for me to walk by. When I do, Koch will say something casually, and I was to say something nice in return, then we could settle it.

"Well, I walk by and Koch was standing there. He said something like, 'See what trouble your big mouth caused.' I got mad and we started all over again."

Manes and Koch didn't talk for several months, while LoCicero, whose Italian is better than his Yiddish, tried to be a peacemaker. Finally, LoCicero was able to break through with a little humor.

"He knew we were both acting like children," Manes remembers of LoCicero. "One day, talking with his hands like he always does, he says to me, 'Koch calls you a *burvan*, you call him a *prusta Yid*. I'm supposed to fix it up, but how can I when I don't even know what the hell you're talking about?' "

Manes and Koch shook hands.

Koch's first years in office were the most active period of his tenure, his nonstop ideas giving birth to some of his more lasting accomplishments and biggest battles. Revamping the poverty programs led to his first heated confrontation with minority group political leaders. "I feel like I'm in a sewer," he announced at a meeting in which a holdover poverty commissioner from the Beame administration futilely tried to explain what his agency did. He ordered the creation of a system under which teenagers were selected for federally funded summer jobs by lottery instead of favoritism. When a fire destroyed an entire block of homes in a solid working-class Brooklyn neighborhood, Koch, at the prodding of *Daily News* reporter Martin Gottlieb, stepped in and helped rebuild them in a minor gem of urban preservation.

Koch also dramatically changed the way new judges were selected and appointed. For years, virtually the only route for a lawyer to take to the bench was through the clubhouse. Without political connections, no matter how good a lawyer you were, you had no chance of becoming a judge. But with the right connections, no matter how much of a hack you were, the black robes were yours for the asking. Koch did something about it, opening his appointment process to any qualified attorney, regardless of their political resumé.

As generally impressive as his beginnings were, Koch was hampered by the cumbersome palace guard he had set up around himself. He solved that in the summer of 1979 when he summarily demoted or dismissed five of his seven deputy mayors. Only Peter Solomon, the Deputy Mayor for Economic Development, and Haskell Ward, Deputy Mayor for Human Services, survived. They too were soon to go, of their own choice, leaving a total vacuum that Koch filled with two newcomers, Nat Leventhal and Bobby Wagner. But before Solomon left, he had a memorable disagreement with Koch. It happened during a large meeting in the Mayor's office called to plan a crackdown on street peddlers.

"At one point," Solomon remembers, "Koch turned to me and said, 'What do you have against peddlers?' I said, 'Ed, you know we all agree that something has to be done. They block the streets, they cause litter, they don't pay taxes, and the merchants are upset.'

"He said, 'You rich German Jews, what's wrong with peddlers?'

"I said, 'Well this is not the place to discuss it. But you know my family is from Russia and Vilna. I'm not German.'

"He said, 'I don't care if you say you're poor and Polish, you'll always be rich and German to me.' "

Solomon was miffed and met with Koch privately after the meeting. "If you insist on saying those kinds of things," Solomon told Koch, "there's nothing we can do to protect you, and the public will know just how crazy you are."

He remembers that Koch turned his palms up and shrugged his shoulders as if to say "that's me."

Wagner and Leventhal would anchor the administration for the better part of five years, setting longevity records for deputy mayors. Their talents, credibility, and steadiness would allow Koch to indulge himself in fights with minorities, quests for reelection and higher office, his foreign policy contretemps and the ribbon-cutting ceremonies that were filling up his schedule.

Leventhal, a one-time Lindsay administration whiz kid and Koch's first housing commissioner, was named Deputy Mayor for Operations, a job that required him to ride herd on the commissioners on a day-to-day basis. That is to say, he ran the government, making sure the commissioners met their deadlines for reports, stayed within their budgets and did what they were told.

Wagner, son of the former mayor and Koch's first planning commission chairman, was named Deputy Mayor for Policy and Planning. His job was to think for Koch, at times coming up with ways of putting a rational explanation on remarks Koch had made, at times advocating directions the administration should take. This latter task was especially difficult, for Koch preferred instinct to planning. But Wagner kept pushing for a greater commitment to a long-range plan for the city, until an exasperated Koch turned to him at one meeting and said sharply, "When you develop it, I'll present it." So much for planning.

Mayoral whim was often more like it, and Koch began to bring that special quality to bear on a range of problems. Prostitution was among the first. Fed up that no one had ever found a way to stamp out the oldest profession, Koch devised a new, unique way to attack the vice in 1979. His campaign led him to WNYC, the municipal radio station, where he took to the airwaves personally, much as his idol La Guardia had decades earlier. The only difference was that La Guardia had used the station to read the funnies to children during a newspaper strike while Koch went on the air with the "John Hour," broadcasting the names of men arrested for patronizing prostitutes. The first episode of the program, a one-minute-fifty-five-second segment in which Koch named nine Johns, provoked a furor among civil libertarians. Koch scoffed at them, said he planned to continue the broadcasts, and urged the city's media to disseminate the names of the Johns he singled out. Most of the newspapers and television and radio stations refused. And Koch finally dropped the idea when even the director of WNYC, his old friend Mary Nichols, balked at extending the John Hour's run. Still, Koch pronounced the escapade a grand success, asserting that his one radio program alone had cut down on prostitution. But neither he nor the police nor anyone else could prove it.

Koch had his next major flight of fantasy in 1980, when he returned home from a trip to Peking determined that millions of New Yorkers should make like Chinese and ride bicycles instead of cars. He'd long been fascinated with the bicycle as a means of mass transportation, and had even proposed legislation when he was in Congress to promote it. He'd gotten nowhere with the idea then, but now he was Mayor and could act on his own. He ordered parts of Broadway, Fifth, Sixth, and Seventh Avenues closed, had concrete barriers installed and created bike lanes stretching from Greenwich Village to Central Park in the middle of those major arteries. For some reason, New Yorkers stubbornly rejected the idea, and the lanes wound up clogging the streets even more. Koch backpedaled, ordering the barriers scooped up by bulldozers. The cost of the brainstorm? A mere $400,000 or so. What's a mayor to do?

What Koch did was forge ahead, turning his attention to the nagging problem of graffiti on the subways. No one had ever been able to stop vandals from spray painting the trains, but Koch approached the problem undaunted. He called on the Transit Authority to build fences around all their sprawling subway yards and have them patrolled by vicious German shepherds—if necessary, he said, wolves. That way the vandals would never be able to get to the trains. It sounded great, a real common-sense approach to the problem. Why hadn't anyone thought of it before? The answer was simple: Because it wouldn't work. The city's

top transit officials knew that and they also knew that i
cost tens of millions of dollars to do what Koch wanted
rally, they resisted, but he bullied them into fencing th
anyway by ridiculing them in the press. There were ju
problems when the job was finished. The dogs got pregna
all the trains didn't fit inside the fences. That was no surp
transit officials because the yards had never been big eno
hold all of the trains in the first place. Many of them had a
been stored on spare tracks outside the yards and still wer
result: The fences are still there and so is the graffiti.

Despite Koch's whimsical tendencies, Leventhal and W
brought stability to his administration. City Hall even seem
catch its breath and settled into an ordered existence th
cused on the nuts and bolts of government. The response
for ambulances, for example, was cut significantly. A pro
for rebuilding the city's "infrastructure"—its aging water m
bridges and highways—was pushed along. And the admini
tion followed through a 1977 campaign promise to build hou
in the Bushwick section of Brooklyn. And after years of try
Koch also switched the sanitation department to the two-
sanitation truck.

This last is quite important. Since Lindsay, mayors had war
to change the department from three-man to two-man crew
saving money and increasing productivity—but had been ste
fastly rebuffed by the powerful sanitation workers union. Ko
however, managed to win the change by giving the workers ab
$12 a day for the extra work. In discussing why he focused
much in his book on personality rather than on the nitty-grit
of government, Koch answered, in effect, "Who would want
read about the two-man sanitation truck?" Still, the two-man tru
is a clear institutional reform, a personal triumph for Koch th
will stand the city in good stead for years.

That is not to say that the new Mayor turned New York int
the shining city on the hill. Ed Koch's New York remained a cit
bedeviled by crime, terrible transit, and a housing shortage tha
was nothing less than a crisis. And racial tensions grew. Indeed
by most objective measurements, New York was a better place
to live and work in before Ed Koch became Mayor. Some examples:

In 1977, the year before Koch took office, a total of 517,554 felonies—murders, rapes, robberies, burglaries, thefts, and as-

t would
. Natu-
e yards
ıst two
ınt and
rise to
ugh to
ılways
e. The

agner
ed to
at fo-
time
gram
ains,
stra-
sing
ing,
man

ted
s—
ad-
ch,
ut
so
ty
to
ck
at

o
y
t

ice. Koch had deplored that level of
by the time he finished his first term
ned for those good old days. For by
the city, leaping 23 percent to a record
surge of nearly 117,000 serious crimes.
e streets became more dangerous they
ration Scorecard, which seeks to mea-
s, rated 68.1% of the streets acceptably
first year, the rating fell to 63.1% and
980, when it bottomed out at an all-time

ngs were worse still. On the city's decay-
es increased by 267 percent between 1977
alone, collisions and derailments jumped
rain breakdowns increased more than 200
ayor's first term in office and youthful van-
a mind-boggling 120,000 panel windows in
ch year.

tistics and reams of others like them, Koch
g conviction that he was a good mayor, maybe
were his commissioners. Robert McGuire, who
oom in crime as police commissioner, was the
as—better even than Teddy Roosevelt. Frank
was the schools chancellor for five years, was
ever. Norman Steisel, the sanitation commis-
, first-rate. And so on. Why? Because Ed Koch
l, he appointed them.

had attacked his predecessors for the city's fail-
cted such criticisms as scurrilous and unfair when
his direction. He rejected the notion that he should
on an absolute basis, saying everything was rela-
ıublic that bumped along over roads cratered with
ıere so touched by fear that many people were pris-
r homes, he answered, in effect, "You gotta under-
ut budget deficits and doing more with less. About
major accomplishment simply getting the most for the
about how bad it would be if somebody else were
d about how things were even worse in Detroit.
ıtive standard is the one by which Koch insisted from
ning that he be judged. It gave him the best of two
Vhen things were worsening, he could say that he was

doing the best job that he—or anyone else—*could* under the *circumstances*. When matters improved, Koch could—and did—take credit. Blame or even responsibility rarely entered his equation, and when they did Koch reacted as though his critics were ungrateful.

Someday he would get a better job, Koch would say defiantly, but New York would never get a better Mayor.

11

A CHIP ON HIS SHOULDER

Haskell Ward wiped the sweat from his brow and stared uncomfortably at 300 angry blacks who had gathered in the state office building in Harlem. It was a hot July night in 1979, and the crowd had come to hear Ward outline the Koch administration's plan to close two city-run hospitals that served the area. A soft-spoken young black man from Georgia by way of the State Department and the Ford Foundation, Ward had been named a deputy mayor and chairman of the hospital system. The titles, given as a reward for acting as Koch's point man in reforming the poverty programs, were impressive but they were of no help in his making himself heard over the booing and jeering crowd. His message—that closing Sydenham and Metropolitan hospitals and replacing them with outpatient clinics would actually improve health care in Harlem—was not being well received, to put it mildly.

"He'll close these hospitals over our dead bodies," said Lillian Roberts, a union leader, expressing the sentiment of the crowd.

Still, Ward pressed his case, but not with gusto. Indeed, he had privately disagreed with Koch's plan to close Metropolitan because he was convinced the hospital provided important health care to Harlem. That made his task all the more unpleasant.

"This is not one of my easiest hours," he said without a trace of a smile, "particularly with this audience."

Many in the crowd had long grown accustomed to being on the short end of the government stick, and they did not consider it coincidental that two of the four city hospitals Koch planned to close were in Harlem. Those hospitals had provided the only medical care many poor New Yorkers had, with the emergency rooms their equivalent of a doctor's office. Harlem residents believed that, without the hospitals, the area's already tenuous health care system would collapse. Moreover, many local people worked in the hospitals and they feared losing their jobs.

From Koch's point of view, the hospitals were a drain on the city treasury. Their soaring vacancy rates—as many as one in four beds were empty on a given day—coupled with the inability of many patients to pay for their care resulted in the hospitals constantly running large deficits. Moreover, Sydenham was, by most accounts, one of the city's worst hospitals. City officials buttressed their plan for closing it by saying that cops assigned to the area had told their colleagues that, even if they were shot in Sydenham, they were to be taken to another hospital for treatment. Metropolitan, officials said, was not a bad hospital, but was too expensive to keep open. As for the loss of jobs, Koch said that hospitals were designed to take care of sick people, not to provide work.

A collision was inevitable between the white Mayor and black Harlem. When it came, the battle was played out in newspaper headlines, and dragged on for more than a year as Koch and his black foes traded verbal punches and insults. Neither side seemed capable of stepping back, or even of looking for a way to compromise. Demonstrators gathered outside Sydenham and engaged in battles with club-swinging cops who had encircled the building. One group of protesters occupied the hospital for twelve days in a last-ditch effort to keep it open, but to no avail. Koch ordered the police to evict them in a tense drama that threatened to erupt into a riot.

In the end, cooler heads prevailed. Sydenham was closed and Metropolitan was kept open through a federal subsidy of $17 million a year. Koch had achieved most of what he sought, getting one hospital closed and federal money for another, but at great cost. An exhausted Haskell Ward, the top black in Koch's administration, resigned because of the Mayor's attempt to close Metropolitan.

The price the city paid for Koch's victory was even dearer, for the hospital battle marked a point of no return for Ed Koch and black New Yorkers. Many blacks had first begun to sense some antipathy from Koch when he attempted to reorganize the poverty programs, but the hospitals turned their simmering resentment into a boil. At the same time, many whites, fed up with what they viewed as favoritism to blacks, found in the constantly battling Mayor a spokesman for their frustration. Koch became the lightning rod for both races, with most whites supporting him and most blacks attacking him. The battle scars and mistrust on both sides were permanent as Koch's relations with blacks became the constant and dominating problem of his administration.

It was to remain so, despite periodic attempts to make peace at well-publicized summit meetings to which Koch invited minority leaders. The sitdowns—sometimes featuring sweets baked by Koch's chef—would result in uneasy periods of truce that would invariably be shattered in days, weeks, or months with new charges and countercharges. After a while the salvos took on a familiar ring. Koch was often labeled a racist. And the blacks were either corrupt or out to dethrone him.

For Koch, who viewed himself as committed to equal rights for all, the charges were a source of confusion. He believed that his administration had treated everyone equally and he could not understand why blacks were not praising him. Sometime in late 1979 or early 1980, Koch took his problem to Stanley Fink, the Democratic speaker of the State Assembly.

"One day, Ed said to me, 'You get along with blacks and Puerto Ricans. I don't understand why I have such a problem.' He then gave me his litany of how many he has hired and that sort of thing," Fink recalls. "I said, 'Suppose I bring down a group of legislators and we'll talk about it and see if we can't work some things out.' "

So Fink got together what he remembers as eight or ten black and Hispanic members of the state legislature and went with them to meet Koch at City Hall. The meeting began on a friendly note, with Koch being "very open" about wanting to solve the problems he was having with minorities and professing to be puzzled about why he was not getting along with them at least as well as his two predecessors had.

"Lindsay and Beame never had problems," Koch said to those present. "Why should I?"

"He made a point of saying how he believed in treating everybody the same and not playing favorites," Fink said. "I see my colleagues getting a little restless. Turned off, you could say."

After the meeting ended, during which Koch had done most of the talking, the others filed out and Koch approached Fink.

"How did I do?" he asked.

"Ed," Fink answered, "I got two sons. I love them both the same, I really think I do. But when one is sick, I love him more. I do, I have to because he's sick. That's the way it is with Puerto Ricans and blacks. Because they have problems, we have to love them a little bit more. They didn't get that feeling from the conversation here today."

Koch's response?

"He just looked at me a little quizzically," Fink said.

To liberals like Fink, Koch's approach represented something of a blind spot, a failure to understand and respond to the special problems of blacks. City Comptroller Harrison Goldin thinks there's more to it than that.

"It is disingenuous to say everybody will be treated alike and everybody is alike," he says. "That is simply not true. It is an excuse and a rationalization for not helping those who may have a special problem."

Other whites criticize Koch for his use of such phrases as "poverty pimp" and say that his reckless statements demonstrate an insensitivity to blacks. Still others think the Mayor's problems are largely ones of style.

Yet to many blacks, such explanations of Koch's behavior do not suffice, if only because what he says and does seem so crude. They ask whether whites would forgive a black who was guilty of such mistakes of "insensitivity" and "style." Thus many blacks who were initially willing to give the Mayor the benefit of the doubt soon began to suspect that his continued battles were intentional and that he had some fundamental reasons for his actions. There was nothing similar going on with white groups, they said, and they came to believe that Koch was courting the backlash vote by practicing a double standard that favored whites over blacks.

"He happens to be bright, he is witty, he is a politician, and he knows how to win—you put all that together and you get a sense that this son of a bitch is not just insensitive," said Harlem Congressman Charles Rangel. "He knows exactly what he's doing. He has consciously cultivated the backlash."

To many, the first indication that Koch had a double standard for the races came in late 1978, when 3,000 Hasidim overran a police station house in Borough Park, Brooklyn, following the murder of an elderly Orthodox Jew. The demonstrators, who said they were disturbed by insufficient police protection, wrecked the

66th Precinct stationhouse, inflicting mostly minor injuries on about sixty cops; four rioters were also hurt. Koch, who was not far away, raced by car to the scene. On the way, he turned to Dan Wolf and said, "So now it will give grist for the blacks to do the same." When they reached the stationhouse, a group of Hasidim saw Koch and began chanting, "Liberal, Liberal, Liberal." After entering the building through the rear entrance, Koch spent a few minutes learning what happened, then went out the front door to speak to the thousands of black-garbed Hasidim gathered there. Using a bullhorn, he made a short speech scolding the crowd for tearing up the stationhouse, then promised an investigation into the murder and said more cops would be assigned to the area. After his comments, which were laced with Yiddish expressions, Koch urged the crowd to disperse, then asked good-naturedly "How'm I doin'?" as he climbed into his car. When the crowd pushed forward against the car, which was surrounded by cops, Koch rolled down his window, leaned out, and, with a wave, said, "Bye bye." As the car sped away, Koch exclaimed, "What a great life." His destination was Maimonides Medical Center. He was going to visit the injured demonstrators.

Koch's action and comments did not sit well with black leaders, who asserted that, had the same thing happened in Harlem, the police would have opened fire on the demonstrators and the Mayor would have applauded. It was, they insisted, simply a case of white criminals getting kid gloves treatment. Koch responded to their complaints by saying he would make sure that if the investigation of the riot identified any demonstrators, they would be arrested. Hardly the sort of answer blacks were looking for.

"Everything is geared to whites, even his reaching out to blacks," said Herman Denny Farrell, a black assemblyman and a 1985 mayoral candidate. "His coalition is the conservative ethic. He appeals to people's fears. That's what the death penalty is all about."

Said Basil Paterson, a prominent labor lawyer and the first black named a deputy mayor by Koch: "I think Ed Koch is the personification of what has been described as institutional racism, that system by which people are victimized almost indifferently."

That Koch had engaged in public brawls with blacks almost from the day he took office surprised many New Yorkers, black and white. After all, he was widely regarded as a solid liberal who had served a brief stint as a freedom rider in the South and had an impeccable voting record on civil-rights legislation in Congress. But as the battles wore on many people concluded that Koch approached race relations with a chip on his shoulder. They viewed him as all too willing to engage in fights over issues that seemed minor compared to the racial tensions they produced. And there is plenty of evidence that they were right. For, despite his public image, Koch for years had been privately expressing animosity toward blacks.

One of his targets was Ron Dellums, a black congressman from Berkeley, California, who had advocated a Palestinian homeland and consistently voted against aid to Israel. He and Koch clashed bitterly over the Middle East in Congress.

"I was having lunch with Koch, I guess it was 1975 or '76," recalls *Village Voice* writer Jack Newfield. "And he kept referring to Dellums as a Watusi, the Watusi from Berkeley."

Another journalist, David Schneiderman, had dealt with Koch over the phone regarding some pieces Koch had written for the Op-Ed page of *The New York Times* when Schneiderman worked there in the mid-1970s. Schneiderman said he viewed Koch as a "decent congressman with liberal tendencies," or did until the night he first met Koch. That was in the summer of 1976 when President Gerald Ford won the Republican nomination for the race against Jimmy Carter. Schneiderman, his date, Koch, and several others gathered at the Fifth Avenue apartment of Howard Blum, a *Voice* writer, to watch the convention on television.

"Koch was just ranting all night, telling stories about the life of a politician that he thought were funny," says Schneiderman, who is now the editor of the *Voice*. "He kept referring to Bella Abzug and her fat ass." Schneiderman says he was appalled, thinking Koch seemed so vicious. Yet more appalling to Schneiderman was Koch's account of a meeting with Dellums.

" 'There was a debate on the floor of the House,' " Schneiderman remembers Koch saying. " 'And Ron Dellums came over to me. I looked up and there was this Zulu warrior standing before me.' "

A third journalist, who works for one of the city's major daily papers, recalls a social evening he spent with Koch not long after Koch became Mayor. Incensed over a now-forgotten battle he was having with blacks, the journalist remembers Koch using the pejorative Yiddish word for blacks.

"He constantly referred to them as *schvarzes*," the journalist says. "It shocked me. It was 'The *schvarzes* this, the *schvarzes*, that.' He did refer to them as *schvarzes*."

Another feeling that Koch secretly harbored about blacks was contained in his oral memoirs, which he taped in 1975–76 and gave, sealed for twenty years, to Columbia University. He allowed Ken Auletta to read them in 1979, and Auletta unearthed a statement that shocked the political establishment.

"I find the black community very anti-Semitic," Koch had said. "I don't care what the American Jewish Congress or the B'nai B'rith will issue by way of polls showing that the black community is not . . . My experience with blacks is that they're basically anti-Semitic."

Koch later complained that Auletta had printed the passage in his *New Yorker* profile without giving him a chance to explain it. Auletta says there was no need to.

"I spent the better part of six months with him preparing that profile," Auletta says. "We must have had lunch thirty times together. The passage accurately reflected his feelings."

To Goldin, Koch's psychological reason for accusing blacks of anti-Semitism is clear. "That is his justification for not liking them," he says. Conversely, Goldin believes, "Nobody is allowed just to dislike him. It always had to be because he's bald, or because he's a Jew or whatever. But nobody can ever dislike him just because they dislike him."

A theory offered by Denny Farrell for Koch's behavior—that "maybe he was beaten up by the black kids who sat next to him when he was five years old or something"—is given credence by many blacks who find Koch ill at ease around them even when not fighting. But, according to Harold Koch, it is not true. For although the Newark of Koch's formative years had a sizable black population, it was essentially a segregated society.

"Neither one of us was ever beaten up by a black," he says, adding that there was no particular antiblack feeling in the family. "I think our family had the normal negatives and positives. Our parents were not enlightened people, nor did they have any great fears. If we had any problems, they came from other places. When my father lost a job, he did not lose it to a black."

Indeed, it was not until 1964 when Koch went to Mississippi and Alabama as a civil rights worker that he became actively involved with blacks. His efforts boosted his reputation as an ultra-liberal and gave him the credentials necessary to launch his political career. Yet many other young reformers in the Village suspected that Koch was not as liberal as he allowed people to believe, that he was a chameleon who conformed to the political landscape. They were right, for already taking root in him was a feeling of resentment that, coupled with his tendency to personalize all issues, would soon lead to hostility—a chip on the shoulder, as it were—toward blacks.

The resentment, which Koch did not openly express until years later, was born out of the feeling that blacks deserved no more help once they had been given equal rights. His commitment to the civil rights movement was based on a conviction that it was unfair and illegal to deny blacks the right to vote and other fundamental freedoms enjoyed by whites. But they should get nothing more, certainly not any advantage over whites. His family had made it up from poverty on its own and blacks should be able to do the same. That they should be given any extra help so they could catch up to whites was an abomination to him.

Two telling incidents illustrate Koch's thinking. The first occurred while Koch was in the South in 1964, and involved the beating of a group of white civil rights workers in the area. Koch left Mississippi and raced to Atlantic City, where that year's Democratic convention was being held. Joseph L. Rauh, a prominent liberal and civil rights attorney, was at the convention leading the fight to prevent the seating of the all-white Mississippi delegation. Koch approached him with news of the beatings, in hopes that Rauh could use the information for his convention fight.

What happened next is a matter of dispute between Rauh and Koch. First, here is Koch's version, which he cited angrily to Auletta in 1979 as evidence that to liberals blacks were more equal than whites.

"What color were the civil rights workers?" Koch remembers Rauh asking.

"White," Koch said.

"Can't use it," Rauh said.

Rauh says the incident never happened that way, and has produced transcripts from the convention showing that he, in fact, did use the testimony of white civil rights workers who had been beaten. He calls Koch a "damn liar."

The second story comes to light through a letter Koch wrote to then-Mayor John Lindsay in 1970. In it, he expressed his growing identification with the white middle class and endorsed their perception that blacks were being favored over whites. Koch wrote:

Dear John:

I write to you urging that you take whatever measures are necessary to undo the horrendous damage already inflicted on 69 families in Corona whose homes will be torn down as a result of the Board of Estimate's decision to build a high school and athletic field in their place.

It is perfectly reasonable for you to inquire why a Manhattan Congressman interests himself in a matter taking place in the Borough of Queens. The answer is a simple one. What is occurring in Corona (a failure on the part of the City administration to recognize the needs of a vital community) is exactly what took place in Manhattan not long ago to a comparable Italian community in the South Village. In 1964, because of what was then termed the "mess on MacDougal Street," I organized the MacDougal Area Neighborhood Association. You must remember it—it sued you for failing to enforce the law . . .

The problems on MacDougal Street are still there, albeit in diminished form. I rake over these old coals to illustrate the tie between Corona, MacDougal Street and every other middle class community. It is kinship of bitterness and frustration caused by the callous indifference of City officials.

The resentment felt in these communities toward City government can best be illustrated by two quotes. In 1965, Mrs. Dina Perini Nolan, one of the really great women in this town, put it this way: "If we could get them to think of us as blacks, they'd be down here helping us." In 1970, Mary Moramarco living in Corona said, "If I leave here, I go on welfare. I can't afford to pay rent. I know how to make a Molotov. Maybe I can't say it right, but I can make it. I've tried it already in my bathtub with sand. We'll get the kids from Stony Brook with the beards, and they'll help us defend our homes."

Proud of his letter, Koch sent copies of it to various people, among them William F. Buckley, the conservative and editor of the *National Review*. He mailed it with a cover letter that referred to the election to the U.S. Senate of Buckley's brother Jim. The cover letter said:

Dear Bill:

Knowing how you feel about the Mayor, I thought you might be interested in the letter that I sent to him regarding the Corona, Queens situation.

Congratulations on the victory of your brother. I would very much like to work with him on matters affecting the city and state where we are in accord—namely, improving the quality of life.

Sincerely, Edward I. Koch

In addition to the resentment both incidents reflected, there was another common thread between them: Koch waited until the political climate changed before discussing them openly. That would be fifteen years after his exchange with Rauh and five years after Mrs. Nolan's remark. The timing of his 1970 letter is particularly significant because it was part of his courting of the white middle-class vote as he prepared for his first mayoral run in 1973.

Yet there was another factor, beyond political opportunism and philosophical shifts, that was emerging as an important element in Koch's attitude toward blacks. It was the personal factor.

In the late 1960s, the tensions between whites and blacks in New York City came to be dominated by clashes between Jews and blacks. These two groups had long had a double-edged relationship. While many Jews had forged alliances with blacks by funding and leading the civil rights movement, others drew black resentment because of their ghetto presence as merchants and landlords. In 1968, even the alliances were strained during the ugly battle involving the attempt by black communities to wrest control of their schools from the heavily Jewish education hierarchy. The resulting school strike was followed in a few months by a photo exhibit at the Metropolitan Museum of Art, entitled "Harlem on My Mind," that contained expressions of anti-Semitism. An introduction to the show in a catalogue put out by Random House, for example, included the opinion of a sixteen-year-old black girl that "behind every hurdle that the Afro-American has yet to jump stands the Jew who has already cleared it."

The disputes over both the schools and the exhibit occurred as many blacks, frustrated at their inability to translate legislative equality into economic and social progress, became more militant toward white institutions. Espousing slogans that ranged from the revolutionary "Black Power" to the peaceful "Black is Beautiful," blacks everywhere demonstrated a growing sense of racial pride and identity. Regardless of whether they received white support, blacks were more determined than ever to claim their rights and, if necessary, take them.

The reaction among whites varied. Some resented black "uppityness," while others jumped on the bandwagon of radical chic. Still others turned inward to their own ethnic groups and sought in them the confirmation that they, too, were beautiful. The result was an ethnic identity explosion that is still going on, leading Hispanics, Italians, Asians, Irish, and every other group to sing its own praises.

The social changes were not lost on Ed Koch. During his early years in Congress he began to identify more strongly with his own heritage. Though raised as a Jew, he had never been religious and once said that he'd had to go to a library to do research so he could deliver a speech on Judaism without embarrassing himself. That would change in the late 1960s when he made a conscious decision to celebrate his roots. As a congressman, he says in his autobiography, he "made the Jews one of my priorities." He pushed constantly to allow Russian Jews to emigrate and sharply increased his efforts on behalf of aid to Israel.

The first domestic display of Koch's newfound identity—and the first time he was called a racist—came simultaneously in 1971 in the battle over the Forest Hills housing project. Koch would have had sufficient political reason to join the fray if it had been any white middle-class group fighting poor black interlopers. But Forest Hills offered even more, for these were not just any whites who believed their way of life was endangered. These were Jews. Koch felt a strong kinship with them, sharing their sense of betrayal and outrage at what they saw as Lindsay's callousness to their values. And he shared their belief they should not be asked to sacrifice their neighborhood so blacks could get out of the ghetto. He argued that the Jewish homeowners had pulled themselves up by their bootstraps, and they should be able to keep what they had earned.

He put the idea into his own words in a statement entitled "Speaking Up For The Middle Class In Forest Hills," which he distributed on December 1, 1971. Angrily, he wrote: "If you have worked hard all your life, as most Forest Hills residents have, to give your family a safe home and a decent education, you rightfully worry about the possible deterioration of your neighborhood. And it is an understandable fear that a large infusion of poverty-stricken people, many on welfare, will pose a threat to the way of life in a middle-class community."

Koch's two-page statement never mentioned the race of the

protagonists, but the code words were obvious: "Middle class" meant white Jews while "poverty" and "welfare" were synonyms for blacks. As a result, Koch was hit for the first time with the charge of racism. "Outrageous," was his response, and he hit back at his accusers, saying they were the ones polarizing the city, a refrain that would become the trademark of his defense.

It was about then that Koch began telling a story—no one knows whether or not it was apocryphal—that captured in a few sentences his feelings about liberalism and social responsibility. Not incidentally, the protagonists were a Jew and a black. The story goes like this: Koch, still a liberal, is going up Eighth Avenue in a taxi when he notices an empty cab in front of him drive past a black man who had hailed it, presumably to go to Harlem. This disturbs Koch, who, deducing that his cabbie was Jewish from the name posted on the hack license, leans forward and asks, "You'd pick that man up, wouldn't you?"

"Never," answers the driver, which prompts Koch to lecture him on how Jews, having suffered so at the hands of others, should always fight discrimination against anyone. At this point, the cabbie shoots back: "With my ass, you're a nice guy!"

Koch approved of the cabby's response and concluded his tale with a moral: Liberals are too quick to demand unreasonable sacrifices from the middle class. It is noteworthy that Koch told the story publicly many times as a congressman, but never as Mayor. Perhaps that's because city law requires cabbies to pick up passengers regardless of race and presumed destination. What would Mayor Koch do if the drivers of the city's 12,000 licensed taxis announced that, like their colleagues in Congressman Koch's parable, they refused to go to Harlem?

Later, Koch would describe his personal sense of responsibility toward blacks. When a magazine interviewer asked whether Jews, because of their history of oppression, should feel a special obligation to help blacks, Koch answered: "I have no guilt complex. My father didn't own slaves."

Two years after Forest Hills Koch was in the middle of another black-Jewish battle, this one over the Middle East.

For years, Arab countries had sought, without much success, to disrupt the good relations Israel had enjoyed with many black African countries. Israel was respected throughout much of the continent, both because of its aid programs—Israeli technicians

and doctors were in thirty African countries in 1971—and because it had established a good track record as a trading partner.
The relationships, however, buckled after the 1973 Arab-Israeli
war when Arab nations exploited a worldwide oil shortage by
threatening to cut off shipments to African countries that did not
break with Israel. Of the thirty-one African countries that had
diplomatic ties with Israel, twenty-six severed them over an
eighteen-month period.

Both the war and the subsequent diplomatic ruptures caused
battles on the floor of the U.S. House of Representatives. While
Koch joined the majority in voting increased military aid to Israel, he was furious at those who opposed it. That camp included some blacks, among them Ron Dellums, who also supported a Palestinian homeland. Dellums, of course, was the
congressman Ed Koch would later call a "Watusi" and a "Zulu
warrior," according to Jack Newfield and David Schneiderman.
They say Koch made those comments in 1975 and 1976, about
the same time Koch was recording his oral memoirs, including
his assertion that blacks are anti-Semitic.

Meanwhile, the mainstream effort to help blacks had continued without Koch, and part of it was a growing acceptance of
racial quotas as a means of redressing past discrimination. The
idea, which was sanctioned by the U.S. Supreme Court in the
Bakke case, was to reserve a certain number of spaces in college
classes, fire departments, and assembly lines for blacks and other
minorities, thus insulating them from the full rigors of open-
market competition.

Koch opposed quotas, and said so loudly. He remembered well
the time when *quota* meant a limit on the number of Jews allowed into colleges and professional schools. And he found the
new definition—a guarantee of a minimum number of spaces for
minorities—similarly abhorrent. It was still a form of discrimination, he argued, and this one was bad because it gave blacks
an advantage over whites. Affirmative action meant to Koch that
blacks and whites should have equal opportunity, but did not
guarantee equal results. If five whites and five blacks applied for
the same five jobs, it would be OK if the whites got all five jobs—
as long as they were hired "on the merits."

The 1977 mayoral race, and his desperate desire to win, put
Koch's opposition to quotas to the test, and he failed. During the
eleven-day campaign between the initial primary and the runoff

election with Cuomo, Koch met with Rangel, Farrell, Paterson, and other black leaders to solicit their support and made them two promises: not to use such offensive terms as "povertician" and to have more blacks in top positions in his administration than his three predecessors combined. Koch admitted later that he had no idea how many jobs he would have to fill to keep that promise—27 percent was the most common estimate—but no matter what the number was, it was still a quota. And there was no denying that he had used the promise of one when he needed votes. Apparently he hated losing more than he hated quotas.

By casting aside his opposition to quotas and holding his tongue, Koch was able to get his administration off to a good start with blacks. His selection of Basil Paterson as his Deputy Mayor for Labor Relations added to the harmony, for it marked the first time in memory that a black had been appointed to a substantive job at City Hall. Blacks had been given impressive deputy mayor titles in previous administrations, but had not been given major responsibilities. They had been window dressing, without real influence or power. Paterson was different.

But two weeks into the new administration—January 15, 1978, to be exact—Koch found his black deputy deficient in a crucial way. The setting was the Convent Avenue Baptist Church in Harlem, where the two men went to a service marking the birthday of Martin Luther King, Jr. There were several hundred members of the congregation in the church as Koch and Paterson joined a group of ministers near the altar. The congregation was predominately black, with Koch and two white reporters among a handful of whites there. After preliminary remarks by one of the ministers, Koch was about to speak when a voice rang out from a balcony at the rear of the church.

It was Charles Kenyatta, and according to Edwin McDowell's account in the *Times*, he shouted, "I say in the name of Martin Luther King, let Basil Paterson speak first, let the black man speak first. We can't go into the synagogue and speak, the rabbi won't let you come into the synagogue and speak first."

Immediately, according to McDowell, many in the congregation and the minister who had introduced Koch called on Kenyatta to be quiet. At the same time, the pastor of the church, the Reverend M.L. Wilson, went up into the balcony and calmed Kenyatta, who then left the church.

The incident over, Koch told the congregation that he would

never silently tolerate racial, ethnic, or religious slurs. The congregation burst into applause, and the Mayor left seemingly pleased with his reception. He got into a car with Paterson who took him on a tour of Harlem, pointing out many of the community's problems, including the long stretches of vacant, abandoned buildings that blight the neighborhood. Paterson thought the tour went well, and not once did they discuss the incident in the church—then or ever.

Paterson had no way of knowing that Koch was seething inside. Indeed, no one would know until Koch's book was published more than six years after the episode. It was only then that it became clear that Koch's version of what happened differed sharply from all others. First, he painted himself as the only white in the church. Second, predisposed to find blacks anti-Semites, he heard Kenyatta say much more offensive things than anyone else had. In his account, Kenyatta pointed down at him and shouted, "Don't let him speak. Send the Jew back to the synagogues!" Third, he remembers a sluggish, halfhearted effort to silence Kenyatta from only a few blacks. And fourth, his version does not contain any reference to the crowd's enthusiastic applause for his speech.

Koch's recollection, unfortunately, is the version he has incorporated into his world view. Similarly, his statement that he never got over that incident, as he saw it, must be taken at face value. The result is that, fifteen days after taking City Hall, all his preconceptions about blacks were confirmed. His mind on the subject was closed, and the chip on his shoulder was bigger than ever.

Open rancor between the Mayor and blacks emerged quickly enough, turning largely on his decision to clean up the city's poverty programs and close municipal hospitals. In both cases, black protests stemmed as much from Koch's rhetoric and attitude as from his actions. For example, Bobby Wagner would later admit that how the administration went about closing Sydenham was one of its biggest mistakes. He said City Hall should have opened the clinics before trying to close the hospital, a move that would have blunted the fear that Harlem residents would be without health care.

By September 1979, when Haskell Ward called it quits, the break with blacks seemed beyond repair. After months of fighting Koch's battles with blacks and being labeled an Uncle Tom, Ward left disappointed and drained. Yet to this day, he believes that Koch carried out his policies with the best of intentions.

"I quite often said to Ed that I would be with him so long as his motives were honest and he did not aim to affect blacks negatively," Ward says. That makes him an anomaly—a black who believes Koch's problems stem mostly from unfair charges by black politicians desperate to protect their turf and patronage systems.

"The real point was that blacks had decided that Ed was a good target to mobilize against," says Ward, who still sees Koch from time to time.

For Koch, Ward's resignation was apparently traumatic. Ward was as close to Koch as any black has ever been—they often had lunch or dinner together on the weekends, sometimes in Harlem—and his leaving demonstrated to many that Koch couldn't even keep a black that he liked, let alone one that Rangel and the others liked. With Ward out of the way, Koch became the direct target of all the attacks from blacks. In his book, Koch puts it this way: "After Haskell Ward's resignation, it was abundantly clear to me that it was I the ideologues were after."

Koch's response to his own assumption was to freeze blacks out of his inner circle. Though Koch denied that race ever played a part in anyone he hired, five years would pass before another black would get a major job in his administration. That came in 1983 when Koch, stung by his single most heated confrontation with blacks, named Benjamin Ward (no relation to Haskell) police commissioner.

The appointment followed highly charged congressional subcommittee hearings into allegations of widespread police brutality against black New Yorkers. Ward, the city's first black police commissioner, was chosen "on the merits," Koch insisted over and over again, citing his long career in government and law enforcement. Koch added that Ward's race was just an incidental plus. No one believed that, including Ward, who once said that, after all, Koch was a politician.

Most blacks, however, had no desire to reach out to Koch. An illustration of how they feel about Koch comes from a description by Paterson of the Mayor's surprise appearance at a Harlem Week Celebration in 1983:

"Koch got out of a car about Fifth Avenue and 135th Street, in the block, and walked up the block, past the crowd of about 3–4,000 people, down toward the other end of the block, crossed the street and walked back to the other side. I watched him. Three people stopped him. People just stood there looking at him. Nobody was looking to confront him. They're just people. They didn't want to talk with him. That's the worst—to treat you like you don't exist. I've never seen that happen to a public official."

"AT HOME" WITH ED KOCH

By 1980, his third year in office, many things could be said of Ed Koch. Some were good, such as how he was restoring fiscal credibility. Some were bad, such as how he had increased racial tensions. But one thing that could not be said, ever, was that Ed Koch was invisible. Quite the opposite.

New Yorkers who listened to the radio could expect to hear Ed Koch's voice. When they picked up newspapers, there he was. When they turned on the evening news, he was often the star. It was unquestionable that whatever he did or said, or didn't do or didn't say, was news. With all his battling, humor, and controversy, how could it be otherwise? Trailed by a bedraggled band of reporters and technicians wherever he went, he quickly became the Media Mayor. He was good copy, his funny features made for catching photographs, and he made himself available all the time. And why not? He loved it. He was the first to listen and watch and read about himself, making mental notes to improve his delivery or sharpen his language. His aim, it seemed, was to get his picture on Page One *and* the quote of the day. Every day.

And many times he did. Yet of all the images inspired by the one-man media machine, none were as powerful and captivating as those he transmitted from the city's streets and bridges during the 1980 transit strike. For eleven long days in April, when the buses and subways stopped, Koch became a traveling press conference. On each day of the strike, he appeared on the Brooklyn Bridge, the Williamsburg Bridge, and the 59th Street Bridge, and at the Staten Island ferry terminal to cheer on workers streaming to their jobs in Manhattan. He took to singing

"Everything's Up to Date in Kansas City," where a strike by firemen had been beaten back. The press followed him, notepads, cameras, and tape recorders at the ready, as he paraded, danced, and sang his way through the city. There were times that his ebullience seemed to have taken control of the city, as though the strike was nothing but a stage on which he could display himself. He rallied the city, shouting encouragement to people walking to work ("Go out and make money!") and denouncing supporters of the striking workers as "wackos."

While negotiators from the Metropolitan Transportation Authority and the Transport Workers Union attempted to achieve a settlement to end the walkout, Koch emerged on the sidelines as a cheerleader. The walking workers were not disposed to back the transit strikers and Koch swiftly seized on the mood of the citizenry. It worked. Koch was the voice of the little guy, the scrappy New Yorker who was telling them off in the newspapers and on radio and television. It was a rapturous event for the first-term Mayor, consummating his bond with the city. From the office of his Police Commissioner, Robert McGuire, Koch recalled in his book, "I could see thousands of people streaming across the Brooklyn Bridge into Manhattan. I thought: There are the municipal workers coming to save the city. It was like the Russian Army coming over frozen Lake Lagoda to save Leningrad."

It was no wonder that reporters were all over him, and not just then. It was that way every day, in times of crisis, in times of quiet. Wherever he went, there they were, swarming all over him with questions. He couldn't even poke his head out of his office to walk across the hall to the men's room without being "ambushed" with questions outside the bathroom door. Sooner or later they'd be waiting for him inside—the female reporters included. As it was, the circus was driving his press staff crazy. Not only couldn't they keep up with his pronouncements, but they also seemed to spend half the day fending off the anger of the reporters who'd been scooped because they hadn't stood sentry at the men's room.

After a while, even Ed Koch began to think things were getting a bit out of hand. Not that he ever thought that he was in the papers or on TV too much, it was just that he was spending so much time dealing with reporters. Something had to be done. Tom Goldstein, who took over as City Hall press secretary in

January 1980—after an exhausted Connelly packed it in and went back to work with Garth—had an idea.

An affable ex-*Times* reporter, Goldstein sought to make order out of chaos and devised a whole new way for Koch and the press to interact. What he came up with was given the rather strange name of the "At Home"—as in "at home" with Ed Koch in his office. Although it seemed of little import at the time, it was one of the most significant decisions of the Koch administration regarding the press. It fed Koch's ego, altered how he was covered, and—eventually—sped the transformation of Koch from the press's co-conspirator to the reporters' distrusted and disliked target.

Instead of watching for reporters lying in wait outside the men's room, Goldstein would now have a member of his staff walk down the marbled center hallway of City Hall at a few minutes before eleven virtually every day, and into Room 9, the press room, where it would be announced, "At home in ten minutes." Instead of chasing the Mayor, the reporters were now being summoned—conveniently—to an audience in his office.

A jumble of video display terminals, typewriters, mounds of newspapers, filing cabinets, coffee cups, beer bottles, debris, books, government reports, and seventeen desks jammed together, Room 9 has been used by reporters since 1897. A plaque on the door that might have been nailed to a war memorial records the names of 23 newspapers that have folded over the years under the heading, "No Comment." Inside the room, another sign counsels the inhabitants to check their hatchets at the door. Some do. But regardless of whether they worked for a wire service, radio station, or the *Post*, the *Daily News*, or the *Times*, they would rise en masse at the summons of Goldstein or one of his minions and troop down the hall to Koch's office on the first floor of the building.

To get there one must first be admitted through a waist-high metal gate that is guarded around the clock by city cops. Then comes a short hallway, a turn to the right through a jumble of secretarys' desks, then a left through another outer office, where Dan Wolf, Diane Coffey, and several others sit, and finally into Koch's sanctuary through a door that looks as though it was cut out of the wall as a side entrance—as was done years ago. The actual main entrance, a few steps away around a corner, is used less often.

Since 1980, the reporters have made that trip almost daily, sometimes two and three times a day. It all depends on how much Koch has on his mind and how much the press wants to talk with him. If anyone from Room 9 asks to see Koch, he's certainly willing to oblige. If no one does, he sends for them anyway, no doubt having something he wants to get off his chest. Sometimes it seems he just wants to see them to make sure that nobody else is making news. He simply can't stand to have a whole day go by without a press conference. That's why Mondays are often bad—a weekend without talking to reporters is sure to leave Koch filled with quotable quips.

When they arrive in his office, the reporters invariably find Koch seated—not behind his cherished La Guardia desk, but in a low-slung black leather armchair situated off to one side of the room. "Well, look who's here," he often jokes as the press takes up positions around his domain.

The office is modest by most executive standards, measuring less than 400 square feet, though the high ceilings and the kitchenette off to the side add charm and convenience. It has four windows with bulletproof glass, four telephones, eleven chairs scattered about, and a chandelier that hangs from the center of the ceiling. The glass desk top is clean of documents and the papers Koch keeps stacked in the IN and OUT boxes at each end of the desk have been turned over to keep their contents confidential. There is a small figure of La Guardia on the desk top, two brass lamps, two crystal apples, and a small sign bearing the latest slogan in fashion with the Mayor. In 1980 it read, IF YOU SAY IT CAN'T BE DONE, YOU'RE RIGHT, YOU CAN'T DO IT. Later that was replaced by BE NOT AFRAID, a phrase from a hymn Koch heard at a Roman Catholic service for a slain police officer. And that, in turn, was superseded by THE BEST IS YET TO BE.

The office is dominated by a large oil portrait of a stern-looking La Guardia that hangs on the wall opposite Koch's desk, seeming to peer down at it. To the left of the desk, there is a fireplace flanked by the flags of the United States and New York City. A Matisse hangs above the mantelpiece. The office walls are decorated with paintings and photographs, nearly all of them of Koch. There he is leading the All-City Band, there he is with Pope John Paul II, there he is with Hugh Carey, there with Abe Beame and Jimmy Carter, about to give Carter a letter on American policy toward Israel. There are even cartoons featuring—guess who?—including a popular one from *The New Yorker* that shows a man coming home at the end of the day and saying to his wife, "Guess who Mayor Koch called a wacko today." Even the deep window sills are dotted with bric-a-brac. On one sits a framed letter written by Koch outlining the terms under which his small and struggling law firm agreed to represent *The Village Voice* in 1966. ("We will represent the Village Voice, Inc. on the basis of a monthly retainer of $50.00".) The only technical equipment in the office, beyond the phones, are a well-used Sony television set and a videocassette recorder stationed along the wall to the right of the desk.

The routine of the "at homes" is always the same. As Koch waits patiently, the reporters spread out around his office. If they like, they even sit at his desk. Television crews set up near the doorway. Radio reporters, their mikes thrust up toward his mouth, surround Koch in his chair, literally kneeling at his feet. Every cough and comma is recorded, every word pored over. Koch is in his glory. People—better yet, reporters—actually seem to hang on his every word, and it is important to him. For increasingly Koch, without family or many close friends, has come to measure himself not by the love of a wife, say, or the affection and development of a child, but by what is written and broadcast about him.

"Not bad for a guy who had to fight to get his name mentioned in the papers," he said one day to Peter Solomon, a deputy mayor, as he gazed joyfully at a picture of himself on the front page of the *Times*.

Koch finds it all endlessly fascinating, particularly his own image on television. Tony Guida, the political reporter for WCBS-TV, witnessed one telling scene after he interviewed Koch in his office. It was a busy day and Koch had agreed to the interview only after Guida promised to limit it to thirty minutes so that Koch could get on with an exceedingly crowded schedule. As the crew was preparing to depart, Guida's cameraman asked Koch if he could use the office videocassette recorder to check the final minute of the tape, just to make sure the interview had indeed been recorded properly.

"My guy checks the tape and Koch says, 'Wait a minute, can I see that?' So the guy turns it back on. We watch the last portion. It comes to the end and Koch wants to see more," Guida remembers.

The Mayor happily pulled a chair up to the television set and began to review the entire tape of the interview.

"It was like he had gone to the movies. He's totally enraptured," Guida continues. "He was laughing when he was funny, looking at himself, saying, 'That's good.' His press secretary came in because of this busy morning schedule Koch has got. I hear the press secretary say at one point, 'So-and-so is waiting.' And Koch said, 'Let him wait.' "

At the same time, as Koch became accustomed to being always at center stage, some of those around him say they began to notice that he was changing personally. That the self-absorption that they accepted—and even found charming—when it was leavened by powerlessness was starting to show itself as, well, brattish behavior.

Ken Auletta, who spent about six months with Koch preparing the profile for *The New Yorker* magazine, recalls the night he took his wife to dinner with Koch, Connelly, and Connelly's date, who happened to be the deputy mayor of Paris. Fascinating company, all. Koch regaled the group with funny stories for about thirty minutes but when the conversation shifted to Connelly's date, Auletta noticed a drastic change in the Mayor.

"As the deputy mayor is talking, Koch is literally sinking in his seat. I mean sinking—literally, physically sinking below the horizon of the table. Maureen then becomes the center of attention, and I'm telling you, Koch's head is literally level with the table. I couldn't believe it," Auletta recalls.

Fearing Koch's possible disappearance, Auletta turned the conversational spotlight back on the Mayor. "He perked up immediately," Auletta says. "He doesn't care about other people. He's totally self-absorbed."

Still, Auletta marveled at the near-total openness Koch displayed to him while he worked on the profile. Koch allowed Auletta to be with him virtually any time he wanted—even to sitting in on almost any closed-door meeting. The result was an exceedingly thorough, vivid, and balanced portrait of Koch. The Mayor, however, was not thrilled with it.

The profile made him look like an egomaniac, Koch complained to Auletta.

"Well?" Auletta replied.

If the coverage Koch received was a measure of his success, he'd come a great distance. It was not so long ago that a *Times*

reporter in Washington sent a memo to the main office reminding all that the congressman from the silk-stocking district was
not "Edwin" Koch. Nor was the time that far gone when Ed Koch
would go to "any press conference and any group with three
empty chairs and an invitation," as a former aide recalls, in a
compulsive search for publicity and public favor. His battle for
recognition took strange shapes in those days. One veteran television reporter remembers first laying eyes on the Mayor-to-be
years ago, when he was scanning some stock footage of Greenwich Village and was puzzled by the persistent reappearance of
one man, talking and gesticulating to the cameramen. "That's Ed
Koch," a technician explained. "He does that all the time."

In those days, Koch could always rely on *The Village Voice*—
owned by his friend Dan Wolf—to lionize him, much the same
role the *Post* would later assume under Murdoch. KOCH: THE NIGHT
THE NICE GUY FINISHED FIRST read the front-page *Voice* headline
over a story about his 1965 defeat of Carmine DeSapio written
by Jack Newfield. The love affair between the left-wing newspaper and Koch came to an end in the 1977 mayoral campaign.
By then Wolf had long since sold his interest in the *Voice*, and
Newfield and several other key writers were among the few
journalists in the city whose outlook led them to write critically—and sometimes extremely so—of Koch. No matter for Koch,
though, because a bigger, more powerful bulletin board was
available—the right-wing *Post*.

Once the *Voice* no longer had kind things to say about him,
Koch grew to detest the paper. So much so that he has refused
to grant personal interviews to its reporters while denouncing
Newfield and his *Voice* colleague Wayne Barrett, demonstrating
that the vaunted accessibility extends only to those who write less
critically of him. Newfield, a former Koch friend, says the Mayor
is so angry he won't even talk to his wife: "In 1978, she ran into
him at Balducci's [a gourmet food store], stuck out her hand and
said, 'How are you doing, Ed?' He made a nasty remark and
walked away."

Koch has also dumped Auletta into his personal gulag of reporters to whom he will not grant interviews. Auletta's 1979 profile of Koch in *The New Yorker* certainly made the Mayor unhappy, but Auletta's banishment did not come until sometime in
1981. Why? Auletta himself is uncertain what article or articles
prompted Koch to cut him off.

During his years in the Village and in Congress, Koch had been a source for reporters, a co-conspirator in the game of journalism. He continued right along that way when he got to City Hall, attacking his own government the way the reporters themselves loved to. He made the job easy. And the extensive coverage he got brought a subtle change in perception to New York City. In pre-Koch years, the city had a big, complex municipal government that included a mayor. No longer. Under Koch, it seemed, it had only a mayor.

"Whatever is good or bad about the city is an Ed Koch story," says a television executive. "You are not aware of city government in New York. There is hardly a story he doesn't play a part in. He just feeds on himself. He isn't a human being anymore. He's the Mayor."

Koch has a childlike delight in making news. Former Deputy Mayor Robert Wagner, Jr., for example, recalls Koch picking up the phone in his limousine and feeding a quote to a press aide at City Hall that would be typed up, photocopied hundreds of times and distributed. "There goes another forest," Koch smiled as he hung up the phone. Every night Koch would go out—or send out—for the early editions of the next day's papers, read them and then reread the later editions in the morning. He noted with interest how the papers changed through the various editions and, of course, searched out how he was played personally, something that he still does fastidiously to this day. One City Hall reporter saw this firsthand as he rode with Koch late one night in his car. Anxious to see the next morning's papers, Koch ordered his chauffeur to pull up at a newsstand, picked them up, and began poring over them right away.

"Koch started reading the papers in the back of this darkened car. I couldn't believe it," the reporter says. "I couldn't see anything. I asked him how he did it but he didn't even hear me." A top mayoral aide later unraveled the mystery. "His name lights up in the dark," the aide explained.

After reading the papers, Koch was immediately ready to respond if he didn't like something, all set to do battle with the press as he battles with everyone else. Lee Dembart, then the City Hall bureau chief for the *Times*, got some insight into how Koch operated when confronted with even trivial news items that displeased him. Dembart recalls a conversation with Koch in the Mayor's office in which they discussed a forgettable movie starring John Travolta and Lily Tomlin.

"Koch said to me, 'When they make a movie of my life, I want John Travolta to play me and Lily Tomlin to play Bess Myerson,' " Dembart says. "I said, 'Oh, you're a teenage sex symbol now?' He smiled and liked that idea."

Dembart included Koch's casting desires as a one-paragraph item in his City Hall Notes column on Sunday. The *Times* was hardly off the presses before Koch phoned the newspaper to deny that he'd ever made such a remark, and the paragraph was deleted from later editions of the newspaper. Dembart was furious—with Koch *and* his editor.

"I got into City Hall first thing Monday morning and said to Maureen Connelly, 'Do you remember when Ed said what cast he wanted?' She said, yes, he wanted John Travolta to play him and Lily Tomlin to play Bess. Subsequently, Koch calls me and says, 'I'm terribly sorry. Maureen tells me that I said it.' I said would you do me a favor and call my editor Sydney Schanberg. He did, and said, 'Well, I guess I was wrong. Maureen tells me that was what I said.'

"A few days later, I was in the car with him, and he brought it up again. He made some passing reference to John Travolta and Lily Tomlin. I said I thought it was a dead issue, but would you mind putting it in writing since the only thing a reporter has to go on is his reputation for honesty."

The letter Koch wrote to Dembart is dated January 25, 1979, and says:

Dear Lee:

I truly regret that I did not recall my comment to you on Travolta and Tomlin and insisted that the *Times* editor delete the items reporting my comment because it hadn't occurred. As you know, as soon as it was recalled to me by Maureen, I called Sid Shamberg (sic) and told him of my error and of your exemplary accuracy in reporting.

I regret the distress I caused you. It was unintentional.

Sincerely, Edward I. Koch, Mayor.

Yet the issue was still not really dead. Koch later told Dembart he didn't mind John Travolta playing him but thought Myerson would be mad about Lily Tomlin playing her.

All through the early years, the press marched forward with Koch. There were a few rough spots along the way, but no major conflicts. Did *Newsday* need a full-page ad featuring the Mayor to promote its New York City edition? No problem. Would the Mayor appear in a promotional film for *The New York Times*? Of course. The Mayor also stood ready to assist local radio and television stations with various promotional schemes. And needless to say, the Mayor was more than willing to defend the *New York Post* against charges of sensationalism and vulgarity. "What? Its headlines? 'KILLER BEES COMING TO NEW YORK CITY'? I believe the bees are coming, ultimately. They're working their way up an inch at a time from the Yucatán," he told an interviewer from *Playboy* magazine. But why should people call the *New York Post* vulgar unless they want to call 1,000,000 *Post* readers vulgar? Koch also thought the tabloid newspaper worthy of the ultimate award for journalists. In 1981, he wrote a letter nominating the *Post* for a Pulitzer Prize for a series of articles on gun control.

But these favors were mere bagatelles, for Koch had developed a finely tuned sense of meeting a paper's editorial needs. In 1979, for example, the papers and airwaves were filled with news of a crime wave in the subways. There had been a rash of murders, but the surge in underground violence was actually more apparent than real. It was largely the creation of one person— Morty Matz, a public relations man whose clients included the Transit Police Union. Matz decided to beat the drums for the underground cops and arranged to have them call him every time there was a serious subway crime. He quickly passed the information along to news desks around the city. The result was an instant subway crime wave. Statistically—except for the rash of murders—there was no significant change in the amount of lawbreaking, but you couldn't tell that by watching television or reading your local newspaper.

Reporters began to press Koch about crime in the subways and what the city was going to do about it. The Mayor replied time and again that he understood the fears of straphangers but that the problem was more one of perception than fact. As the horror stories continued to appear, a *Daily News* editor dispatched a reporter to ask the Mayor yet again what he was going to do about the problem. After all, whether crime was increasing or not, it was still a plague on the subways. You only had to talk to the mugging victims or the families of those murdered to understand that. The reporter told press secretary Connelly that the *News* needed something fresh on subway crime. She went in to see Koch and returned with a statement that repeated what he'd been saying all along. The reporter looked at it. "No story," he thought to himself unhappily. Then he looked at Connelly. "This isn't good enough. I've got to solve subway crime by deadline," he said, implying that the highest echelons of the tabloid newspaper were unhappy with the Mayor.

Connelly arranged for the reporter to see Koch personally. "He wants you to come up with the ideas," she told the reporter. The reporter had none. He quickly surveyed a group of City Hall police officers. They had no ideas either. The reporter, lacking any proposals to smash subway crime, then met with Koch in his office. The conversation did not go well at first as Koch simply repeated what he'd said before. At last, the reporter said, "What about a task force?" Ah, now there was an idea. Koch picked up on it right away. "I've got to get the best minds in to give me their suggestions," he said with deadline urgency.

It wasn't much, but it was something, and the *Daily News* heralded it on March 16, 1979 as an impending showdown with subway thugs. The headline on page one blared, KOCH: BATTLE SUBWAY CRIME. The headline over the brief story reporting Koch's remarks on page 3 promised even more: BATTLE PLAN ASKED BY MAYOR TO CURB TRANSIT VIOLENCE. That night, Connelly was flooded with calls from other news organizations demanding information on the battle plan. The next morning, none too pleased, she greeted the reporter with "You don't know the trouble you caused! The story was all right, but after that headline, how could we say we weren't battling subway crime?"

Koch leaped into action immediately, convening a summit meeting with the Police Commissioner, the Transit Police Chief, the Manhattan district attorney and other officials. The results, announced late in the day at a news conference, were gratifying enough to warm the heart of the crustiest union leader. The Mayor's "battle plan"—assembled, as he had told readers of the *Daily News*, with the "best minds"—called for beefing up subway patrols, reorganizing the transit cops, shortening the trains at night to make them safer, and pushing for get-tough-with-crime legislation. The cost was estimated at $7.5 million.

"Is that enough?" Connelly asked the reporter who'd started it all. "Seven-point-five million dollars?"

"OK, who's got the first question?" the Mayor asks to begin an "at home," his six-foot one-inch frame slumping deeply into the chair. The funny face is mobile, puttylike; the expressions flit from anger to laughter to disgust to disbelief to a smirking self-satisfaction. The mouth always moves quickly, but the slouching body sometimes seems to be slowly deflating in the armchair during routine discussions. A hostile question or a threatening topic and suddenly Koch is on the edge of the chair, his body taut.

Arms flail in a variety of directions for emphasis and are occasionally extended outward with palms upraised heavenward in a "What do you want me to do?" gesture to the press. Hand and arm movements combine with facial expressions and a raspy, nasal voice to create a multimedia effect. ("Do you really expect me to do that? It's ridiculous! It's stupid!")

If others in the office speak for more than a minute or two, the body again melts into the chair but does not—and seemingly cannot—remain at rest. Impatience and boredom cloud the face. His hand reaches upward to cup his chin or clamps onto the top of his bald head with fingers pointed outward. He taps on his teeth with a finger; looks upward with raised eyebrows and furrowed forehead; puffs up his cheeks; and lists to one side or the other in the armchair like a child trapped in a new suit.

Reporters are free to ask anything they wish. So much so that, as a joke, a newsman once jumped into a particularly rambling "at home" to ask Koch to name his favorite color. To his surprise, instead of laughing, Koch launched into a fairly lengthy discourse that disclosed he was partially color-blind and favored blue—though not at the expense of other colors. There were follow-up questions from other reporters.

Like a late-night television talk show host, Koch sometimes invites guests to his "at homes." They may include other city officials, show business personalities, foreign dignitaries, or even animals. Like the time Archie, a dog with a strong resemblance to Old Yeller, disappeared from Gracie Mansion for several days. The missing mutt, which is owned by Koch's chef, though Koch has "adopted" it, became the subject of stories in the tabloids, television, and even the staid *Times*. The return of the pooch rated a news conference in Koch's office and a battery of microphones and cameras were at the ready when Koch looked at Archie and commanded, "Talk! Talk! Talk! Talk!" Archie passed up an opportunity for instant immortality by declining to speak; perhaps he knew better than to open his mouth and upstage the chief executive of the World's Greatest City. Nevertheless, the return of the canine who called the Mayor's official residence home was news, news, news.

And it was wonderful, wonderful, wonderful. Whatever it took to get into the papers and on television, Koch was more than willing. Dress up like Michael Jackson in a black silk bomber jacket, white glove, and sunglasses and for no reason at all suddenly appear on the steps of City Hall? No problem. Try on hats, ride a camel, wear a gold lamé jumpsuit, call Carol Bellamy "a pain in the ass." Happy to do all that and more. The more outrageous, funny, and cruel he was, the more likely it was that he'd be news. It worked.

Koch now appears on television more than 300 times a year, and is heard on radio even more often. A routine memo from his press office outlined his pre-scheduled media appearances for a Sunday and Monday in January 1985: "The mayor will appear on 'CBS News Sunday Morning,' . . . He will also appear on 'International Dateline,' Manhattan Cable . . . He will also appear on 'Off the Set,' WNEW-TV, Channel 5 . . . He will also appear on 'The Law in Action,' WOR radio . . . He will also appear on 'The Michael Jackson Show,' WABC Radio . . . He will also appear on 'Albany Report to Long Island,' Group W Cable."

Koch has been on television so much that he has even developed his own distinctive video style—one in which he breaks a cardinal rule and looks not at his interviewer but right into the camera. Gabe Pressman, of WNBC-TV, likens the technique to "a lawyer arguing eloquently in the courtroom, who might look away from the judge and the witness and aim a couple of shots at the jury."

"That's what he does," Pressman says. "He sort of half-answers your question and then turns to the camera and says—'Isn't that R-I-D-I-C-U-L-O-U-S?' He looks at the jury—the public."

Koch also writes weekly columns for three small daily newspapers in the city and other mayoral musings are packaged and mailed for publication to dozens of weeklies. Mayoral newsletters jammed with pictures of Koch and personalized photo captions ("Here I am with Captain Gneckow on the sparkling deck of the U.S.S. *Iowa*") are periodically sent out by the thousands. And in 1984, his office issued more than 500 press releases, a figure that does not include mayoral letters, schedules, reports, and assorted other documents that pour forth from his press aides every day.

How important is the coverage to Koch?

Well, in 1984 when Channel 2 stopped inviting Koch to appear as a guest every Friday on its late-afternoon news broadcast, the station management was surprised to receive a detailed lawyer's letter about the matter from Koch's counsel Patrick Mulhearn. Although several news reporters at the station had complained bitterly that there was no journalistic justification for having Koch as a weekly guest, news director Frank Gardner says his appearances were terminated as a matter of fairness in what was a presidential election year with a hot Democratic primary contest in New York State. Koch responded to the cancellation of his appearances with Mulhearn's "opinion," arguing in detailed legal prose that his guest spots would not obligate Channel 2 to provide equal time to anyone. "It was sort of a legal exercise," Gardner said. "I read it with amusement and discounted it."

When Koch strides into a formal press conference in City Hall's Blue Room, he immediately counts to himself the number of television cameras present, a fact that came to light when a reporter made an offhand remark to him before the start of one such session. Koch had called the press conference to announce that he was endorsing Walter Mondale for nomination as the Democratic candidate to run against Ronald Reagan, but he had scheduled the announcement for a day filled with major world events.

"I guess you picked a day when you didn't want much coverage," the reporter said.

"I don't know," Koch answered without hesitating. "I guess this is a story. There are eleven cameras here."

Indeed there were.

And even seven years into his mayoralty, Koch still badgers his top aides into watching his performances on television so that they can review his performances—all terrific, of course. Once a reporter happened to be in Deputy Mayor Stanley Brezenoff's office when a call came in from Koch. The reporter could only hear Brezenoff's side of the conversation, but there was no question what Koch was saying.

"No, I didn't see it, Ed," Brezenoff said.

Pause.

"No, I don't have a TV in my office."

Pause.

"Yeah, yeah, I will. I'll go to the press office. They probably have it on tape. Talk to you later."

At some point, as far as many in the press were concerned, it all became overkill. There was just too much Koch, too many attacks on too many things. On one day alone in 1983, Koch managed to denounce the policies of Ronald Reagan, banks, doctors, lawyers, contractors, unions, landlords, Britain, Saudi Arabia, the stock market, and Albany. And, in the end, too many "at homes." The old adage came true—familiarity bred contempt—and as Koch's administration wore on, the tone of the exchanges between Koch and the press changed markedly. The good-natured arguments of the early years were replaced by thinly veiled hostility.

A reporter who asked a challenging question or one relating to a sensitive or politically charged issue could expect Koch to turn it back on him in a verbal assault. In early 1985, for example, when reporters asked Koch about his decision not to declare the birthday of Martin Luther King, Jr. a city holiday because, he said, it would cost too much money, Koch answered that city employees "already get three more holidays than you do. I'm now talking about the reporters' contract on holidays gotten through collective bargaining."

King's birthday, the Mayor lectured the reporters, was a "holiday that *you're not getting.*" The veins in his face bulged a bit and his voice rose to a near shout as he stood behind a podium at the front of the room.

"Are you getting Martin Luther King holiday?" Koch asked William Murphy of the Associated Press. "You are not," the Mayor answered with finality. "Anybody in this room from the media getting Martin Luther King holiday? Anybody?"

There was silence from the thirty-odd reporters and the Mayor moved to pick off individual tormenters. "Gabe [Pressman of WNBC-TV], are you getting the holiday? You are not. I know you are not. I know you are not getting the holiday." He looked around the room. *"Why don't you get your bosses to provide it?"* he asked, sneering at the journalistic shrugs.

Koch was riding high when Goldstein began the "at homes."

As far as the press was concerned then, he was a fun mayor—open, candid, invigorating. His credibility was unrivaled by any politician. That was all to change, however. Koch's credibility with the press would plummet dramatically. In the midst of a controversy with Defense Secretary Caspar Weinberger he would be caught in a lie with a reporter. He would break a solemn and oft-repeated vow never to run for any other office but Mayor. And with the publication of his autobiography, he would be forced to admit to the City Hall press corps that he had misled them on a number of occasions by answering their questions with statements that were, at best, half-truths: About a key political strategy in his 1981 reelection campaign. About his feelings after he lost the 1982 Democratic gubernatorial primary to Mario Cuomo. About why he performed so poorly in taping a television commercial supporting Cuomo against Republican Lew Lehrman after his defeat in the primary.

It all came out in an extraordinary press conference in February 1984, the day on which Koch first answered questions about his controversial book. Facing obviously angry questioning by reporters, Koch finally explained, "I am not required to tell you everything I know." And if the public was misled, he said, the fault rested not with him, but with the reporters who failed to ask him questions that were "sufficiently pointed." That politicians do not always tell the truth is not, of course, news. But Ed Koch had promised to be different.

WHOSE SIDE IS HE ON?

During his first two years in office, Koch's madcap, thumb-in-the-eye style led many people to conclude that he didn't care who he offended, that he could not walk away from a fight even if the consequences were that he would not win a second term. Koch said he regarded such conclusions about his behavior as flattering, assuming that people who said he acted like a one-term mayor believed he was an honest man who was putting the good of the city above personal ambition.

But Koch never said he intended to be a one-term mayor. Far from it. Having fulfilled his life's dream, he announced soon after he was elected that he expected to stay in office for twelve years. And Koch had no sooner taken the reins of government than he began plotting ways to hold on to them. Even his public fights were calculated—never did he pick on anyone who could do him real damage. As Koch himself said, blacks don't vote, so they were safe targets. So were the unions, for Koch knew that most New Yorkers shared his belief that the city was not getting a full day's work for a day's pay. The same was true with other traditional liberal causes, such as improved services for the poor. Koch knew the public mood had changed, that the white middle class was feeling threatened and abused. So he took on their enemies. Maybe they deserved to be taken on, but there were many other entrenched groups making money off the city's hide that he did not take on. Real estate developers had been having their way with the city treasury and city policy for decades, and when the fiscal crisis hit, the banks did not lose a penny. Koch knew all that, but he did not excoriate them, call them names, or threaten to take away their "patronage." Koch is many things, but dumb is not among them. He knew the big rollers could hurt him by giving money to a candidate against him. No, Ed Koch was not out of control with his fights, even for a second. He knew exactly what he was doing. He had one goal in mind, and everything was geared to achieving it.

"Ed doesn't have a theme, or an ideology," said Peter Solomon, who served as a deputy mayor under Koch in 1978 and 1979. "His only goal is to be reelected."

To what end?

"Forever," Solomon said.

Why?

"Because that's his ultimate."

Koch was not going to give up the top of the heap without a fight. And so he began preparing for his 1981 reelection campaign in 1979. Yet even Solomon underestimated what Koch had in mind. He thought Koch just wanted to be reelected. But a number of his predecessors had already achieved that. La Guardia had three terms. So did Robert Wagner. Even John Lindsay, Koch's favorite scapegoat for all that was wrong with the city, had managed two terms. So just getting reelected was not good enough. What Koch had in mind was a victory so total and overwhelming that he would be the undisputed King of New York. He wanted a coronation, and he would settle for nothing less.

His strategy was simple. He would become a Republican. Not that he would stop being a Democrat. He would stay one of those, too. He would be both. That way just about everybody who went to the polls would have to vote for him. There his name would be at the top of the two big columns on the ballot—Democratic and Republican. That's about as close as democracy can come to banana-republic politics. There would be other lines on the ballot, as well, but only two other parties had even a remote claim to credibility—the Liberals and the Conservatives. In his quest for dominance of the political scene, Koch considered trying to get the endorsement of those parties as well.

"We almost tried a parlay across the board," Garth says with a smile. "All four—the ideal campaign."

But the stir that would have caused might well have cost more votes than it gained, and so the idea was dropped. The Democratic and Republican lines were the two biggies anyway and in the end, Koch decided to limit himself to them. One hundred and four men had been mayor before Ed Koch, and not one had ever achieved the two-party endorsement he had in mind. While many mayors ran for reelection with the endorsement of two parties, one of the parties had always been a minor one. La Guardia ran as a Republican and as the candidate of something called the City Fusion Party. None had ever had the backing of both major parties. Then again, none of them was named Ed Koch.

Koch's plan started to unfold in late 1979, when he held secret talks with New York City Republican leaders. In December of that year, he attended a quiet dinner with twenty prominent Republicans, all members of the Columbus Club. Given by Vincent Albano, the Manhattan Republican leader, the dinner was a way for Koch and a few big-time Republican bankrollers to rub elbows and feel each other out. The outcome was a foregone conclusion, though, for Koch had captured the attention of conservatives everywhere with his call for the death penalty and by fighting with blacks and the municipal unions. Such positions enabled Koch to pass the "litmus test" of conservatives, and so it came as no surprise when Albano, after several hours of eating and drinking, told Koch that Republican backing was his for the asking in the 1981 campaign.

"Don't worry, you'll get plenty of support from us," Albano told Koch. In saying that, Albano was reflecting the reality of his party's weakness as well as his admiration for Koch. Roy Goodman, a Manhattan state senator, was the Republican nominee against Koch in 1977 and got only four percent of the vote. Albano did not have to be a genius to know that his party, outnumbered by Democrats among registered voters in the city by 1.8 million to 340,000, had little chance of electing a mayor on its own. But there were possibilities for a party that could help a man become king. Jobs, maybe, perhaps a few judgeships, too. In a word, patronage, the glue of party and personal loyalty.

Armed with the knowledge that Republican support was within reach, Koch put his plan into high gear. A few weeks later, he startled even the most grizzled politicians when he had a very public lunch with two other city Republican leaders. The two—George L. Clark, Jr., of Brooklyn and his Bronx counterpart, State Senator John Calandra—broke bread with the Mayor at Luchow's, a famous old German-style landmark on East Fourteenth Street. Newspaper accounts said Koch picked up the tab, but Clark says he doesn't remember that.

What he does remember is the subject, which was whether
Koch could get the endorsements of the Republican and Conservative parties in his reelection bid twenty months hence. Although a lifelong Democrat—the endorsement of John Lindsay
in 1965 the only stain on his record—Koch emerged from the lunch
and announced that he wanted to be a "fusion' candidate who
could unite the city's various parties. Clark and Calandra suggested the Mayor would get their blessings, although they made
no commitments.

The move brought immediate criticism not only from Democrats, who viewed Koch as disloyal, but from some Republicans
as well, who did not want a Democrat, especially one with liberal roots, defiling their party. There were many suggestions that
Koch was more interested in a coronation than reelection, suggestions which Koch rebuffed with the rudest denials. His only
goal, Koch said repeatedly, was to strengthen the city's position
with Republicans in the state and federal governments. Being
endorsed by both parties, he said, would work to the advantage
of all New Yorkers because Albany and Washington would have
no partisan reasons for not helping the city out of its financial
straits.

It sounded good—very altruistic—but the campaign was still
secretly worried that Koch would be hit with the charge that he
was about to switch parties. Garth made a commercial to deflect
the issue.

"I am a Democrat," Koch says in the commercial, "and I'll always be one. But I also sought the Republican nomination to show
Washington and Albany we're united behind our city government . . . I wanted to make a strong case for New York in
Washington and Albany to fight the Reagan budget cuts."

Much later, long after he'd won the election, Koch said his real
reason for seeking the Republican nomination was that he had
been afraid that the city's Democratic voters would reject him in
the party primary. Having the Republican line, he said, was an
insurance policy that guaranteed him a spot on the ballot in his
general election. It was when he made that revelation—in his
book—that reporters who cover Koch on a regular basis came to
realize that Koch had a different definition of honesty than most
people. For all during the campaign he had denied that he had
any reason, other than the good of the city, for seeking both
nominations.

But Koch's closest confidants question whether the notion of an insurance policy was the real reason for Koch's pursuit of the Republicans. What they say he was motivated by was, plainly and simply, his ego—vanity. After years of nervously asking "How'm I doin'?" he wanted to answer the question for himself once and for all.

"It was something he kept pretty much to himself, but it was clear he was interested in it as a confirmation that he had been a good mayor," said one confidant. "Not just a good Democratic mayor, but a good mayor, period."

Said another insider: "Despite what he said in his book that he wanted the Republican line as an insurance policy, 90 percent of the reason was vanity. In his wildest dreams, he didn't believe he could lose the Democratic primary. He wanted to be special, to be different. That's all."

But to get the Republican nod, Koch had to prove that he was one of them. So he set about doing just that, methodically putting together a puzzle that only he could see. Like a clever real estate developer who quietly assembles a huge site one lot at a time at bargain prices, so as not to alarm the neighborhood, and drive up prices, Koch went about his work without much public ado. Consider just a few developments that took place over the eight months following the Luchow's get-together:

Koch accepted an offer from William Simon, a supporter of Republican presidential candidate Ronald Reagan, to form a Republicans for Koch campaign committee in 1981.

Koch threw his support behind the reelection bids of four Republicans: Goodman, Calandra, a third state senator, John Marchi of Staten Island, and Bill Green, who had succeeded Koch as the silk-stocking district congressman.

Koch became the first Democrat ever to address the Republican Party's National Platform Committee, where he attacked the urban policies of his fellow Democrat, President Jimmy Carter.

And finally, with the November presidential and congressional races approaching, Koch invited Ronald Reagan and Alfonse D'Amato, a Long Island Republican running for the U.S. Senate, to Gracie Mansion for a chat—and pictures. He praised Reagan, saying his policies on Israel were better than Carter's. Reagan responded that he would support Koch.

Democratic officials, already depressed about Reagan's commanding lead over Carter in public opinion polls, were livid.

Koch's message was that he could live with Reagan, D'Amato, and Republicans in general. His position was particularly significant because, as New York's Mayor and the best-known Jewish politician in the country, he was also sending a signal that Ronald Reagan was OK for Jews. That was especially irksome to President Carter, who was already under fire from Jewish groups for his yes vote on a United Nations resolution rebuking Israel for its settlements on the West Bank of the Jordan River.

Koch had roundly criticized Carter for the vote, and labeled Cyrus Vance, the Secretary of State, and other top State officials the "Gang of Five." He called them Arabists, a polite way, in Koch's lexicon, of accusing them of being anti-Israel. Later, it was widely assumed that Koch's criticism had contributed to Carter's defeat in the 1980 New York State presidential primary at the hands of Senator Ted Kennedy. On top of that, Carter was still upset at Koch for calling his brother Billy a "wacko." And, of course, there had been the first incident between then, back in 1977 when Koch, in the midst of his third race against Cuomo, had publicly embarrassed Carter by handing him a letter criticizing American policies toward Israel. Reporters and photographers were at the ready because they knew what was happening, but Carter didn't. It must have still rankled Carter that when Koch had later apologized, he had made his beg-pardon in private, away from the glare of the cameras.

Meanwhile, Koch kept repeating that his dealings with Republicans were not political, that they were for the good of the city. How good they were for Koch became more evident in 1981. Early that year, John LoCicero, Koch's reformer companion from the Village and now the Mayor's patronage dispenser, began calling Republican leaders. Koch wanted their support and, more specifically, their permission to run in the Republican mayoral primary. As a registered Democrat, Koch needed the approval of a majority of the five county leaders before he could enter the Republican race.

The Bronx leaders, headed by Calandra, quickly got in line, as did Albano from Manhattan and the Staten Island group. That gave Koch the required backing of three counties, but Koch said he wanted Brooklyn too, where Clark reigned. Without Clark's support, Koch said, he would not enter the Republican primary.

So Clark got his first call from LoCicero since the Luchow's lunch, nearly a year earlier. LoCicero, an earthy, warm guy who is a walking dictionary of political history and factions, said he'd be grateful if Clark would come over to his apartment one night and talk to Koch. LoCicero didn't say what Koch wanted to talk about, but he didn't have to. Clark, also the state Republican chairman, had been reading the papers and the tea leaves. He knew Koch had contributed to Reagan's good reputation among Jews and helped D'Amato, Calandra, and the others get elected over Democrats. It was not outrageous, nor even surprising, that Koch was now calling in the chits.

Clark, a diehard Brooklynite whose family had lived in the borough for four generations on his Irish father's side and for three on his Italian mother's side, appeared at LoCicero's Greenwich Village apartment on the appointed night. Koch was waiting, along with Pete Piscatelli, Koch's chief lobbyist, LoCicero and his wife, Jo. Clark sat on a chair opposite Koch. After some brief pleasantries about how cold it was, Koch got down to business. He told Clark he wanted his party's nomination, that having the backing of both Democrats and Republicans would make him independent of partisan labels and could lead to a united city. Besides, Koch threw in, he liked Ronald Reagan.

Clark had expected something like this, and was prepared with a little speech of his own. He said he suspected that Koch was still a liberal who was masquerading as a conservative because the country was moving to the right. Then he went on to complain that Koch was operating the city like a liberal—judges and the cops were soft on crime and landlords, including Clark, were being beaten out of rent payments by welfare families.

Clark remembers that Koch responded by saying he was interested in improving the criminal justice system and by spouting some statistics about how many apartments his administration had rehabilitated for middle-class families. The conversation went on like that for about thirty minutes. Koch never demanded a yes or no answer about the nomination, and Clark never offered one. They promised to meet again.

Afterward, Clark started meeting with other Republicans in Brooklyn, telling them that Koch reminded him of himself when he was a conservative Democrat. In 1969, Clark switched parties because he felt that he was no longer in tune with the Democrats. And, despite lingering suspicions about Koch's motives, Clark had a feeling the Mayor was now in the same position— that he was finding himself drifting further away from mainstream Democrats. Clark started putting out some feelers to Washington, asking Republican bigs there how they felt about the Mayor. The signals he got back were mostly positive. Party loyalists were grateful for the way Koch had helped elect Reagan and D'Amato in 1980. And Washington was appreciative, if confused, over the fact that Koch was less critical of Reagan than he had been of Carter, even though Reagan's budget cuts were wreaking havoc on city programs. Moreover, in all his fights over money and legislation in Albany, Koch had never beaten up publicly on Warren Anderson, the upstate Republican who controls the state Senate. Democrats Koch would fight, even brawl with, but not Anderson. His restraint had not gone unnoticed in Republican camps. So now Koch was asking for something in return—half a king's crown, as it were—and Clark was being told Washington had no problems with granting it.

Meanwhile, Clark got another call from LoCicero, who opened the conversation by asking Clark what he drank. Clark said J & B. LoCicero said, OK, why don't you meet us at Koch's apartment in the Village. Clark arrived at the scheduled time, carrying a small drinking glass filled with Ronald Reagan's favorite candy, jelly beans, as a gift for the Republican convert. When he walked in the door, there on the table was the J & B—a pint bottle.

"I thought it was really cute," Clark says. "I mean they had run out and bought it just for me. The cheap son of a bitch. A lousy pint."

Garth, Connelly, and LoCicero were there. Someone fixed Clark a drink—"the weakest, smallest Scotch I've ever had"—and they got down to business. Clark gave the same speech he gave before, to test Koch, about how he didn't like what was going on in the city. He still had some anxieties that Koch was pretending to be a conservative because that's what the public wanted. He was afraid Koch was the kind of guy who sees a parade and jumps in front of it so he can claim to have led it to where it was going anyway, the kind of guy who wears plaid socks because a Garth poll says they are in vogue with the voters.

Clark remembers that Koch reassured him. No, that's not me. I'm a new guy. I believe these things, he recalls him saying. So Koch passed the first test, again, but Clark had some other things on his mind as well. He knew that Koch didn't need the Republican nod—that he was going to win the Democratic primary in a walk. He also knew that John Esposito, a loyal Queens Assemblyman, wanted to run for Mayor on the Republican line. Esposito had no chance of winning the election, but Clark considered him a friend who, after all, had been a Republican all along. Then, there was the question of what was going to happen in 1982, the big statewide political year.

The polls were showing that Hugh Carey, the second-term Democratic Governor, was slipping in popularity, and Clark thought the Republicans had a chance to capture the statehouse. Suppose, just suppose, Koch decided he wanted to jump into the race himself? Clark had seen Republicans reach out to Democrats they liked—Richard Nixon with Pat Moynihan, Nelson Rockefeller with Hugh Carey—only to have those Democrats haunt the Republicans later by winning offices the Republicans might have won. Clark did not want to be remembered as the Republican who built up Ed Koch. Yet he also had to think of the present. He reasoned that no Republican was going to beat Koch and that the party might salvage something by helping Koch get elected. He looked at Koch, who was sitting alone on a two-person love seat, and remembers telling him:

"You've got to promise me that you will never run for another office. No City Council, no Assembly, no Governor, no nothing. I don't care what happens to Carey, even if he gets hit by a bus on Madison Avenue, you've got to promise me you will never run for any other office if I support you for Mayor."

Koch slid forward on the sofa and answered Clark firmly, repeating a promise he made to God at the Wailing Wall in Jerusalem—never to seek another office. Koch subsequently boasted of the pledge to aides.

"I give you my word of honor," Clark recalls him saying. "I want to be Mayor for twelve years. I then want to retire and I want to go make some money because I have never made serious money as a lawyer. But after twelve years, I think I could make some money as a lawyer, and that's what I'd like to be able to do."

All the while he was talking, Koch kept sliding forward on the sofa, so by the time he finished, his right knee was almost touching the floor. Clark was struck by the posture. "This is obscene," he thought to himself. "I mean, it's like he's begging me." It occurred to him that Koch was more desperate than he had realized. But he didn't have time for reverie, because Koch, pushing his case, sought to impress Clark with his Republican spirit.

"I've got to tell you this story because then you'll know why I think Ronald Reagan is so great," Clark remembers Koch saying. "It is a combination of the fact that I think Reagan will make a great President, and I had to make sure that Jimmy Carter never got to be President again. I met him at the heliport once, and I'm riding in the car with Carter, and Jimmy Carter is very angry at me. He says to me, putting his finger two inches from my nose, he says to me, 'Nobody has done more to hurt me in my political career than you have, Ed Koch, and I'm not going to forget it.' I did not want to see my body floating in the East River, and I thought some hit man will get me or the CIA will find me or the FBI."

Clark remembers Koch then running through the alphabet names of all the government security and intelligence agencies, and concluding: "I decided then that Carter cannot be President again because I was scared for myself."

Clark says it was the strangest thing he ever heard. And he insists that Ed Koch, the Mayor of the City of New York, appeared to truly believe that Jimmy Carter, the President of the United States, was capable of having him murdered.

Koch's ramblings caught Clark off guard, but he kept his senses by focusing on the one issue that was critical to him: that Koch not run for anything else, especially for governor. Koch repeated his pledge not to. Satisfied, Clark then suggested that Koch should also try for the Conservative Party nomination. The Conservative Party is even smaller than the Republican Party and often attempts to increase its influence by endorsing Republican candidates. Here is the conversation as Clark remembers it:

GARTH: He can't take the Conservative line.
CLARK: Mr. Mayor, why can't you?
KOCH: Because the blacks wouldn't stand for it.
CLARK: Wait, a minute! Are you saying the blacks would feel the Conservatives are antiblack, because I don't know any Conservatives who are antiblack?
KOCH: Let me tell you, I'll take the Conservative line in my next administration. But I can't do it now because they are part

of the problem, and if I took the Conservative line, it would seem like I was siding against them.

CLARK: Mr. Mayor, I've got a problem with that . . . The Conservatives are not antiblack and you are wrong if you think they are.

GARTH: Believe me, I've seen the numbers. He can't take the Conservative Party line, but he'll take it in the next administration.

Garth says that there was talk of the Conservative line, but that he does not believe Koch said anything about blacks because he was not concerned that taking the Conservative line would have cost Koch black votes. Rather, Garth says the concern was that taking the Conservative line would have cost Koch liberal white votes.

At any rate, Clark said he was troubled by Koch's answers, but dropped the subject and returned to the question of the 1982 gubernatorial election.

CLARK: Would you not campaign for Hugh Carey in a reelection effort?

KOCH: What I may want to do is one thing, what I may have to do is another . . . I can't give you a commitment on that.

Clark accepted Koch's answer and the deal was cut. He had done Koch a favor, a big one, and Koch owed him. Clark remembers that Koch acknowledged his debt immediately.

"By the way," he said as Clark headed for the door, "I intend to have a bipartisan administration including Republicans who are qualified. I am going to be depending on you to tell me who they are so they can be part of it."

Clark left, confident he would have the Mayor's ear and would be able to get a few of his people jobs at City Hall. Not bad for a kid from Brooklyn, he thought. In exchange, Clark ran interference for Koch with the other Republican leaders, who agreed to let Koch run in their primary. That caused the Republican leaders a lot of flak from their rank and file, some of whom felt they were disgracing their party. But they stuck to their bargain. Many Democrats were unhappy, too. They felt on principle that Koch's alliance was an unholy one that amounted to a sellout.

Since the days of Roosevelt, the party had prided itself on being a haven for the disaffected in American society while the Republicans were seen as the party of the rich. Now Ed Koch had gone and said there wasn't any difference between the two.

One Democrat who publicly criticized Koch was Stanley Fink, the speaker of the state Assembly. Fink, from Brooklyn, was besieged by complaints from upstate Democrats who had voted money for city programs numerous times since Koch had become Mayor. The rivalry between upstate and downstate, between rural and urban, was a tradition in New York, but it had grown sharper in recent years because of the fiscal constraints on both the city and the state. The city always seemed to be needing more to avoid collapse, and upstate and suburban legislators were tired of being told that the city was facing yet another emergency. Every dollar they gave the city was a dollar that their own constituents would not get, but they had gone along because Fink was able to persuade them that Koch was doing good things for the city and had control of expenditures. They always paid for those votes, when every two years the Republicans ran candidates against them with the charge that they were neglecting their own districts to vote more money for that sinkhole known as the Big Apple. So now they, too, felt betrayed by having Koch say there was no difference between a Democrat and a Republican.

"It was very insensitive of him," Fink says. "It had nothing to do with survival. He did it only for self-aggrandizement. It was grandstanding."

Meanwhile, the field for the Democratic primary was taking shape. Or more precisely, shaking out.

The action started when a group of influential New Yorkers generally of liberal persuasion, people such as Theodore Kheel, Arthur Schlesinger, Jr., and John Lindsay, sought to find a candidate to run against Koch. Their ranks included some bitter Koch enemies—Herman Badillo, who had broken with Koch after resigning as deputy mayor in 1979, and Bella Abzug. They made much of their efforts to find a liberal intellectual with academic credentials who could take on Koch. They felt the Mayor had moved so far to the right, and had so polarized the city along racial and class lines, that a compassionate healer could pull off an upset. Koch despised them all, said so, and launched a series of vituperative, personal attacks. He said they were all afraid to run themselves, called them elitists, radicals, nuts, and even did a little redbaiting—some of his enemies might be Communists, he said. Koch was going for the jugular right off the mark—indeed, the campaign hadn't even started. Coupled with what seemed a very high popularity, Koch's vicious attacks took the wind out of the group's sails and it eventually ceased to be a factor in the campaign.

At the same time, however, a ragtag band of candidates was getting ready to run in the Democratic primary with or without organized support. After several false starts, three candidates emerged with enough money and energy to stay around to the end—Frank Barbaro, a longshoreman-turned-assemblyman from Brooklyn; Melvin Klenetsky, a wide-eyed adherent of Lyndon LaRouche's U.S. Labor Party; and Jeronimo Dominguez, M.D. The latter two distinguished themselves chiefly through their bizarre statements. Klenetsky repeated over and over his charge that the problem with New York City was that Hong Kong banks were somehow laundering money that was being used to import narcotics. Dr. Dominguez, too, focused on crime, but came down hard on the punishment angle by calling for the forced amputation of criminals' limbs. Literally an eye-for-an-eye man, he was dubbed Fingers Dominguez.

Naturally, if Koch was to be given a real race for the Democratic nomination, Barbaro would have to supply it. A gruff, burly man who seemed more suited to his stevedore background than to kissing babies and debating fiscal policies, he waged an uphill battle from the start. He was reluctant to run, knowing he was unlikely to beat Koch, but his liberal background raised some hopes—albeit slim—among Koch haters that he could pull off an upset. Even Barbaro didn't like his chances.

"I was praying somebody else would run, but nobody else would," he says. "I was hoping for somebody like [Councilmember] Ruth Messinger or Carol Bellamy, but nobody would run."

Yet run he did, in part because he had found Koch unpalatable both politically and personally. He had had only minimal contact with him before the 1977 mayoral campaign, when Koch visited him in Brooklyn to ask for his support in the primary. Barbaro had already made it clear that he was going to support Abzug, but Koch wanted to see him anyway.

"We went for coffee," Barbaro remembers. "He said to me it

would be in my best interest to support him. He never said why. But I made it clear that I was not going to change. Before that, he was very conciliatory, friendly, but as soon as I made it clear I was going to support Bella, he turned icy cold, and there was no more conversation."

Barbaro had a similar experience soon after Koch took office in 1978. As chairman of the Assembly Committee on Government Employees, Barbaro had authority over a package of bills that would increase the Mayor's power to hire, fire, and promote outside the civil service system. Barbaro did not like the idea—he felt it did not give the workers enough protection—but he met with the Mayor prepared to see if they could address each other's concerns.

"We have to push through this package," he remembers Koch telling him over breakfast at City Hall one morning. "If you do this, you'll be a hero, you'll go down in history."

"Mr. Mayor," Barbaro said, "I'm not interested in going down in history." He added that he was willing to work with Koch if the Mayor would support the added protection for workers if they had a grievance. Koch suddenly turned cold and silent, Barbaro remembers, and the meeting ended abruptly. Koch would not even discuss it.

In the end, Barbaro agreed to let one of the bills out of committee, though he would not support it himself. He then told Koch that he wanted to discuss something that was bothering his constituents—a city plan to redraw the borders of all of the city's planning, police, and sanitation districts. Known by the ultimate government word—co-terminality—the plan was creating fears among residents in some areas, including Barbaro's, that they would lose contact with local officials to whom they had been addressing their complaints. Barbaro wanted Koch to at least delay the changes.

"I told him I wanted to talk about it with him," Barbaro remembers. "He evidently had to show his macho. He said, 'If you think that your letting this bill out of committee is dependent on this, you can fuck off.' I just looked at him and thought to myself, this guy has either got to be very neurotic or insecure. That's the first I got an insight into the fragile character of this guy's personality. He strikes me as a very frightened little boy, trying desperately to be liked and to come across as a tough, macho guy."

Barbaro had other problems with Koch's politics as well. He believed that Koch was antilabor, antitenant, and was perhaps a racist. The latter was fixed in Barbaro's mind during another of Koch's periodic visits to Albany. The subject was housing and one legislator asked Koch at a private meeting about trying to find a way to get developers who were operating only in midtown Manhattan to build housing in such places as Spanish Harlem.

Koch's response to the request infuriated Barbaro.

"He very flippantly said, 'Who's going to go up there?' " Barbaro recalls. "In other words, who would want to live among poor blacks and poor Latinos."

When the campaign got under way, Koch did his by-now familiar media blitz, with Garth working the controls. The theme this time was that Koch had saved the city from fiscal ruin and that he deserved four more years to get services on track again. The contribution pipeline from the fat cats was stuffed with millions of dollars, and the Koch juggernaut rolled on. Barbaro, on the other hand, was eking out a virtual hand-to-mouth campaign that hinged on the possibility of a miracle. Barbaro fought hard, probing Koch on several fronts. He pulled no punches in accusing the Mayor of being a union buster and of causing racial divisiveness. And he scored perhaps his most impressive gains by raising to new levels the charge that Koch was giving away millions of dollars from the city treasury through reduced taxes to real estate developers, who were in turn making hefty contributions to Koch's campaign. Though the actual price tag of the giveaways was never discerned—estimates would eventually reach $500 million—nor proof of a *quid pro quo* for the contributions ever established, Barbaro had enough circumstantial evidence to make a credible case. To this day, he believes Koch essentially bought campaign contributions by giving away millions of dollars that could have gone to make the city a better place for all New Yorkers, not just the developers and their lawyer friends who negotiated the deals. Time after time, Barbaro paraded out two sets of charts, one showing the names of landlords who got the biggest tax breaks and the other showing the heaviest contributors to Koch. Not surprisingly, many names appeared on both lists. They were many of the same people who would pay $1,000 or more to come to Ed Koch's birthday party.

In the end, Koch romped home with 60 percent of the vote,

Klenetsky and Dominguez shared 4 percent, and Barbaro snared 36 percent, a surprisingly respectable showing considering his meager resources. Many were convinced that had he been better known and financed, he might have made a contest of it.

Meanwhile, Koch did even better against Esposito in the Republican primary. He pulled 66 percent of the vote against the Queens assemblyman, who is remembered mostly for his anger at Koch's chutzpah in entering the Republican primary. At one debate, Esposito showed up with a paper crown from Burger King for Koch and a tiny American flag. So the anti-Koch forces were weak with one exception: black New Yorkers voted against him by a margin of two to one.

Thus it came to be that in the general election for mayor of New York in 1981, the voters who bothered going to the polls found Ed Koch's name under both the Republican and Democratic lines. Against a host of minor-party candidates, including Barbaro, who ran on the Unity Party line, and Councilwoman Mary Codd, who ran as a Liberal, Koch got 75 percent of the vote, a record. Other mayors, such as Wagner, had received more votes in the days when the turnout was heavier, but none had ever gotten such a high proportion of the votes cast. So Koch had what he wanted—a coronation. He was jubilant, or at least seemed so publicly. During a round of appearances the day after his election, including his traditional visit to shake hands at the subway stop at Lexington Avenue and 77th Street, where he had gone after every election victory, Koch talked in grand, sweeping terms of his plans for the next four years. He would immediately convene meetings of black and Hispanic leaders in an attempt to heal the city's racial wounds. Moreover, he would stop blaming the subway crisis on other people, saying he would take charge of making things better.

"It does me no good or does you no good for me to say that I cannot run the subway system, that the state law gives that responsibility to someone else," Koch said. "I accept that responsibility."

But the new Koch was not the real Koch, and so the Mayor soon forgot his promises. His plan for the subways was to be carried out by a special transit advisor, Ross Sandler, whom Koch appointed. Koch had hoped to get Sandler on the board of the Metropolitan Transportation Authority, where Koch controlled four seats. But David Brown, the former congressional aide, friend, and deputy mayor, refused Koch's request to give up his seat and so Sandler was reduced to an advisory role. Before long, Koch abolished Sandler's office altogether in a budget-cutting move, a fact Sandler did not learn until a reporter called him for a comment.

The plan to heal the racial wounds met a similar fate. A few days after his conciliatory speech about meeting with all top minority leaders—a speech suggested and written by Deputy Mayor Bobby Wagner—Koch began ticking off the names of people he would not invite because he did not like or trust them. Badillo was one, and Al Vann, a black Brooklyn assemblyman, was another. When an aide suggested to Koch in private that barring some people was at odds with the purpose of unifying the city as well as with the initial statement, the real Koch shot back: "That statement was Bobby's. This is mine."

⟫⟫⟫ 14 ⟪⟪⟪

BEYOND THE DREAM

A few weeks after his smashing reelection victory, Koch summoned his Kitchen Cabinet to Gracie Mansion for a strategy session on how they were going to make good on his pledge to improve municipal services in his second term. Garth and Connelly were there. So were David Margolis, Dan Wolf, Allen Schwartz, and Bobby Wagner. They assembled in the mansion's spacious living room and chatted among themselves as they waited for Koch to join them. When he finally strode into the room about twenty minutes late, he apologized for his tardiness, and explained that he'd been held up by a long magazine interview. Knowing Koch as well as they did, that was an excuse they all understood.

"It was with *Playboy*." Koch smiled—a national magazine with a big readership. Very impressive. He was going to be their monthly interview subject.

"How long was the interview?" someone asked.

"About eighteen hours," Koch said, explaining that it had been spread out over several visits by the reporter.

Silent warning bells rang simultaneously inside Garth and Connelly. What had Ed Koch talked about for eighteen hours with *Playboy* magazine, of all things?

"How was it? How was the interview?"

"Fine," Koch answered. "It went well."

"Was there anything hot in it?" Garth asked warily.

"No." Koch shrugged. Everything had gone smoothly.

Garth was skeptical, but he let the subject pass as the group got down to the business of charting the course of the second Koch administration. What would it look like? What would its goals be? How could Koch improve the quality of life in New York

City? The conversation had barely begun when Schwartz said he had an idea he wanted everybody to hear: He announced that Ed Koch should run for governor.

The proposal took everyone in the room by surprise. After all, Koch had only just won the mayoralty again. Was Schwartz serious? Yes, he insisted, he was. In fact, he'd thought the idea through quite thoroughly. Hugh Carey's popularity had plummeted so far in his second term that the governorship was, for all intents and purposes, up for grabs. In fact, it seemed only a matter of time before Carey would announce he was not running again. And who better to replace him than Koch, still riding high from his reelection, the most popular Democrat in the state? The governor's mansion could be his for the asking. On top of that, the action was shifting to Albany anyway. Koch had done all he could for the city by balancing the budget and avoiding bankruptcy. But the chances of actually being able to improve services seemed slim because the budget would be tight for the foreseeable future. Albany, on the other hand, would be on the receiving end of President Reagan's plan for the New Federalism, which would give states a greater say in how money earmarked for local governments would be spent. If Koch really wanted to help the city, Schwartz reasoned, he could do it better in Albany than in City Hall.

The reaction to Schwartz's surprise proposal among the rest of Koch's advisers was overwhelmingly negative. They argued that Koch had won big because he'd forged a bond with the city as the straight-shooting mayor who loved New York. Who loved his job. Who had promised Clark and everyone else—including God—that he would never run for anything else. How could he turn around after pulling in 75 percent of the vote and say that he was packing to leave? Better that he set his mind to keeping his electioneering promises while he had a mandate to make his mark on government and the city for years, perhaps generations. Besides, he'd hate living in Albany, something that he once described as a "fate worse than death."

Koch seemed a little taken aback by the idea—perhaps even annoyed. He listened as the debate bounced back and forth, and although he never responded with a direct yes or no, many of those present gauged his reaction as one of disapproval. When the meeting ended, they thought the idea of Ed Koch running for governor was mercifully dead.

A month or so later—in early January of 1982—two very powerful people independently broached the subject again with Koch. The first was Rupert Murdoch, the publisher of the *New York Post*. His paper had become a virtual Koch bulletin board, and he now was suggesting that it might be a good idea for Koch to step up to the governorship. Koch reportedly told Murdoch that, while he was flattered, he was inclined against the idea. Still, he told the publisher he would think about it on an upcoming eight-day vacation to Spain.

Next came Stanley Friedman, the Bronx Democratic boss, who met with Koch in his office and urged him to think about running. "He was negative about it," Friedman remembers.

The overtures were made privately, and so, publicly at least, Koch was not generally viewed as even a potential gubernatorial contender. That crown was worn by Koch's old nemesis, Mario Cuomo. In 1978, a year after he was defeated by Koch for the mayoralty, Cuomo was selected by Carey to run for lieutenant governor on his reelection ticket. They'd won without much trouble, but Carey's popularity dwindled badly during his second term, pushed downward both by the perception that he had become bored and ineffective in the job and by the laughter that his personal life had begun to generate.

An enigmatic man whose moods vacillated from brilliant to brutal, Carey, a graying widower with twelve kids, got remarried toward the end of his second term to Evangeline "Engie" Gouletas, a wealthy, exotic woman whose family was heavily involved in the New York real estate scene. Their romance made the gossip columns sing, with the loving couple seen arm in arm here, there, and everywhere. Much comment was directed at the color of hair—but not Engie's—after the newly youthful Carey took to dying his and the tint came out close to orange.

The marriage itself was a social extravaganza, but the fun did not last. While the newlyweds were on their honeymoon, it was disclosed that Carey was Engie's fourth husband, not her third as she had said. And she was not a widow, as her official biography had said. The event was a juicy scandal, all the more so because Carey found out about the extra husband as well as the resurrection of the "dead" one the same time everybody else did. Must have been some honeymoon.

Whatever popularity Carey had left dissolved in the sneering mirth. In political circles it was widely believed that he couldn't possibly win again and thus wouldn't run. Meanwhile, Cuomo was obviously and publicly aching to take a shot at becoming governor, regardless of what Carey did. Quite naturally he became the focus of attention, the number-one Democratic contender for taking over the executive suite.

When Carey finally threw in the towel on January 15, saying he would return to private law practice when his term expired at the end of the year, the field was open. Cuomo immediately called Garth and set up a meeting for the next day. Their friendship went back a long way, though it was interrupted by the 1977 campaign, and Cuomo wanted to hire him for his quest. Garth, according to Cuomo, said yes, but warned him there was a remote possibility Koch might take Schwartz's advice and run. If that happened, all bets would be off. "Garth thinks he's unpredictable enough to consider it," Cuomo wrote in his diary.

That same day, Garth, Koch and the others took off for their vacation in Spain. Away from New York and in a country where he is not immediately recognized, Koch loosened up. The vacation was great fun, and to this day Garth swears that never once on the trip did he and Koch discuss a possible gubernatorial race— an indication, he says, that at that point Koch really wasn't thinking of running.

Meanwhile, back in New York, Murdoch, repelled by Cuomo's liberalism, was all business. He launched a "Draft Ed Koch for Governor" campaign in the *Post*, and day after day, while Koch was abroad, it trumpeted him as the right man for Albany. The idea caught hold in the press. When Koch's plane landed on his return, a public relations aide raced to meet him, a copy of the day's *Post* in hand. Murdoch had gone as far as to run a clip-out coupon asking the paper's readers whether Koch should run for governor. Cleverly, the coupon had only one answer box—yes. Garth grimaced at the sight of the paper. "If you are going to run, the last way you want to start a campaign is with a write-in in the *New York Post*," he says.

Koch was immediately thronged by reporters and cameras. The question on everyone's lips was simple: Are you running for governor? Koch's answer was simple, too: maybe. Surveying the media battalion that had trekked out to Kennedy Airport to meet him, Koch professed himself flattered by the excitement the idea had generated. Based simply on that, Koch said, he would be foolish to rule out a run. The next day he announced that he was giving himself thirty days to decide.

Koch would later say that he postponed a decision because he wanted to milk the situation for all the publicity it was worth. If the public was that interested, why not build up the drama? It also gave him time to consider the idea—to see where everyone stood on the race. What about it? Why shouldn't he run for governor? Maybe he'd given Schwartz's initial idea short shrift after all.

A man without an intimate relationship with any one person, Koch often turns to his inner circle of supporters and aides when decisions have to be made. He will summon them to Gracie Mansion, and, treating them as a cross between an extended family and impersonal sounding boards, will ask their opinions. The run for governor was no exception. One by one he asked his closest supporters what they thought, and a clear majority of them advised him not to run. Garth led the opposition.

"I felt he would snap the strongest muscle he had, which was integrity," he says. "I was petrified of breaking that promise which he had reiterated a hundred times. That broke the subliminal bond that he had created."

More important to Garth, however, was Koch's inability to articulate a reason for making the race, even in private.

"We sat on the porch at Gracie Mansion one day," recalls Garth. "I asked him, 'Why the hell do you want to run for governor?' There was a big pause. I said I knew all the mental reasons. But what do you want it for? He couldn't answer."

The faction of Koch's advisors who advocated his running was led by Schwartz and included, significantly, Dan Wolf. What they lacked in numbers, the two men more than made up in closeness to Koch. Both went way back with him—to his Greenwich Village days—and Koch has described them both with superlatives: Schwartz as the best lawyer he has ever known and Wolf as the wisest man he has ever met. Together, they were a potent combination.

The behind-the-scenes battle to sway Koch one way or the other continued intensely throughout the thirty-day period he'd set for himself. Toward the end, Garth met with Koch on a Friday night and made what was an extraordinary offer: If Koch stayed out of the race, Garth would not work for Cuomo or anybody else, thus bypassing the chance to pull in at least $250,000 in fees and commissions.

"You feel that strongly about it," Koch asked him, clearly impressed by the financial sacrifice Garth was willing to make.

Garth said he did and would even put the promise in writing, proof that his advice was straight from the heart. "It's wrong for you," Garth said.

When Koch left the meeting Garth thought he had him convinced, but he wasn't sure. They were scheduled to get together again at 2:30 that Sunday afternoon. So Garth and Connelly began preparing a written list of all the reasons why they thought it was a bad idea for Koch to run. They were set to give it to Koch as soon as he arrived on Sunday, but before they could, Koch short-circuited everything.

"I'm going," he said ebulliently as he walked in the door.

His second term as Mayor was less than two months old, but he was ready for a change. Time to move out and up again. Or so he thought.

Koch had made perhaps the worst decision of his political life, one that irrevocably damaged his image, his mayoralty, his relationship with the city. Why did Ed Koch, perhaps the most popular mayor in the city's history, risk it all to try for a job he really didn't want?

The answers certainly aren't to be found in the Schwartz-conceived rationalizations that Koch offered publicly: the New Federalism; that people told him he could be a good governor; that Albany was where the "power" was going to be. In his autobiography, Koch offered another answer: hubris, excessive pride. That's closer to the truth, but it glosses over much deeper emotional currents that some of Koch's closest friends believe swept him into running for governor.

By the assessment of those who know him best, Ed Koch, in 1982, was a man haunted by his own success. Almost all his adult life he'd invested virtually every waking moment in his single-minded quest to become mayor and then to be reelected by a wide margin. He'd achieved both—at the expense of every other facet of his life—and now he discovered that life at the top was not as richly satisfying as he thought it would be. At the age of fifty-seven, with his every dream come true, there was nothing further to look forward to—except more of the same.

"God help you if all your fantasies come true," Garth says. "That's what happened to Ed Koch."

Garth and other confidants describe Koch's emotional state following his reelection as akin to postpartum depression. He seemed to them suddenly bored and uninterested in the job that had been so fascinating before. One insider says that he sensed that Koch regretted that Barbaro and the others hadn't put up a stiffer fight, that his victory would have been sweeter if the race had been tougher.

"You come off that 75 percent victory. It's heady stuff," one confidant said. "But what do you do next? What do you do for an encore when you've done it all and somehow it is not as totally satisfying as you want?"

"What are you going to do, get 80 percent of the vote the next time?" Garth said. "It can't be done."

Koch was also following a predictable pattern. Throughout his career, he had never passed up an opportunity to seek higher office, and now the governor's chair was empty. He had felt no loyalty to the Democratic Party in 1981, and he felt no loyalty to the city now. In the words of an aide, Koch is not really a Democrat, a Republican, a liberal, or a conservative. "He is a Koch," the aide says. "One of a kind."

Moreover, Koch believed the job was his for the asking. The increasing media attention he had been getting after his big re-election had turned his head so far around that he began to believe he was as good as his own press clippings. Everybody was telling him he was invincible, so it must be true. Political pros, like Stanley Friedman, thought it would be a good move. Rupert Murdoch was solidly in his corner. And Cuomo? He was no real threat. Koch had sent him packing in '77, demolished him in their debates. Koch's newfound popularity would make it that much easier to vanquish him again, and wouldn't that be sweet, especially after the "Vote for Cuomo, not the Homo" episode of 1977? This time he could bury Cuomo for good. All he had to do was throw his hat in the ring and the election would be over.

"He believed it was just like a ripe plum," says Marty Mc-Laughlin, Koch's campaign press secretary in 1982. "He thought all he had to do was reach out and it would fall into his hands."

And once he had Albany, there was no telling how much further he could go—perhaps even to the vice-presidency in 1984 as the first Jewish American on a national ticket. Exactly which of Koch's advisors first raised the notion that Koch was vice-presidential timber is a matter of debate. Several members of the inner circle say it was Allen Schwartz. However, Schwartz said the only time he talked of national issues was to argue that, as governor, Koch could be a much more effective spokesman on issues he cared about, such as American policy toward Israel.

In his book, Koch indicates that Garth first raised the idea of national office in an effort to keep him out of the gubernatorial race. Garth, according to Koch, contended that Koch had a better chance for national office as a popular mayor in the city than as a governor isolated in Albany. For his part, Garth acknowledges that he did discuss the subject, but only in response to others who were trying to sell Koch on the idea that winning the governorship would lead to the vice-presidency.

"I said to him, that if in fact being vice-president is out there, it could happen here, in the city," Garth remembers. "I was trying to allay the fantasy they were feeding him."

Finally, while Koch was deliberating, his father Louis Koch passed away in Miami at the age of eighty-seven. His body was flown to New York and he was buried in the family plot in New Jersey. Ed Koch is not religiously observant—he attends synagogue only on the High Holy Days—but out of respect for his father he followed most of the Orthodox traditions of mourning. For three days—instead of the usual seven—he sat shivah. In accordance with Orthodox practices, he did not shave, wore only slippers on his feet and covered the mirrors in the house so as not to see his grief. Scores of people came to visit, to pay their respects and participate in the twice-daily prayer for the dead conducted by Rabbi Arthur Schneier, of the Park East Synagogue. Many visitors also talked politics with Koch, and most encouraged him to run.

It was a time of great reflection for Koch, both as to his past and the future. His father—the Polish immigrant who came to America through Ellis Island; who had struggled to support his family during the Depression; who had taught his children by example the nobility of hard work—had meant a great deal to Koch, both as a man and as a symbol of his heritage. Koch had come a long way from the apartment on Crotona Park and begging for dimes at Krueger's Auditorium in Newark. He'd started with little—the poor Jewish kid, the outsider—and had beaten them all at their own game. Even the "richies," as he liked to call them, of the silk-stocking district now were afraid of him. Koch was immensely proud of that, and his father had taken great joy in his success. Perhaps he could raise the family name to greater heights.

"There was probably an inner restlessness that he wouldn't admit publicly," says one of Koch's closest friends. "A feeling that being Mayor of New York is terrific, but here is a job that has been held by a Rockefeller, two Roosevelts, and a Lehman. Now it can be Louis Koch's son."

On Monday, February 22, Koch announced that he was running, and how the public—or at least the press—felt about it became clear immediately. He had barely finished reading his prepared remarks when reporters came at him with a fury he had not expected. In biting tones, they besieged him with questions about his honesty, about his pledge at the Wailing Wall and to the people of New York. Their meaning was clear: The guy who had vowed to be different had exposed himself as just another politician who put personal ambition above everything. Koch's decision quickly became the talk of the town, and regardless of whether people felt that Koch was right or wrong, the feeling they shared was one of "What chutzpah!"

That was, however, much kinder than what George Clark had to say after he found out in the newspapers that Koch was running. Without so much as a phone call, Koch had broken his word—and he'd never made good either on his other pledge to hire qualified Republicans. Koch had also promised that to Goodman and Marchi and they'd all complained about it, but to no avail.

"I still feel like a jerk, the jerk from Brooklyn," Clark says. "I trusted him. I took his word."

The next time Clark and Koch saw each other was at a political dinner on Staten Island. Clark remembers Koch walking over to him, sticking out his hand and saying, "George, let's be friends." Clark says he responded, "Mr. Mayor, if I shake your hand, I'm going to have to go wash mine. I'd rather not."

Even though the press conference at which he kicked off his campaign went poorly, Koch was still riding high in the polls around the state. Of course, he had strong backing in the city, but even upstaters and those in the suburbs loved Koch for his feistiness and willingness to take on the blacks and unions. His promise not to run for another office notwithstanding, once he had broken the promise Koch seemed invincible. So much so that many other pols who had thought they had a chance to be governor—both Democrats and Republicans—thought better of entering a battle they were sure to lose. Stanley Fink, the assembly speaker, who thought he could count on backing from Koch for his own candidacy, was one of those who quietly folded his tent.

"It's no secret that I was making plans to run myself," Fink says. "He had been urging me to run—that was before Hugh Carey announced he wasn't running." Fink smiles when he thinks of Koch's maneuvers.

"He'd get into fights with Carey, and then he'd say to me, 'Why don't you run. You'd make a great Governor. We'll make a great team,' " Fink says. "That was his attitude until such time as there was a vacancy. It's easy to urge somebody else to run when there's an incumbent. As soon as there's a vacancy, he rushes to fill it. It's almost humorous."

So Fink was out of the way. Another to drop out was Bobby Abrams, the state Attorney General. And Carol Bellamy, the Council President, who had been contemplating a run, pulled back because Koch's election as governor would make her Mayor under the City Charter's provisions for succession. Even Ned Regan, the Republican state comptroller, decided not to run for Governor because, he said, he and Koch would be trying to tap the same people—Wall Street and the banks—for contributions. So strong did Ed Koch seem that those who weren't busy running away from him were getting in line to jump on his bandwagon. The only exception was Cuomo, who said he was in the race to stay. Pundits felt sorry for Cuomo, likening him to a man who did not know enough to come in out of the rain. But Cuomo, looking like an oxcart trying to run over a freight train, would not budge.

Cuomo may not have been politically smart, but he sure was lucky. For it was said about Koch in those days that only Koch could beat Koch, and that is exactly what was going to happen. Indeed, it already had happened. There was a ticking hidden bomb in the Koch campaign, one that, when it exploded, would bring the campaign down around the candidate's ears. The bomb was the *Playboy* interview.

Given in the flush of his mayoral victory back in November, in what Garth calls Koch's "I-don't-give-a-shit" phase, the interview had been virtually forgotten by everybody in the Koch camp. That was understandable, for while there would be concern about any long interview if Koch had been in a campaign, the *Playboy* writer had talked to Koch before the decision to run had been made. Indeed, the final segment of the interview had taken place the same day Schwartz had first suggested that Koch move on to Albany. So nobody ever gave another thought to what Koch had said, or how the interview would be played in the magazine.

The bomb went off as soon as Koch announced his candidacy. Within hours, Koch was given an advance copy of the magazine. He knew right away he was in deep trouble. So did Garth.

While the interview ranged far and wide, from Koch's army days to his feelings for Israel, the explosion came from what Koch said about the suburbs and rural life. "Have you ever lived in the suburbs?" he had cracked. "It's sterile. It's nothing. It's wasting your life." When the interviewer had asked him about wasting time on the subways, Koch had answered, "As opposed to wasting time in a car? Or out in the country, wasting time in a pickup truck when you have to drive twenty miles to buy a gingham dress or a Sears Roebuck suit?"

In New York City, those were funny, even hilarious remarks—Koch, the witty put-down artist at his best. Virtually every New Yorker had felt the lash of his tongue at one time or another. So now he was giving it to those outside the city. It was the essential Koch. But it's not the kind of act that sells well everywhere, and Koch's remarks in *Playboy* bombed in all the Peorias around the state. The man who had offended many city residents during his first term, then compounded the offense by breaking his vow never to seek higher office, had now managed to offend virtually everyone else in the state. Talk about a clean sweep! Casey Stengel would have called him amazin'.

The *Playboy* remarks were picked up by newspapers and televisions everywhere, and soon there wasn't a "sterile" suburbanite or a hick in a pickup truck who didn't know what Ed Koch thought of him. His comments so rankled the editor of the *Oneida Daily Dispatch* that the paper printed a mail-in ballot parodying the *Post*'s "Draft Koch" campaign. "Tell Ed Koch You Don't Want Him," the *Dispatch* ballot said. Koch complained that the remarks were taken out of context and insisted that, on balance, the interview was a positive statement about the city, not a criticism of life elsewhere. But his credibility wasn't what it used to be, and few people bought his explanation. The interview spoke for itself and there was no way he could explain it away. How devastating the incident was became clear to Koch and Garth when they took another poll of potential voters around the state. What they saw astonished them. In just a few days, Koch's positive rating dropped 25 points, while his negative rose 28—a fifty-three-point swing, the biggest, fastest plunge Garth had ever seen in politics.

For the next six months, Koch tried gamely to recover while also making at least a pretense of running the city. While his administration drifted rudderless, he sleepwalked his way around the state. "Just feed me three times a day and I'll do whatever you want," is how one campaign official remembers Koch's attitude. But at every opportunity he shot himself in the foot. At one campaign stop a radio reporter armed with a question of beautiful simplicity stuck his microphone in Koch's face as he was about to get into his car.

"Mr. Koch, what county are you in?" he asked.

After the briefest of pauses, Koch answered, "Oneonta."

Not even close. Koch was in Otsego County—in Cooperstown, the home of the Baseball Hall of Fame. What was even funnier was that Oneonta is not even a county, it's a town.

"How bad is that?" Koch asked Marty McLaughlin as they pulled away in the car.

"How about every paper and wire service in the state?" McLaughlin answered. "Is that bad enough?"

The blooper led to a change in the routine of the Koch campaign. Thereafter, the last thing Koch was told as he got out of his car or plane upstate was where he was—both the town and county. Even with that, campaign aides said, at least once, he sat down for an interview and then suddenly got a look of sheer panic on his face. It disappeared the moment an aide whispered in his ear where he was.

Getting lost on the campaign trail was not difficult. The Koch campaign, convinced it had a solid base of support in the city, and, to a lesser extent, in the suburbs, concentrated much of the candidate's time in the relatively rural upstate areas in an attempt to get out of the hole created by the comments in *Playboy*. Just as he had in the Village when he was accused of making anti-Italian remarks, Koch went out of his way to make inroads with the people he had offended. He would, the strategy went, spend so much time with the hicks and suburbanites that they would forgive him.

"We were in places that hadn't seen a gubernatorial candidate since Roosevelt," one campaign worker said. "We spent more time in Penn Yann than we did in the Bronx."

A typical weekday trip for Koch would have him leaving City

Hall in the afternoon, helicoptering to Long Island, where he would board a chartered twelve-seat plane for a flight to a dinner gathering two hours away and maybe another stop or two at rallies or civic meetings. Then he would get back on the plane, and arrive home at Gracie Mansion around midnight. Never much for small talk, he was so uncomfortable outside the city that he would not even eat in restaurants at the end of a long day.

When he got aboard his plane, a plate of sandwiches, usually egg salad or tuna salad, would be waiting, along with a supply of the Diet Pepsi Koch favors. The Mayor would take the Walkman headset belonging to Victor Botnick, put the earphones on, turn on Carly Simon or Simon and Garfunkel, read his briefing papers for that night's stop and maybe doze. When they got back to the city, he would invite those who accompanied him to Gracie Mansion, where Mitchell London, his chef, would throw together a late supper. The meal, often a Caesar's salad, was usually eaten in front of a television set turned to the news to see what Cuomo was up to as well as how Koch's candidacy was being perceived. Though he is fascinated by watching himself on TV, Koch was sometimes so exhausted he fell asleep in front of the set, with his aides tiptoeing out so as not to wake him. As for staying overnight somewhere, forget it! Koch only spent one night during the campaign outside the city and that was at the nominating convention in Syracuse, where he had little choice.

"You don't run for Governor that way," said one aide who worked hard on the campaign.

More importantly, you don't run for Governor by taking Ed Koch to picnics, car shows, and laundromats in small towns. Bobby Wagner tells of a day trip he won't soon forget.

"We flew up into Batavia, where we nearly collided with a small plane," Wagner recalled. "Then we drove in a trailer to some kind of motorboat race outside of Buffalo which was attended all by Canadians. Everybody was drinking beer. They sort of knew Ed but only as a character. It was very strange. His antennae are terrific, but not for motorboat races. This was totally new and he quickly picked up that none of these people lived in the state of New York.

"Then we went to a Democratic picnic in a room next to a laundromat—I don't remember which town it was—and they had a woman dressed in a gingham dress joking about *Playboy*. Up front there were TV cameras around Ed, but in the back of the room, nobody was applauding. They were sort of glowering at this guy who beat up on them. Then we went to a Polish picnic somewhere in a Buffalo suburb, where he tells them he is Polish. It was fine and then we ended up at the Classic Car Show in Olean because people said that was one of the great draws of upstate New York. It was a bucolic setting with probably fifty people, if we were lucky. He had to go out and try to reach them. The whole thing was a mystery to me and it was probably even more of a mystery to Ed."

Other times the crowds were larger, but no more fun.

Marty McLaughlin tells a story about a Sunday that started before daylight when he met Koch at 5:45 A.M. at the Mansion. They flew way upstate to Messina, where Koch spoke to a breakfast group. As soon as he was done they climbed back on the plane, flew to Long Island, took a helicopter to the city and raced, with police sirens wailing, to a midtown march and rally for Soviet Jewry. After the parade, Koch and McLaughlin boarded the helicopter again for a hop to New Jersey, where the Mayor was appearing at a fund raiser for a Jersey politician. From there, they rode the helicopter to Kutsher's Country Club, in Monticello, where Koch was to speak to a Rotary Club.

"As soon as the helicopter lands on the lawn outside, our advance man, Kevin Frawley, comes over to us," McLaughlin says. "He has a glazed look in his eyes, and I know right away he doesn't like what he's seen. I feel this is going to be a bad stop.

"We go inside, and I see why. Half the men in the place are loaded. Women and children are there too, and they're all wearing cowboy hats. As Ed comes in, they mob him. Kids are putting ice cream cones on his blazer, people want autographs. They're pawing him, and he hates it. He's tired, his neck is turning red. He's gritting his teeth. He gets to the front of the room, and the guy making the introduction is like a nightmare version of a Borscht Belt comic, complete with stuff like 'Eddie BAAAby.' He sounds like a bad Jerry Lewis. Finally, Koch slides the microphone away from the guy and says, 'I'll speak now.'

"He starts talking about the campaign, and some drunk stands up and says, 'That's boring. Talk about the Rotary Club.' Koch just looks at him and says, 'The Rotary is great.'

"Anyway he finally finishes, we start to leave, the pushing and shoving starts again, the kids with the ice cream cones and everything. We get into the 'copter, the engine starts up, and Koch leans over to me and says, 'Marty, when this fucking thing gets off the ground, I want napalm.' We all cracked up."

But Koch wasn't through. Over dinner at the Mansion that night, he wanted to know who had arranged the schedule that way. When McLaughlin said Jerry Skurnik had done it, Koch got him on the phone, though it was near midnight.

"Ed starts with, 'Hello, Jerry, this is Ed Koch. Jerry, I'd like you to take two weeks off, and spend them in one of my work camps. The ones with the barbed wire and the guard dogs.' " McLaughlin says, imitating Koch's nasal whine. "We're all breaking up, wondering what Skurnik must be thinking. Finally, Ed says, 'Jerry, just one more thing. The only rotary I want to see the rest of the campaign is the one on top of the helicopter.' "

Despite *Playboy*, not being able to say where he was, and lacking any real reason for running, Koch maintained a lead in most of the public opinion polls into the summer. He always had the biggest lead in polls conducted by Murdoch's *Post*, of course, usually in the 20 percent range. Yet others had the Mayor ahead also.

An indication of how strong Koch was came in late June at the Democratic nominating convention in Syracuse. Koch got 61 percent of the delegate vote to Cuomo's 39 percent. However, because there was much speculation that Koch could prevent Cuomo from reaching the 25 percent threshold needed to force a primary, Cuomo's showing was regarded as a victory. The underdog was gaining.

Then, in July, came the second major turning point in the campaign, one that, in a different way, was perhaps as important as *Playboy*. It was the first debate between Koch and Cuomo and, more than anything else, it showed that Cuomo had come a long way since 1977. His campaign then had self-destructed, but he was hungry this time, and the debate showed how formidable Cuomo had become. Held in a midtown hotel, the verbal showdown was sponsored by Murdoch, who had invited 600 guests to watch his candidate demolish Cuomo over breakfast. Remembering how inept Cuomo had been in most of the debates in 1977, Murdoch calculated that a public thrashing by Koch might finish off Cuomo for good. Kingmaker that he is, Murdoch volunteered to provide the forum for his candidate to showcase his fire power.

That is how Koch viewed the debate, also. He was so sure he

would run right over Cuomo that he spent little time preparing. Meetings scheduled to ready him were a waste of time, for Koch would not rehearse his answers to expected questions and would only glance at the extensive briefing books prepared for him. Aides say his mind seemed to wander during rehearsals and they could not get him to focus on the issues that were likely to be raised. In short, through a combination of arrogance, disdain for Cuomo's ability, and a lack of real desire for the office he was seeking, Koch was not giving a hundred percent. It was light-years from 1977, when he went about the mayoral campaign like a man on a mission. Even in 1981, against weaker opposition, he had campaigned as though he were the underdog.

Cuomo, on the other hand, had prepared thoroughly, going so far as trying to counter the fact that the crowd, given the sponsor, was likely to be packed with Koch supporters. He declined to show for breakfast, and made a dramatic appearance at the last minute. When Koch won the coin toss that allowed him to answer last, Cuomo got in the first quip, saying, "No wonder he's for casino gambling."

From the outset, Koch, who had been saying that he was a proven administrator while Cuomo had no record, was on the defensive. Cuomo hammered away at the level of services in the city and suggested that Koch's tax abatement policy was fattening the already fat cats of the real estate industry at the expense of ordinary New Yorkers. Throughout the session, Cuomo was sure of himself, impassioned and persuasive. Koch was off his game.

The reaction was unanimous—Cuomo won. Even Koch agreed. Moreover, the same day a poll was released showing that Koch's lead was down to eight points. Although most of the polls would eventually be proven wrong by the outcome, the candidates and the public counted on them during the campaign for measurements on what was working and what wasn't. The poll showing Cuomo only eight points behind was significant because it meant that with more than two months of the campaign remaining, Cuomo was rapidly narrowing the gap. The debate performance plus the poll gave Cuomo the boost he needed, while Koch's effort continued to sag, like a balloon slowly losing its air.

Not that Koch ever quit. After the *Post* debate, Garth and Koch had a head-to-head session at which Garth told him either to make a complete effort or drop out. Koch promised to try harder, and from there on, prepared assiduously for the debates. With members of his City Hall staff playing Cuomo, mainly Deputy Mayor Nat Leventhal, Koch rehearsed his answers to questions about his relationship to the real estate industry and attempted to poke holes in Cuomo's campaign. His performance at subsequent debates improved sharply, but none ever received the attention that the first one had. Most turned out to be a draw, and none played a significant role in the campaign.

Meanwhile, Garth was mounting his standard media blitz, using the millions in contributions that were pouring into the campaign coffers. The single theme was that Koch had a proven track record. As Mayor, he had balanced the budget, saving the city from bankruptcy, and had given New York its spirit back. Others featured a lineup of testimonials—Representatives Geraldine Ferraro, Mario Biaggi, and Robert Garcia and boxers Floyd Patterson and Hector "Macho" Comacho. The commercials also hammered away at Cuomo, with the best one of these showing a stopwatch where the second hand is moving. "You have twenty seconds to think of one major accomplishment of Mario Cuomo as Lieutenant Governor," a voice says as the seconds tick off. "Time's up. Maybe that's the reason you should vote for Ed Koch for Governor. He's got a record to run on."

The one thing the commercials could not do, the one question they could not answer, was why Koch was in the race. One spot tried, with Koch delivering a line that he had done his best for the city, but that the remaining problems "can only be solved in Albany." The commercials, however, could not create a reason where none existed, save the candidate's ego. How little Koch really cared for the race was revealed in a comment he made to McLaughlin during the campaign.

"If I lose this time, I won't kill myself," Koch said to him. "If I had lost in '77, I would have."

Cuomo, on the other hand, was as hungry for victory as Koch had been in 1977. Exhibiting for the first time some of the public-speaking skills that would make him famous later, he was able to touch a nerve with his traditional Democratic promise of government help for those who couldn't help themselves. Because he seemed genuinely appalled at Koch's conservative Republican leanings, Cuomo was making big inroads among minorities, the unions, and liberals. He did well with his accusations that Koch was guilty of the "politics of death" when the Mayor brought up the death penalty, which Cuomo opposed. And Cuomo adopted an unusual but brilliant slogan: "When you vote for Cuomo, you get Koch for Mayor." The idea was to appeal to the people who only a year before had voted overwhelmingly to re-elect Koch as Mayor. Cuomo even had two buttons made up that he wore, one on each lapel: "Cuomo for Governor," read one. "Keep the Mayor Mayor," read the other.

On Primary Day, September 23, 1982, Cuomo pulled in 52 percent of the vote to Koch's 48 percent. While Koch had won the city, the margin was far less than the two-to-one margin the campaign believed would be necessary to offset the effects of the *Playboy* interview upstate and in the suburbs. The city vote turned in large part on the vote of minorities, with Cuomo carrying virtually every district where blacks and Hispanics predominate. Two of every three blacks voted for Cuomo. He also did well among white liberals, union members, and Italians.

Cuomo's victory was one of the great upsets in modern New York politics, and the new champ celebrated well into the night. It was, he aptly said in his book, *Diaries of Mario M. Cuomo*, the "little guy against the big guy, the underdog against the favorite." Ed Koch, who only five short years before had been the upstart outsider, had been viewed by many voters as the bloated Goliath who needed to be taken down a peg.

Koch was not ignorant of that perception and so, in the final week of the campaign, had written both a concession and a victory speech. The concession speech was gracious, in which Koch thanked everyone and said he stood ready to help Cuomo in the general election. But both sentiments were temporary. Koch made one TV commercial for Cuomo, and it was so bad and stilted that it was run once and pulled off the air. Koch later said it was probably his subconscious way of getting even.

Similarly, his thank-you's to his staff were soon lost in a hail of recriminations. When he got back to the business of running city government, Koch blamed Leventhal and the others for the high labor settlement he had agreed to during the campaign. In what now seems a flagrant attempt to buy union votes, Koch had agreed to raises of up to 16 percent over two years for city workers. Critics thought the settlement was about twice as high as it should have been, and Koch dumped the blame on those who had been running City Hall in his absence.

In addition, he later faulted the way his staff handled the campaign. Although he said his heart probably wasn't in the race, he did not accept the responsibility for the loss. Instead, he blamed everybody from Garth to LoCicero.

The 1982 Democratic gubernatorial primary was a watershed in a long, unusual and frequently bitter relationship between two politicians whose orbits began crossing in ever-tightening circles a decade earlier. They encountered each other in a significant way first in 1972 when Cuomo met with Koch as he was trying to work out the Forest Hills compromise. The deal he eventually structured was much the one Koch and many others proposed. Cuomo won great praise for it, and Koch the everlasting enmity of the liberal supporters who felt betrayed by what he had done. The episode is noteworthy for two reasons. First, it offers an early illustration of how different Koch and Cuomo are in their approach to government: Cuomo, the talking, behind-the-scenes mediator and Koch the confrontational, upfront bully. Second, the widely differing results for each man at Forest Hills were the start of a pattern that has recurred time and again ever since: When Koch and Cuomo are mixed politically one of them will suffer and the other prosper—unless they are extremely careful.

Their political ambitions brought Koch and Cuomo together again in 1973 when Koch sent an emissary to sound out Cuomo about running for City Council president on his doomed mayoral ticket. Their relationship then was one of good will and mutual respect, but all that dissolved in the heat of political conflict in 1977, when Koch dispatched Cuomo three times. If Cuomo had lost again in their fourth battle in 1982, his political career would quite likely have been over. That was not to be, however, and his victory set the stage for new dimensions in what was already one of the more interesting political phenomena of our times.

There have, of course, been plenty of famous feuds among top New York politicians, and many of the most bitter have come when both men were members of the same party. Thus, Nelson Rockefeller as Governor and John Lindsay as Mayor were at each other's throat constantly despite the fact that, at least for one of Lindsay's terms, both were Republicans. And Hugh Carey and Abe Beame were always trying to pull the rug out from under one another despite being fellow Democrats. Yet the Koch-Cuomo relationship is different because the two men have developed such a reservoir of personal animus.

In addition to their four showdowns, Koch and Cuomo have each written a book that, in good part, is devoted to attacks on the other. Perhaps it is too much to say that they hate each other, perhaps not. Certainly they are sworn enemies, each constantly vying to be one up on the other. "It will be that way to the death," says a man who knows both well. An illustration of how the two feel about one another comes from a Cuomo confidant, who remembers Cuomo saying that, "Despite being elected Governor, and despite giving the keynote address at the 1984 Democratic Convention, nothing can ever be as satisfying as beating Ed Koch."

And what about Koch?

"Ed thinks Mario is not trustworthy," says one Koch confidant. "Mario tells you one thing, then does another."

The seeds for the bitterness that flourishes between Koch and Cuomo were planted in the 1977 mayoral election. For Koch, it was the "Vote for Cuomo, not the Homo" campaign. For Cuomo it was a suggestion by Koch that Andrew Cuomo, Mario's older son, had invented a story about a sound track going around the city in 1977, saying that "A vote for Cuomo is a vote for the Mafia."

"I don't believe that ever happened," Koch says in his book, while blaming Cuomo directly for the fact that the homosexuality issue was raised in 1977 and, to a lesser extent, in 1982. "I hold Mario Cuomo responsible for what happened."

In both campaigns, Koch believes, Cuomo took a step back and allowed others to do the dirty work. Neither time, Koch wrote, did Cuomo admonish or fire those responsible. Koch thus concludes that, even if he did not encourage the smears, Cuomo at least condoned them.

Cuomo, of course, denies the allegations, even going so far as to say that rumors of a smear were started by Garth so Koch would get a sympathy vote. That would be typical of Koch, says Cuomo, who believes that Koch has a character defect that permits him to function only when he sees himself under attack.

"Koch is *always* painting himself as victim," Cuomo writes. "In every campaign he's in, at some point his opponent is accused of dirty tricks. He never misses the opportunity even if he has to create the opportunity."

According to a Cuomo confidant, Cuomo had debated how critical to be of Koch and specifically whether to leave that attack in the final draft of his book. But Koch had the misfortune to publish his book first. When Cuomo saw the reference to his son Andrew, he was furious and decided he would pull no punches.

"You don't understand," Cuomo reportedly said in justifying the "Koch as victim" theory. "I don't have to be nice to Ed Koch. He called my son a liar."

However, the state and city governments of New York are so dependent on each other that Koch and Cuomo have no choice but to live with each other. Well aware of each other's political power and penchant for revenge, they've generally settled into a no-first-strike kind of existence, like two nervous superpowers. When they meet personally it is usually in a private unpublicized summit meeting arranged by an intermediary—Garth often serves the purpose. But that is not to say that they don't skirmish or that their aides don't conduct their own little border wars.

Cuomo, for example, did his utmost to personally plant the idea with reporters that Koch was in the pocket of George Klein, a major real estate developer and Koch campaign contributor selected by the city to build a major portion of the Times Square redevelopment project.

"Check George Klein. Check George Klein," Cuomo told a reporter during a telephone conversation.

"Why? What about Klein?" the reporter asked, intrigued at such a tip from the governor.

"Just investigate Klein," Cuomo advised before hanging up without a good-bye.

The warfare between Koch and Cuomo even has its own group of refugees: New York City's homeless. The governor and the mayor pin the blame on each other—sometimes for worsening the problem, sometimes for failing to stop it. In one grenade-tossing episode, state doctors prepared a controversial report on conditions in city welfare hotels that alleged that children living in them were suffering from malnutrition. Koch's aides believed that Cuomo had promised not to release the report or discuss it with the press until City Hall had a chance to study it. The next day's newspapers had stories on the report, along with comments by Cuomo critical of the conditions in the hotels. Koch was furious, particularly because city doctors came up with their own findings indicating that the state report was wrong.

While the war between Koch and Cuomo is primarily personal, there is a philosophical bent to it as well. Koch now finds himself at odds with many of the liberal causes that Cuomo espouses so eloquently. Thus, Koch is viewed as an enemy by the unions, liberals, and blacks, which make up the backbone of the Cuomo coalition. And Cuomo derides Koch's budget-balancing attitude, saying government must serve the people, not the credit-rating agencies.

The issue of the homeless is again the battleground over which these philosophical differences come to the fore. One man who attended a meeting between Koch and Cuomo on the subject described it this way:

"Cuomo was making profound speeches about the root causes, the moral issues, and how something had to be done to better understand why so many teenage girls decide to get pregnant. Ed was talking about how much it costs to keep homeless people in shelters. He wanted the state to put up more money to deal with the immediate problems."

Yet even here the differences between the two degenerate into personality conflicts.

"Ed considers Mario sanctimonious," says a Koch insider. "He believes that Mario is not that far from him politically, but won't admit it."

And Cuomo views Koch as a panderer who will shift his politics to suit the public mood, a weathervane who does not take a position on an issue until he has taken the public pulse.

"Ed perplexes him," says a Cuomo insider. "What does he really believe in? Why is he in the business? He thinks a politician should at least believe in something."

Perhaps the essence of their dispute can be reduced to a single word—jealousy. That would not be surprising, for they are, after all, politicians. So Koch keeps awarding himself raises until his salary of $110,000 is $10,000 more than Cuomo's. But Cuomo is said to have doubled Koch's $50,000 advance for his book. But Koch's book sold more copies. But Cuomo got to give the keynote address to the Democratic Convention on national television, while Koch was invited to speak in the afternoon while the delegates mingled around the convention floor, talking to one another.

"Cuomo sees Ed being successful and it drives him crazy," says a Cuomo man.

"Ed gets angry because he thinks Mario gets away with more than he does," says a Koch man.

15

AROUND THE WORLD IN 80 INSULTS

New York City doesn't have an army or a navy, or even a secretary of state, but Ed Koch has a foreign policy. The Mayor's excursions into statecraft have led to humiliation for Prince Charles, brave challenges to the Eastern bloc ("I'm here! It's me!" he called out across the Berlin Wall), international incidents, and even an episode in which he became an unwitting dupe of the KGB. Koch has also proposed the obliteration of various foreign powers (BOMB IRAN NOW: KOCH trumpeted the *Post*), operated a profit-making foreign aid program, insulted and embarrassed foreign dignitaries visiting his office during "courtesy calls," and tussled with the United Nations.

As a congressman, Koch was interested in foreign affairs. There was a time—before the gubernatorial primary—when he may have imagined himself in the Oval Office, actually in a position to give the Russians and the PLO whatfor, and rearrange the international map to his liking. The Austrians, a favorite mayoral target, would really be in trouble under President Koch. So would the British, who are after all "a little crazy," and all the European governments who play footsie with the Arabs or the communists—the "Red Nuts," as Koch calls them.

The Mayor's foreign policy declarations might pour forth at any moment or in any place; in parks, hallways, elevators, supermarkets, delicatessens, or building dedications; at home, abroad, or from the black leather armchair in the corner of his office, where his mind flits from continent to continent.

But by 1983 it was clear Koch's foreign policy excursions would not be practice for greater things to come. Instead, they were diversions that amused the Mayor and diverted the public from the more mundane matters of poor subways and dirty streets. There is nothing like a war to unify the country. Or, as Koch said, he wasn't just a city manager.

If, as some City Hall observers suspect, Koch's internationalist tendencies peak when he is bored, the boredom in 1983 was at an all-time high. His quest for higher office a bad memory, the time was ripe for expounding foreign policy. He announced plans to violate State Department policy by traveling from Israel to Beirut to meet with U.S. Marines ("Ready or not, here I come"); debated the Mayor of Managua (at least there was a free press under General Somoza, Koch said of his old nemesis); and attempted to save President Reagan from his Secretary of Defense, Caspar Weinberger.

Koch had long considered Weinberger anti-Israel, and he had already sounded the alarm in no uncertain terms. "Let Caspar Weinberger come to the Emunah Women and tell you he has no animus toward Israel," Koch thundered to the applause of a Jewish women's group lunching at a New York hotel. Weinberger not only failed to appear, he seemed to be paying no attention at all to indications he had been placed on the Mayor's lengthy list of "Arabists."

But all of that was mere warmup for the foray Koch took in August of 1983. The Mayor then announced—first to the *New York Post*, of course—that he had previously undisclosed evidence that Weinberger was holding secret conversations with Saudi Arabia, promising them weapons so advanced even America's own armed forces did not have them. The proposal was so secret, the Mayor said, even President Reagan and Congress had been kept in the dark. And what kind of defense secretary would keep such vital information from his president? Koch wondered aloud.

The source of all of Koch's secret information was an English-language translation of a purported transcript of a meeting between Weinberger and the Saudi defense minister that had been published in a leftist Lebanese newspaper, *Al Safir*, a periodical never previously cited by the Mayor during his many musings on the state of the world. Koch, who misspelled the name of the newspaper and misidentified it as a news magazine, was nevertheless happy to assure reporters that *Al Safir* was a reputable journal—a Lebanese *Le Monde*.

He speedily wrote to Weinberger, demanding an explanation. ("The transcript, if accurate, is shocking.") But he did not wait

for an answer. The Mayor showered Congress with copies of the
transcript and letters hoping to provoke official committee inves-
tigations. Victor Botnick, an aide who specialized in health and
hospital matters, became a Koch detective and commenced a
sleuthing operation aimed at unearthing additional evidence of
Pentagon perfidy. Defense officials, meanwhile, immediately
branded the transcript a fake. Weinberger formally responded by
letter eight days later, assuring Koch that the transcript was an
"obvious forgery" and a "very crude attempt at disinformation,"
a common practice among the intelligence services of most countries. He nonetheless invited Koch to write or call anytime he was
again presented with such a document.

But New York's mayor wasn't satisfied. He fired off another
salvo to the secretary, wanting to know why, if the transcript was
wrong, Weinberger wasn't writing to this leftist Lebanese newspaper demanding a retraction. What really went on at those
meetings with the Saudi defense minister, anyway? Finally,
Weinberger threw in the towel, declining to continue the correspondence. He also expressed bewilderment at what Koch was
up to. "I cannot believe you are serious in suggesting that these
allegations, meaning the obvious forgery and disinformation in
some obscure publication, were serious enough to the U.S. to
warrant a reply," he wrote. Weinberger added that he already
said the transcript was false and resented what he called Koch's
clumsy attempt to make political hay out of the matter.

The story was petering out but Koch knew how to revive it.
He turned over his correspondence with Weinberger to top editors of *The New York Times*, with permission—nay, encouragement—to publish the letters. The paper did and the issue became a national story. Everybody was calling Washington,
wanting to know if Weinberger had made the traitorous deal. The
Mayor loved it.

But where had Koch obtained his English-language translation
of the transcript? Was it Israel? No, said Koch, not Israel. But he
would not answer any more questions about it. He was protecting his source, just as any good reporter would.

Then Koch got a visit from FBI agents, who asked him the same
question. The bureau had been asked to track down the source
of the English-language translation of the bogus transcript. The
Mayor immediately obliged the inquiring agents by squealing on
his source, just as any good reporter wouldn't. It was indeed Is-

rael. He had not actually lied the first time around, he later tried to convince reporters, since the transcript had been physically handed to him by Botnick. It was Victor who got it from the Israelis.

So much for Mayor Candor.

Cornered for just a moment, Koch followed the old football adage—the best defense is a good offense. So he attacked again. The target was still Weinberger, but this time the strategy was different. Instead of a direct hit, Koch would go for his flanks. Off went a six-page, single-spaced letter to FBI Director William Webster, charging that the visit by the FBI agents was proof that "others in the Federal government may be attempting to use the FBI to stifle my constitutional rights to comment upon matters of national policy."

The letter was, well, unusual. After recounting for four pages all that had happened—including the fact that the letters had been published in the *Times* and that "various newspapers and television reports" dealt with it also—Koch said that "if the foregoing were all that happened I would not be writing to you." He then cited the visit of the agents, saying he was "seriously concerned as to the motives of those who requested the FBI to make this inquiry." Finally, after driving a few more nails into Weinberger's character by saying that most of what the government knew had been leaked by someone in the "Defense Establishment" to an Arab reporter, he said he was sure Webster would take "the appropriate steps" to find out whether "anyone in the Federal government is seeking to infringe upon my civil rights."

The letter closed on a note familiar to Koch watchers: "Due to the public attention and press inquiry this matter has received, I intend to make this letter public."

Webster's reply was to the point: "I have received your letter of December 15, 1983, expressing your concern that others in Government might be using the FBI to chill your First Amendment rights. After a review of our records, I can assure you, categorically, such is not the case." He added that far from being repressive, the Defense Department was only doing its job in that it was required by law to turn over to the FBI any information on disinformation schemes.

Koch still was not satisfied, and wrote to Webster again, asking that he keep on the case. Webster, a touch of exasperation in his response, promised he would.

Intelligence officials later said the Lebanese transcript was concocted by the KGB to discredit Washington, the sort of thing they do all the time. The only difference was that this time, the Mayor of New York, an avowed anticommunist, had become their unwitting accomplice. Koch finally conceded the document was a fabrication but remained undaunted when asked whether Weinberger had not indeed turned out to be right and the Mayor of New York completely wrong.

"We're both right," he announced. It was not clear just what Koch was right about, but it was clear that being Ed Koch means never having to say you're sorry.

The Weinberger affair did not leave the Mayor chastened. He continued his foreign policy pronouncements whenever the mood struck. The routine is almost always the same. The Mayor takes a legal pad and pen and roughs out his feelings in long hand, or summons his secretary into his office and holds forth. It is always outrage he's expressing. Seldom are there mayoral press releases with good tidings. Statements welcoming Moscow's return to the arms talks or congratulating Argentina for holding democratic elections are not his style. There are certainly no proposals to combat sub-Saharan famine or analyses of the Latin American foreign debt situation.

Once Koch has finished venting his spleen on paper, his press office is alerted to get the statement printed and delivered to reporters immediately. During one particularly heavy blizzard of diatribes, each headlined simply "Statement by Mayor Edward I. Koch," weary mayoral aides began warning Room 9: "Ladies and Gentlemen of the Press: Beware. Another dispatch from the Mayor's foreign desk is on the way."

Some are written in such stinging language that reading them made the hair stand up on your neck. Aides sometimes fight with the Mayor, trying to get him to tone them down, but he wouldn't hear of it. Here, for instance, is Ed Koch on Austria and its Jewish chancellor after a terrorist bomb exploded in Vienna:

"Austria has come full circle. Hitler was born there, and now the PLO receives support from the Austrian government.

"The blood of Jews was spilled by Hitler and his Austrian Nazis. Today the descendants of the Nazis, in the form of the PLO, are allowed to reign again in Austria.

"That it is Bruno Kreisky, born of Jewish parents, who is the Chancellor of Austria, makes the horror even more evil. God, and the State of Israel, will punish the Nazis of today as God punished the Nazis of the past."

In another high-spirited moment, Koch called on the United States to "destroy part of Iran" to even the score for Iran's reported complicity in the terrorist hijacking of an airliner. But outrage did not rob Koch of his humanity. He said the leveling of Iranian real estate by U.S. warplanes should not be directed "at killing people, but maybe bombing an oil well." Koch also showed modesty. The precise nature of the bombing assault, he said, should be decided by Secretary of State George Schultz "and others in government."

The need for the attack was clear in the Mayor's geopolitical mind, for the entire planet was craven. The United States, he warned, should not appeal to the world for justice against Iran "because the world is cowardly."

Much of Koch's outrage is devoted to the enemies, real or imagined, of the "Three I's"—Ireland, Italy, and Israel—the homelands of so many of his constituents and their ancestors. In New York, the I's have it. Every New York mayor has had to play that game—even WASPy John Lindsay did—but Koch has outdone them all, escalating his love of the three I's into international incidents. No wonder he has the nickname Ethnic Ed.

Like the time Koch turned a visit by the Prince of Wales into a minor crisis when he blithely violated protocol and told reporters Prince Charles was looking forward to the day British troops would leave Northern Ireland.

After a luncheon in Charles's honor on the yacht of magazine publisher Malcolm Forbes, Koch returned to dry land and announced to the media that he had taken a private stroll with the Prince on deck and allowed the heir to the throne to unburden himself of his true feelings about the mess in Northern Ireland. Charles, he said, "felt very sad to be the subject of invective" by Irish demonstrators during his visit, and was "very sympathetic to the plight of the Catholics" in the North. Furthermore, Koch said, the Prince hoped that eventually it would be possible to "remove British troops" from Ulster.

None of those sentiments appears very noteworthy in New York, but the Royal Family keeps its job by avoiding any political positions, no matter how mealy-mouthed. Charles, having resigned himself to a lifetime of vapid pronouncements and issue-skirting in the name of national unity, was being undone by a stranger from the Colonies, who breathlessly reported his private pleasantries to an equally avid media.

The British press declared itself shocked that Koch would have made a personal conversation public. A representative of the British government called City Hall, asking that Koch use his influence to keep the matter out of the papers, thus betraying an abysmal ignorance about the workings of the mayoral mind. Koch, of course, reported the phone call to reporters, and volunteered that Britain was "a little crazy."

Koch's interest in Italian affairs has been somewhat thwarted by the fact that peaceable Italy does not have many external enemies to denounce. In one bizarre incident, the Mayor dropped his normal law-and-order posture long enough to demand the Italian government free Sophia Loren from jail, where she had been sent for tax evasion. And when he visited Rome as the guest of Ugo Vetere, the city's communist mayor, Koch called Ugo a "rather charming man," but felt compelled to add that "he is not of a party that I have the highest regard for." His lack of sensitivity to things Italian was further exhibited when he confused Rome with Italy, telling Vetere that the greatest mayor of New York—La Guardia—was a Roman. In fact, La Guardia's parents were born in Italy, but nowhere near Rome.

On the same trip, Koch told Pope John Paul II a long and touching story about a Jewish woman in Poland who turned her infant over to a Catholic family when the Germans invaded in order to save the child from the death camps. The family was tempted to keep the boy and have him baptized, but their priest directed them to send the child to a Jewish relative in America as the mother wished. "That priest was the Pope," Koch said. John Paul, unfortunately, did not remember ever having been consulted in such a case. Nevertheless, Koch told reporters he and the Pontiff "hit it off beautifully."

The meeting was captured by the Pope's photographer, who assured Koch and his party that the pictures would be delivered to their hotel that night. When a messenger arrived, Botnick went to the lobby to get the pictures and handed the man a tip of $10. The messenger just smiled, and said the bill was $110. Botnick reported back to Koch, who took out his wallet with amazement.

"I don't believe it," Koch said, counting out the money. "They have a concession. The only pictures you can get of yourself with the Pope are from this guy." Koch thought a moment about his

own photographer, Holly Wemple, and the possibilities of bill-
ing everybody she photographs with Koch. "Imagine if Holly had
that," he said with a chuckle.

Growing up Jewish in the New York area, Koch has a natural
interest in and love for the third I: Israel. But his stance has grown
more aggressive during his mayoralty, perhaps because he was
secretly chastened by an incident that occurred in 1979. After
voicing some criticism of Israeli Prime Minister Menachem Begin's policy of putting settlements on the West Bank, Koch then
went off to Egypt, where he felt very comfortable with Anwar al
Sadat. In between photo opportunities—including a historic picture of Koch riding a camel at the pyramids, wearing an Arab
headdress—the Mayor continued to criticize Begin's policy on the
West Bank, and his remarks were picked up by both the Arab
and Israeli press.

None of this sat well with Begin, who made his feelings clear
when Koch's party arrived in Israel.

"We went to see Begin," one of Koch's traveling companions
said. "Ed went up to embrace him but Begin would have none
of it. Begin pushed Ed away just as Ed was about to put his arms
around him."

The incident, however, stands in stark contrast to Koch's usual
support of Israeli policy. During the Israeli occupation of Lebanon, when U.S. Marines were in Beirut and it seemed things could
not get much worse, Koch decided to put in his own personal
oar. The Mayor announced he was off to the Middle East on a
"fact-finding" mission that would take him to Israel and then into
Lebanon, where he planned to visit the Marines. The facts involved apparently had to do with Weinberger, who Koch believed was plotting to isolate Israel from her former allies.

The State Department quickly vetoed the itinerary. Americans
were not supposed to go from Israel into southern Lebanon, Department officials said. It offends the Lebanese and compromises
the Marines' role as a peacekeeping force.

"Ready or not, here I come," the Mayor retorted. Although
he, the law-and-order mayor, would never break a law, a rule
was something different, Koch said. "That doesn't mean I'm not
going to violate State Department policy. That's not law."

The State Department finally worked out a compromise plan
involving flying Koch to a U.S. aircraft carrier for a cooling off
period between his flight from Israel and his trip to Beirut. But

all the plans fell through when the Lebanese government refused to give Koch any more official status than a renegade tourist. Going to Beirut without his usual status of special guest, Koch decided, "would not be as productive."

The Mayor did get a tour of southern Lebanon, however, courtesy of the Israeli government. He was even able to interview some of the local officials, but most of them apparently sized Koch up more shrewdly than had Prince Charles. At Sidon, Koch reported, the mayor did not show up for the meeting. A deputy who did appear responded "I don't know" to almost every question. The mayor of another village turned out to be "not very communicative."

Koch's areas of interest in foreign affairs have not quite kept pace with the changing composition of New York's ethnic groups. His only frequently stated position on the non-Arab parts of Africa is that he is opposed to apartheid. He has accepted campaign contributions, however, from a law firm that was registered as an agent for the South African government. "Don't they as lawyers have a right to represent criminals?" he asked reporters. When an organization headed by the Reverend Jesse Jackson accepted a donation from the Arab League, Koch said, that was a different matter entirely since it showed Jackson to be "simpatico" with Arab League efforts to destroy Israel.

The Mayor also has not evinced much interest in Latin America, except for periodic attacks on Colombian drug dealers, fulminations against Fidel Castro, and deep concern about the spreading tentacles of communist subversion south of the border.

He and Samuel Santos Lopez, the mayor of Managua, Nicaragua, cheerfully locked horns at a meeting of urban leaders of the Western Hemisphere in San Juan. Koch said Nicaragua was supplying arms to leftists in El Salvador. He had gotten the information, he said, directly from the mayor of San Salvador himself. The most dramatic moment in Koch's swing through the Caribbean, however, came during a side trip to the Dominican Republic, paid for by the impoverished nation. Koch and Santo Domingo mayor Jose Francisco Peña Gomez sped off on a sightseeing trip that took them to one of the many shantytowns that dot the hillsides along the river.

"All the people who lived there came running over to see us, shouting," Koch told the press, which had not been invited to go along. "They loved Gomez and seemed happy to see me too. He told them who I was. It was very exciting."

Another version of the same story was told by someone on the Mayor's staff who had accompanied the two mayors. According to the aide, the sight of hundreds of residents of the shantytown running toward Koch excited him all right, but not exactly the way the Mayor had said.

"He was scared," said the aide. "He was shaking. And then his shoe got stuck in the mud and almost came off. I've never seen him that scared. The people were running and shouting and clapping. He thought they were coming after him. I think he thought he was going to get killed."

Santo Domingo was also the victim of Koch's money-making foreign aid program. In 1983, the city sold five used garbage trucks to the impoverished Caribbean municipality for $25,000. New York and Santo Domingo were, after all, "sister cities," and as an announcement on the sale noted, the Big Apple's sister to the south was getting "five trucks in good mechanical condition at a reasonable price." How reasonable? Well, the city was planning to get rid of the trucks anyway, and could have expected to get only $1,500 per truck by selling them at public auction. Thus, New York sold them to its smaller sister at a $17,500 premium. In the noblest tradition of American used-car salesmanship, the Sanitation Department threw in a paint job. The trucks shipped south were yellow.

Ed Koch is the first Mayor of New York ever to make the United Nations a personal target. Previous mayors have been proud of the particular status—not to mention the millions of dollars in revenue—that the UN's presence lends the city. Koch's dislike stems mainly from the UN's increasingly Third World outlook, particularly its tough stands against Israel.

Koch's most famous foray involved the Isaiah Wall, a retaining wall across from the United Nations, inscribed with the famous verse from the Book of Isaiah on turning "swords into plowshares." As a protest to the anti-Israeli tilt, Koch announced he intended to add a new inscription. The search for a proper quotation began. Three contenders, all from Isaiah, were nominated. ("I will put my salvation in Zion, for Israel is my glory," one read in part.) The Mayor milked the matter for ten days of nonstop publicity, and even hit the jackpot with a boost from *Pravda*. The Soviet newspaper charged that Koch's campaign was designed to "curry favor with the Zionist lobby of New York." The Mayor responded by denouncing "those Red Nuts" and suggested slashing the U.S. contribution to the UN.

"Why are we the patsies?" he asked. Nevertheless, the Mayor finally decided to leave the wall unscathed. "Silence," he said uncharacteristically, "sometimes is more effective than a shout."

So the Mayor changes street signs to surround the diplomats with names of Russian dissidents. Then, too, what would Koch do without the UN, for it is the magnet that draws foreign dignitaries into his lair. A great many of them find their way to City Hall, giving him unlimited opportunity to issue foreign policy pronouncements, and humiliate guests from any country whose policies, past or present, do not please the Mayor of New York. Billed as "courtesy calls" on the Mayor's schedule, City Hall regulars have, with good reason, dubbed them "discourtesy calls."

Austria, the home of Chancellor Kreisky, is, of course, a pet peeve because Koch considers it anti-Semitic, right down to the last yodeler. So when a group of Austrian dignitaries showed up at his office one afternoon, Koch interrupted the pleasantries and gift exchanging to reminisce about the good old days. "As I recall," says an aide who was there, "one of the questions was, 'We still won't let you have an army, will we?'

"The interrogation went on in a similar vein and Koch's visitor, who appeared too young to have been around during World War II, began to get the panicky look of a man who believes he is having a hallucination. Although he had managed the first part of the conversation in English," the Mayor's aide remembers, "he began turning more and more to his interpreter. His replies became monosyllabic, and he was jittering in his seat, unable to understand how the visit had become a forum for the discussion of the sins of his fathers. Koch chatted on, either not noticing or not caring what the man was going through. Finally, the Mayor stood up, shook his visitor's hand and invited him to stop back any time. The Austrian left looking completely bewildered."

A former Koch staff member recalls a visit by a Polish diplomat: "The guy comes in, pure Eastern European, down to his clothes, which were incredible. He and Ed exchange pleasantries, then Ed says to him, 'I just want you to know how proud we are of the Polish people. Lech Walesa is a national hero to us. We're very proud of you all.'

"The guy looks pale. He mumbles something, I don't know

what, and Ed cuts him off. 'You don't have to respond,' Ed says. 'I know you're a diplomat and that prevents you from speaking out. But it's okay—I'll talk.' Then he goes on to say again what a hero Lech Walesa is, how wonderful Solidarity is. The Polish guy was speechless—he looked awful, like he was about to throw up. The thing about it is that Ed knew exactly what he was doing. He knew the guy worked for the government, and knew the guy had to give the party line about Solidarity and Walesa, no matter how he felt personally. Ed knew all that. But he was torturing the guy. And I could see in his eyes that he loved it."

When a group of Chinese officials visited, Koch inquired about the Gang of Four, opined that Peking Duck was better in Shanghai than Peking, and made a string of jokes about capitalism and communism that apparently did not translate well, because the visitors merely looked confused. The Chinese probably blamed themselves, but reporters comparing notes afterward found they, too, were unable to understand the punch lines.

Western Europeans visit Koch too, but things do not necessarily go any better when the cultural gap is a bit narrower. A British mayor appeared in elaborate, formal garb, including a heavy flowing robe. Around his neck was the solid gold, rope-like chain that held the official seal of office, a round, ornate gold medal. "Ed grabbed the seal," a Koch aide recalled, "and started turning it over in his hands, looking at it. He clearly liked it. Then, in an offhand way, he said to the guy: 'You'd better not wear that north of 96th Street,' " referring to the dividing line between white Manhattan and Harlem.

French President François Mitterrand visited in 1984, and presented Koch with the Legion of Honor, his country's highest medal. The award was made in an official ceremony in an upstairs room at City Hall, and Koch was obviously touched and proud of the award. He gave Mitterrand the key to the city in return, and the two retired to the Mayor's office for a private gathering.

Koch proudly reported later that he used the occasion to chide Mitterrand for allowing Communists to take part in his government. Asked if it had not been ungrateful to raise such a subject just after receiving the honor from Mitterrand, Koch waved his hand. "I did it because I like to cause controversy," he said.

The Mayor seldom gets a taste of his own medicine, but an exiled Soviet dissident did inadvertently put Koch on the receiving end once. While they dined together, 7,500 demonstrators protested outside, opposing proposed municipal hospital closings. At a press conference later, Reverend Georgi Vins said he had been impressed by the demonstrators' freedom to express their dissent, and added impulsively: "I felt these people are demanding something that is just—I had a desire to join them."

Hosts of the Mayor have found Koch's rules for visiting are about the same as his rules for receiving visitors at home, with one difference—they pay the air fare when he visits. But that does not mean Koch will be a gracious guest. In West Berlin, he constantly criticized the West Germans' willingness to consider requests by Saudi Arabia for delivery of advanced German weaponry. The German trip was most notable, however, for Koch's arrival at Checkpoint Charlie. Spying East German border guards snapping pictures of arriving vehicles, Koch immediately began to wave. "I'm here," he shouted. "It's me."

Two of the better stories involve Koch's visit a few years ago to China, where he went to see the Great Wall and try to drum up a little business for the city. Taking a tour of a communal farm, Koch was introduced to the local doctor, who described how he used herbs, roots and other natural medicines. When Koch asked what he had for a headache, the man produced a handful of flower petals. Koch looked at it, paused, then with a deadpan delivery, said, "Do you have anything stronger?"

During the trip, the Mayor was invited to dine in the Great Hall of the People of Peking. The description of the scene comes from various sources, but the punch line comes from Peter Solomon, who accompanied him.

Everything about the opulent, gilded palace bespeaks majesty on a grand scale, and there is a ritualistic formality in the timeless manner of the Chinese hosts as they display their nation's sacred heritage. Koch got the grand tour and first-class treatment. Every courtesy was extended to his party and they were being treated with respect bordering on deference.

But the Mayor had other things on his mind, foremost Joseph Stalin. Probably because there are some huge, imposing portraits of Stalin in Peking, Koch was angry at the dead Russian dictator. No, not angry. Furious would be better. And so he was in Peking, ranting and raving about Joseph Stalin. On and on he went, proclaiming with much animation that the long-dead Russian dictator was one of the greatest mass murderers of all time.

His short, pink-cheeked host said little. The Chinese official occasionally got in a grunt, a groan, or a nod as Comrade Koch explained it all. Finally, out of breath, Koch paused, waiting for a response. The Chinese official turned to his interpreter and, smiling politely but inscrutably, said something in Chinese. But in a departure from protocol, the interpreter did not translate it. Not curious, Koch picked up his tirade again, oblivious to another conversation in the room.

A stunned American diplomat accompanying the group was whispering to Solomon. What the Chinese official said about Ed Koch was: "How much longer do I have to put up with this garbage?"

→ 16 ←

MAYOR FOREVER

The day is dawning on Gracie Mansion as Ed Koch throws off the covers of his king-sized bed. The sun is rising over Queens, the easternmost province of the Mayor's domain, home to nearly two million people and the heart and soul of his white ethnic political base. Light streams in through the large, bulletproof windows of his bedroom, left uncovered at Koch's orders so he can look out over the lush green lawn that slopes down to the East River. The lawn is a playground for squirrels, a picnic spot for the Mayor, and, because it rests on a platform over the East River Drive, shields him from the noise and fumes of the rumbling, congested roadway. Koch likes the view, especially at night, when cargo ships and tugs move up and down the river, in and out of the harbor. He can also see the Triboro Bridge, a spectacular sight when its necklace of lights graces the night sky.

"That's *my* bridge," Koch told a recent visitor who had remarked on its beauty. "And you should see what I'm planning for the garden."

The bright and spacious bedroom was designed by Albert Hadley, a top New York interior decorator. The walls are off-white and the furnishings few, including two reclining loungers and an early federal linen press on loan from the Museum of the City of New York that stands between two windows. The most striking object in the room is a black-and-white, three-foot-high papier-mache rabbit that Koch has dubbed Peewee. The Mayor's nighttime companion since 1978, the rabbit survived a $6 million renovation of the 185-year-old, four-bedroom mansion that is the official mayoral residence.

"I'm keeping Peewee," Koch told a gossip columnist. "When

you get up to go to the bathroom in the middle of the night, it's nice to see a familiar face like Peewee's."

Koch sits on the edge of his bed for a moment, his feet near some of the early editions of that day's papers, which he'd picked up the previous night and read before dropping off to what he once called the "sleep of the innocent." His flabby, 210-pound-plus body needs work but this wasn't one of those mornings for swimming at the chi-chi Manhattan health club he frequents. He has other things he wants to do, among them firing off an angry letter to the *Times*, which lately had been writing editorials criticizing his seeming unconcern for the deteriorating quality of life in the city. Once laudatory in its appraisal of Koch's accomplishments, the paper had begun hammering at his failure to come to grips with some of the most crucial problems facing the city: the accelerating breakdown of the subway system; crime; dirty, rutted, and congested streets; the homeless; the high dropout rate in the schools; and racial polarization.

The *Times* wasn't alone in criticizing Koch. The *News* had been hitting him hard, but these two were pikers compared to the steady barrage aimed his way by the *Voice*. After seven years of unrelenting attacks, a group of Koch's friends decided to do something about it. Howard Blum and Dan Wolf, with David Margolis backing them, sought to buy the *Voice* for about $35 million from yet another friend, Rupert Murdoch. The deal would have permanently silenced such Koch enemies as Jack Newfield, but Murdoch rejected the offer.

Anxious to get to City Hall, Koch stands up and walks through the special vaultlike door of his adjoining bathroom. Although a detail of cops is posted at the mansion twenty-four hours a day to protect him, there have been so many threats against Koch's life, the bathroom has been converted into a bunker. If intruders manage to get past the security detail and reach the locked bedroom door, Koch is instructed to flee inside the bathroom, slam the door, and secure it by snapping into place four long steel bolts concealed inside it. The bathroom contains a small closet, which has a high-tech, push-button combination lock and is packed with communications and survival gear. A mayor under siege can reach inside it and call for help on a special phone connected directly to the Police Department. If the phone fails, there is a two-way police band radio for the Mayor's use. And if that fails, Koch is to take the rope ladder stored in the closet, open the bulletproof window, lower the ladder, and climb to safety. The police had urged Koch to keep a gun in the closet for a last-ditch defense, but he declined.

"If I have to go that far," he once told an aide, "it's no use."

After shaving and showering, New York's Mayor dresses, putting on an Oxford-cloth shirt—blue, the right color for television—and a dark Brooks Brothers suit. Hurrying down the stairs, Koch slips into the large, remodeled kitchen and helps himself to his breakfast of juice and coffee. Unlike the old days, when he brewed what he boasted was "the best coffee in New York" in his little pot with frayed wires, his morning cup now is made by one of the servants employed by the City to make its mayor comfortable.

There had been many other changes in his lifestyle as well. After his first week in office, Koch had complained that Gracie Mansion was "like a hotel" and that he did not feel comfortable with its size and elegance. He'd said that he could maintain "contact with my life and reality" only by living in his apartment. But now, seven years and $6 million later, he finds Gracie Mansion "a wonderful house, just right for me." He visits the apartment, which now has bulletproof windows of its own, "on occasion."

A horde of architects, interior decorators, museum curators, skilled craftsmen, fund raisers and even archaeologists collaborated on the triumphant renovation of the mansion. The centerpiece of the work is a broad hall that provides a dramatic entranceway to the house. The wooden floor is handpainted, with a striking Federal-period diamond pattern surrounding a huge, stylized ship's compass. Stone-colored wallpaper with a striped pattern and border selected from the Cooper-Hewitt Museum collection lines the main staircase, with its marbleized woodwork, to the second floor.

Indeed, the entire house, from the guest bedrooms graced with linens contributed by J. P. Stevens to the numerous modern pieces donated by Tiffany and Co., oozes with elegance and expense. The mansion has been stocked with valuable antique furniture and works of art from the city's great museums. The front porch has been rebuilt with tongue-in-groove planking, eliminating from the Mayor's view all those unsightly rusty nail heads. Furnishings have been reupholstered and new curtains hung. Even Archie, the mutt with the wanderlust, got a new doghouse, complete with a Colonial cupola, shingles, and wall-to-wall carpeting. He won't be running away anymore.

As for the Mayor, he is happy, too, having personally approved everything in his mansion. "Marvelous," he says of an early nineteenth-century mirror in the entrance foyer. "Wonderful," he says of a series of 1830s prints on the stairway landing. "Mine," he gloats over the formal dining room with its 1830 French Dufour wallpaper. "Not bad for a kid who was born in the Bronx," says the man who once got his kicks by excoriating the "richies."

Gulping down the last of his black, unsweetened coffee—he will have about ten more cups before the day is finished—Koch goes out the door, bounds down the mansion's steps, and jumps into the back seat of his waiting Lincoln Town Car. The police driver and his partner in the front seat greet him as the car pulls out of the driveway, past the guardhouse and ten-foot-high security wall that was constructed to further protect the Mayor. Unfortunately, it also blocks from public view the lovely flower garden that passersby on East End Avenue enjoyed under previous mayors. That kind of nitpicking is far from the Mayor's mind, however, as his jet black limousine, accompanied by two more plainclothes officers in a separate car, heads downtown toward City Hall.

Traffic is heavy, so the officers place on the roof a magnetic flashing red light and turn on the car's siren to clear a path. While many motorists find the morning commute a frustrating grind, New York's chief executive, when he is not listening to all-news radio stations, likes to turn his travels into a musical adventure. A former Koch aide tells with amusement of the first time he rode with the Mayor. They were stuck on a traffic-choked Brooklyn-Queens Expressway with thousands of ordinary New Yorkers one day when Koch called out over the sound of the Lincoln's expensive tape deck that he didn't want to be late for his next appointment. The driver stepped on the gas, and with light flashing and siren wailing, the car weaved and veered from lane to lane. The Mayor, more than a little off-key, joined Carly Simon in singing one of his favorites, "You're So Vain."

Pulling into the City Hall parking lot, Koch's car comes to a stop outside the graceful nineteenth-century building that is the seat of municipal government. The back door of the Lincoln swings open and Koch jumps out and bounces quickly up the eleven stone steps leading to the portico. If it is raining, Eddie Martinez or another of his bodyguards will often walk a step behind the Mayor holding an umbrella over his uncovered head. When he gets to the top of the stairs, a police officer swings open the bolted front door and Koch steps into the building's columned rotunda. To his right is a life-sized bronze statue of George Washington atop a stone pedestal. To his left, an airport-style metal detector and fluoroscope that the Police Department recently installed at a cost of $90,000. City Hall had always been an easy, informal, comfortable place that the public seemed able to wander at will, but no more. Now all the doors but one are locked and everyone who works in the building has been issued an identification pass. All others, including Koch's top commissioners, are required to pass through the metal detector.

Koch strides confidently up the carpeted center of the rotunda between the statue and the metal detector, turns left past the sweeping spiral staircase and down the corridor toward his office. He passes the first of the scores of oil portraits of former city officials that adorn the walls of the building, and is ushered through the waist-high wrought iron security gate that is held open for him by one of the dozen or so officers on the morning shift. He acknowledges their "Good morning, Mr. Mayor," and walks quickly by the press office, where a staff of more than fifteen will soon begin churning out the reams of press releases, statements, letters, schedules, documents, and reports that make up the day's propaganda assault.

A few steps beyond the press office, Koch passes another police outpost, turns right at the end of the corridor in front of Deputy Mayor Stanley Brezenoff's office and walks past a police officer watching television monitors hooked up to surveillance cameras around the building. A dozen steps, a left turn, a right turn and he is in his office. He takes off his jacket and hangs it in a corner walk-in closet where he keeps copies of his book *Mayor*, to autograph and distribute to select visitors. The closet also contains assorted other knickknacks the Mayor has collected, including hats and helmets that he often gives to visiting children, including Christian Browne and Scott Goodwin.

It is only 7:30, and one of the few staff members on hand is Mary Garrigan, Koch's personal secretary since his days in Congress and a loyal woman with the patience of a saint. She must always be ready to drop what she is doing and join Koch in his office so that he can dictate to her his latest outpouring, scratched out the night before on a yellow legal pad. It may be a dispatch from the foreign desk, a statement on federal legislation, or a blistering response to any form of criticism, real or imagined. Koch has explained his compulsion for hitting back by saying that a public official should always set the record straight. But there is more to it than that because he personalizes every criticism of his administration and thus must respond with a personal attack.

Issuing statements and writing letters are two of the many ways Koch lives up to his reputation for getting even. He once described his feeling about revenge to Harrison Goldin while the two were riding in a car together in China in 1980. "He was telling me stories about slights he had suffered and relishing how that, as Mayor, he was finding opportunities to retaliate against these people one by one," Goldin remembers. "It was a very long ride and he kept saying how this one had done that, and how he had managed to get back. Finally, he looked at me and said, 'But of course, you understand that the most important thing in life is getting even.' The tone of his voice was such that if I had said, 'Oh, come on, Ed, there are other things in life,' he would have thought I was putting him on."

That is not to say Koch does not have a more tender side, one that shows itself when those whom he likes and respects are troubled. There are many stories of private gestures he has made, with perhaps the most noteworthy involving William Devine, an affable career cop who climbed to become the department's second in command before developing brain cancer. A gift-bearing Koch brought smiles to Devine and his family by becoming a regular visitor to the hospital. When Devine was temporarily well enough to leave the hospital, Koch made him Police Commissioner for two days. Devine has since died. When a close friend separated from his wife, Koch called him virtually every day to make sure he was OK, and invited him to numerous events. When George Arzt of the *Post* and Joyce Purnick of the *Times* suffered the deaths of their mothers, Koch went to their homes to join the mourners.

Invariably, Koch's day follows a detailed schedule of events and meetings, a few open to the press and public but most private. The morning's agenda may include meetings with his three deputy mayors, a budget briefing by his top fiscal aides, a discussion with city lawyers about a legal fight the city is waging, a lengthy phone call with a borough president mixing politics and city business, a rundown on the controversial items up for approval by the Board of Estimate, a review of the stacks of eye-glazing reports submitted by his commissioners, and a bill-signing ceremony for new municipal ordinances. Sipping coffee and nibbling on Danish sent over from Ellen's Coffee Shop across Broadway, Koch works his way through his office chores like any good bureaucrat. He takes a midmorning break to read his "press digest," a daily compilation of every newspaper story containing his name. And he always reserves time for a press conference and some high-profile travels about the city. A trip to a ribbon cutting in Brooklyn, a ground breaking on Staten Island, a midtown speech to garment manufacturers or meatcutters—all these are but a few minutes away in the speeding Lincoln, or, if need be, a police helicopter.

Now in his eighth year in office, Koch is accustomed to being the highest paid mayor in America at $110,000-a-year and the only one with a mansion to go along with the job. But he is not used to changes that have been taking place of late. For one thing those politicians who would deny him a third term have already begun to mobilize their forces. Carol Bellamy, that "horror show" down the hall, and Denny Farrell, the Harlem assemblyman, both entered the race, each armed with their own constituencies and issues. For another thing, the public agenda has changed drastically since Koch first took office in 1978. Then, the focus was overwhelmingly on preventing municipal bankruptcy, and other problems facing the city took second place to balancing the budget.

But now the fiscal crisis has passed, thanks in large part to Koch and his willingness to say no to new spending. That singular achievement, however, has its downside for him because it obviates the need for a mayor who built his reputation by holding down expenses. The embarrassment of riches the city has these days, symbolized by three straight years of $500-million budget surpluses, makes it impossible for Koch to blame an empty city treasury for everything that goes wrong. And plenty is going wrong.

Hardly a month passes without a crisis or major embarrassment of some sort, and many times it seems that city government is under siege. The last half of 1983, for example, began a particularly disastrous series of events that did not make the Mayor look good.

First, the city lost its last professional football team after Leon Hess, the oil tycoon, decided to move his New York Jets out of Shea Stadium to New Jersey. Hess packed the team's bags after being unable to persuade Koch that the shabby city-owned stadium needed extensive repairs. He was particularly upset about the grossly unsanitary conditions that the fans long had to endure in the stadium's bathrooms. The state of the toilet facilities was a far cry from the comfort and safety Koch was used to, but he had no way of knowing that, having made only a brief ceremonial appearance at one Jets game. The Mayor simply does not like sports, nor does he have any hobbies.

Then, after a federal judge ruled that the city's jails were unconstitutionally overcrowded, Correction Commissioner Ben Ward swung open the doors to release more than 600 prisoners. Many of them had long criminal records that they began adding to almost as soon as they hit the streets.

The Mayor's problems with blacks reached new heights because of congressional hearings into allegations that white police officers were being allowed to ride roughshod over black New Yorkers. Koch was able to quiet the storm only by making Ward the city's first black police commissioner, even though he knew of a secret report that found Ward had used his office in a city jail for late-night and weekend trysts with a female friend. Koch's persistent denial that he had been playing racial politics by appointing Ward suddenly was undercut when the report became public, for the straight-laced Koch would not have, under normal circumstances, given the top police job to anyone guilty of such conduct. Ward later showed up drunk at a police convention, and again Koch forgave him. But the top cop wasn't the only one with problems. A little more than a year after Ward took office, the department was rocked by charges of police brutality and other acts of misconduct. Officers driving hit-and-run police cars were involved in two accidents in which one person was killed and two injured. Two cops were charged with murdering innocent citizens, and five others were charged with torturing criminal suspects with an electric stun gun.

Corruption was proven widespread after scores of inspectors were found to be on the take in nine city departments. Everybody from lowly hotdog vendors to wealthy real estate operators was routinely making payoffs to gain favors or buy protection. And the spate of embarrassing arrests led to the joke around City Hall, "What's the the civil service test for inspectors?" The punch line was an extended palm. But the biggest case of all—indeed the largest bribery scandal in the history of city government— came to light with the indictment of Alex Liberman. Responsible for renting space for city agencies, Liberman pleaded guilty to extorting $1.5 million in kickbacks from landlords.

Liberman was an active member of Meade Esposito's local political club in Canarsie, and Esposito says he warned City Hall long ago that Liberman was a crook but was ignored. "I told them. I said, 'This guy's dishonest,' " Esposito recalls. "Why they didn't do anything, I don't know, but I told them."

Yet Koch's reputation for personal honesty remains intact, a fact testified to by mobsters caught in an FBI wiretap discussing bribery of government officials. After suggesting that some officials could be bought, William "Billy the Butcher" Masselli said: "I don't think this Koch, you could do business with him on, ah, on this level. He's not that kind of guy."

One agency whose problems always seemed to be in the headlines was the Human Resources Administration, the city's sprawling welfare agency. Over a few months, it produced, among others, the following scandals: An investigation of twenty-two child abuse cases found city social workers negligent in seventeen, including those that resulted in the deaths of nine children. The first city employee who complained about what was happening was demoted, suspended, and fined and the investigator who wrote a report supporting him was told her services were no longer needed. It was only after reporters pressed Koch in a marathon "at home" that he reversed himself and removed the penalties. Workers in city-funded day-care centers were arrested and charged with sexually molesting children in their care. Another agency employee was punished for disclosing that the Medicaid program was a mess. Later, when his charges were investigated, officials found 7,000 applications from needy New Yorkers requesting Medicaid assistance hidden in a drawer, turning yellow with age. The applications had never been acted on, and the people who filed them were deprived of benefits.

With issues like these, there is always plenty to talk about when Koch sends a press aide to summon reporters for his morning fix of jousting and newsmaking. But that is not to say that Koch is prepared to accept responsibility for these and other ills afflicting his government. Quite the opposite. When a reporter asks a legitimate question, such as why the high school dropout rate remains at 40 percent despite a $4 billion education budget, Koch responds with a verbal knee to the groin—"That's ridiculous," "That's stupid," "You're foolish," or "How dare you."

Reporters who have dealt with Koch over a long period of time have identified what seems to be Koch's three-pronged survival strategy: Rule No. 1: Blame someone else. Anyone else. Rule No. 2: Never be defensive. Always attack. Rule No. 3: Deny the problem exists. This is best accomplished through citing a bewildering blizzard of statistics showing that everything is fine, or at least better than it is in Detroit.

The Patton of politics, Koch does not hesitate to throw everything into a fight if he feels pinned down. No issue has forced him to employ his entire strategic arsenal more frequently than the homeless. When anyone points out that the number of New Yorkers with no place to live has increased under Koch, from 2,000 to an estimated 40,000, the Mayor first resorts to Rule No. 1. In a withering attack, Koch blames federal budget cuts and the wholesale release of mental patients from state hospitals, saying Washington and Albany are following outrageous policies.

If the questioner persists in pointing out that Koch's tax incentives have encouraged developers of luxury housing to destroy the boarding houses and cheap residency hotels, where many of those who are now homeless once lived, Rule No. 2 is unleashed. That kind of muddle-headed thinking can only come from an ideologue who either wants his job or who would have Koch bankrupt the city by subsidizing housing for all the people who wanted it, the Mayor will say.

If the questioner is still standing, and points out that a report commissioned by the Mayor described the city's program for sheltering the homeless as "tragic," Rule No. 3 comes into play. Koch will say that New York is spending $200 million a year on nineteen emergency shelters and is renovating 4,500 apartments to care for nearly 13,000 people. He will say that his New York is the most generous of all American cities and skeptics should visit Detroit, where everything is worse. Moreover, Koch likes to conclude in a flourish, his policies have been so fair and so successful that all segments of the city have benefited. Anyone who says that the city is divided into haves and have-nots just because people live on the streets, in the parks, and over subway grates is nothing but a naysaying cynic.

The Mayor is also hostile to complaints that Manhattan is becoming an enclave of the rich. Rebecca Kaufman, the wife of Michael Kaufman, a *Times* foreign correspondent, remembers a scene at a wedding reception when she and others argued with Koch about the effects of gentrification. They told him that too many ordinary people were being priced out of Manhattan. "We're not catering to the poor anymore," she remembers a bristling Koch saying. "There are four other boroughs they can live in. They don't have to live in Manhattan."

A few days later Kaufman got a letter from Koch in which he said, "I felt abashed because of my contentiousness." He enclosed a report filled with statistics aimed at proving his point that New York was still a good place to live.

Talk stimulates the Mayor's appetite, and many a press conference has ended abruptly with Koch announcing, "I'm hungry. I'm going to lunch." Everyone in City Hall knows better than to try to stop him, for the Mayor has never met a meal he didn't like. Indeed, twice his epicurean habits have been nearly fatal. Once he had to be rescued from choking in a Chinese restaurant by his friend David Margolis, who successfully applied the Heimlich Maneuver. What the Mayor choked on is a matter of debate. He said it was sautéed watercress. But subsequent reports identified the near lethal morsel as pork and suggested the Mayor had covered up what he was really eating so as not to offend his kosher constituents. The day after the incident, Koch said he wanted every school child in the city to learn the Heimlich. It was done.

Illustrating how versatile Koch's eating habits are, his next culinary brush with death occurred in an Italian restaurant, and again Margolis was Johnny-on-the-spot. After gorging himself on hors d'oeuvres and wine with Margolis and his wife Barbara in their East Side townhouse, the three companions feasted at the Parma Restaurant on Third Avenue. Describing what he later called a "monster meal," which included four more bottles of wine, Koch said, "I ordered a half order of spaghettini and I think the waiter brought me an order and a half. (See Rule No. 1 above.) I ordered a veal chop parmigiana. I think he brought me the whole calf." Koch topped the meal off with a hefty chunk of cheesecake and tried to wash it all down with scalding cappuccino. But the assault proved more than his stomach could handle.

Suffering pains and nausea, Koch stood up and staggered among the stunned diners around him to the men's room where he passed out into Margolis's arms. Immediately his bodyguards put out an alert on the police radio, "The Mayor is down. The Mayor is down," provoking a speeding fleet of police cars and rescue vehicles to converge on the restaurant. By the time they arrived Koch was back on his wobbly feet and well enough to announce that he was holding a midnight press conference at Gracie Mansion to tell all. He blamed the whole episode on the coffee. (Again, Rule No. 1.)

Eating can also be unpleasant for Koch if the ambience is wrong—i.e., somebody else is the center of attention. Manhattan Borough President Andrew Stein recalls attending a charity dinner with Koch several years ago. A comedy routine by Red Buttons plunged the Mayor into depression. "Red Buttons was very funny. The place was just breaking up. Even the waiters were breaking up. Ed just sat there the whole time like this [Stein propped a very glum face on his right hand]. For twenty minutes he sat there like that, never smiling or anything."

Stein and his wife also fell victim to the kind of ambience the Mayor prefers at a more recent dinner.

"It was a battle to talk about something other than Koch. It was amazing. Ed did not talk about anything but himself the whole time. Anytime we tried to talk about something else, he would just prop his head on his hand for a minute and then change the subject back to himself. Dinner with him can be exhausting," Stein said.

Sometimes the Mayor doesn't have to announce lunch because reporters can see Mitch London, Koch's chef, standing in the back of the press conference in a white apron, glancing nervously at his watch. When he first took office, Koch was notorious for having a sandwich sent in from a nearby deli and eating it at his desk. These days, Mitch often spends the morning cooking Koch's luncheon repast in the kitchen at the mansion. When everything is just right—smothered by garlic—Mitch brings the meal to City Hall. How does he get there, you ask? Since city cars are now a perk for all of Koch's aides, Mitch simply loads the lunch into one and is chauffeured to the Mayor's office where, if necessary, he reheats the food in Koch's private kitchen. Then the Mayor and his guests retire to the Peach Room, a former conference room that was remodeled into a mayoral dining salon.

If Koch desires, he goes out to lunch, with friends or even with enemies he is trying to make peace with. He once went to Chinatown with Carol Bellamy, who recalls the experience with near revulsion. "It's typical in a restaurant to look at what others are eating and maybe even ask a waiter what it is," she says. "But that nicety was lost on Ed. I recall he simply just walked around pointing at other people's plates and asking 'What's that?' without being invited. The diners looked aghast but Ed didn't even notice. I remember wondering if he wasn't confusing the mayoralty with a personal fiefdom that entitled him to do what he wished with the people he governed. I haven't had lunch with him since. I've lost my appetite for it."

Koch took Goldin, another regular adversary, to the Buffalo Roadhouse, a Greenwich Village restaurant, to try to make peace. They each had spinach salad but Koch ate some crow as well. "I told him he was acting as though he was diminished in some way every time somebody says one of his positions is not the embodiment of perfection," Goldin recalls. "I said, 'You're not a *mensch* [Yiddish translation: A good and mature man]. A man is either a *mensch* or not a *mensch* and you are not.' He was stunned. He was speechless. Then he said, 'I'll try to do better.' "

The Mayor's post-lunch routine is another round of meetings, phone calls, ceremonial events, and press conferences. Much of that time in the first months of his eighth year has been devoted to taking, modifying or, if necessary, reversing positions, to keep pace with public opinion on two major criminal cases with racial overtones.

The more sensational was that of Bernhard Goetz, a thin, quiet electronics specialist who became something of a national hero by emptying a revolver into four black youths who had harassed him on a Manhattan subway car. The Mayor's reaction to the multiple shooting was swift and strong.

"Vigilantism will not be tolerated in this city," Koch said. "We are not going to have instant justice meted out by anybody." The Mayor repeatedly pointed out the dangers to innocent bystanders created by opening fire on a subway car. Koch also expressed sympathy for one of the youths, who was paralyzed in the shooting.

But it quickly became evident that Koch had miscalculated. Popular support for Goetz was strong and growing, in New York and elsewhere across the country. The Mayor received 280 letters on Goetz in a single week. The score was 273 to 7 in favor of the thirty-seven-year-old subway gunman. So Koch switched gears. He dropped references to the dangers of vigilantism and reckless shooting from his statements and said that a grand jury would determine if the gunman was a "victim or villain."

The groundwork the Mayor carefully prepared bore fruit when the grand jury declined to indict Goetz on attempted murder charges. Koch now revealed that that he was sympathetic to the subway gunman. He said Goetz had acted in self-defense and that he was pleased by the grand jury decision, which he called "right." Koch even began emulating his death penalty plebiscites of the 1977 mayoral campaign by asking audiences for a show of hands to determine who agreed with him.

The Mayor's effort to get on the "right" side of the Goetz case suffered a serious reversal, however, when newly disclosed court documents revealed that Goetz had fired a second shot into one of his victims with the words, "You don't look too bad, here's another." Koch's initial reaction to this bit of unwanted news was an uncharacteristic silence. But a day later he began distancing himself from Goetz by announcing that he was taking "a step back" from the case because Goetz had said some "flaky things." The Mayor described a proposal by Goetz to arm 25,000 New Yorkers as "Looneyville." When a second grand jury indicted Goetz on attempted murder charges, Koch had little to say.

Koch's twists and turns were less dramatic in the case of Eleanor Bumpurs, a sixty-six-year-old black grandmother from the Bronx who was shotgunned to death in her apartment by a white police officer named Stephen Sullivan. Police said she was attacking another officer with a knife when Sullivan fired. A grand jury in the Bronx heard evidence in the case and the Mayor announced that he was prepared to accept the grand jury's decision.

But that soon changed. The grand jury's decision to indict Sullivan on a manslaughter charge was "wrong," he declared. The Mayor announced his opinion on the Sullivan grand jury on the same day that he determined that the Goetz grand jury was "right." The racial arithmetic—five blacks killed or wounded by two gun-wielding whites—infuriated many black leaders but the

Mayor airily dismissed charges he was playing to white public opinion and increasing the level of racial polarization in the city. When a judge subsequently dismissed the indictment against Sullivan, Koch was happy.

Despite his mushrooming governmental headaches, Koch has no apparent cause for political alarm. A *New York Times* poll indicates that his popularity among voters is high. They give him credit for the city's strengths, such as its revived economy, but do not blame him for the city's problems, such as high crime. This paradox has led pundits to dub Koch the "Teflon Mayor."

Nonetheless, after a day of jousting over such issues, by four o'clock Koch is showing some wear and tear. His blue shirt is wrinkled and hanging out at the back. His pants have slipped below the paunch at his waist, the cuffs crumpling in folds over his shoe tops. But Koch continues to work as City Hall itself slows down, sometimes turning on the Sony television set in his office to catch the late afternoon news.

About six, Koch calls it a day. He walks through the relative quiet that has settled on the central corridor of the building as evening approaches. It has been a long day and he looks tired. His shoulders are hunched slightly forward and down as he walks, as if they bear a weight, and the curvature makes him seem both rounder than his 210-plus pounds and shorter than six-foot-one. His walk has lost its bounce. With the slightest of gestures Koch bids good night to the plainclothes police officer as he goes through the security gate. It isn't so much a wave as an upward flip of his right hand that he makes in silence.

"Good night, Mr. Mayor," the cop responds as Koch continues toward the front door, surrounded again by bodyguards. Outside, he gets into his waiting Lincoln for the ride home to the mansion. The limousine and the backup car roar off into the rush hour twilight. As they pull out of the parking lot, Koch relaxes, stretches his legs out to the side and catches a quick nap. Just a few hundred feet away on both sides of City Hall, thousands of New Yorkers are pouring down the steps of two subway stations, readying themselves for their own miserable commutes home on the decaying transit system. Koch had promised to devote his second term to improving the subways but his gubernatorial quest had sidetracked his efforts. He rarely talks about improving the subways these days and even more rarely does he ride them.

Koch is headed home. Some evenings he has a friend or two over for a quiet dinner in front of the TV set, but not tonight. Koch is having company and Mitch is already busy preparing dinner at the mansion. It's no wonder Koch's endless diets end in failure. "My cooking is not lean cuisine," laughs Mitch, whose specialty is pastry. London is the fifth cook Koch has had. And number six would be on board by now if Koch hadn't persuaded Mitch to withdraw his resignation in 1984.

Somebody else interested in Koch's food habits is Al Nahas, the Brooklyn restaurateur. After Koch admired a tapered shirt Nahas was wearing, Nahas says that he went out and got the Mayor one just like it as a gift. But Koch's shape is not tapered.

"He called me and said, 'What's wrong with this shirt? I can't put it on,' " Nahas remembers. "I said, 'What do you mean?' He said, 'It's too tight. I can't button it.' "

Nahas laughs at the anecdote and says he once tried to help Koch in the battle of the bulge. He put Koch on a diet that consisted of three low-calorie meals a day. Nahas delivered the food to Koch and said, "Only eat what I bring you." The regimen went on for some time, but Koch failed to lose weight. When Nahas expressed surprise that the diet wasn't working, Koch confessed that he was consuming all three diet meals at once and then eating normally. "God, is he a great eater!" Nahas marvels.

Koch's dinner guests, usually an assortment of his commissioners and aides, political figures, newspaper editors, and developers, begin arriving at the mansion shortly after he does. Typically, seven will be invited because he prefers intimate dinner parties with eight people and eleven bottles of wine. If Koch did not have lamb for lunch, he may well have it for dinner. "I'm serving a lot of lamb these days," Mitch says. The meal is served in the formal dining room, where the most striking feature is a magnificent Duncan Phyfe sideboard. But without doubt, the centerpiece of the evening is the host. The Mayor likes to regale his guests with a travelogue of his life and times, even if his guests have heard it all before.

The dinner is completed when the food and wine are exhausted, at which point Koch invites his guests into the library for a little entertainment.

"Very enthusiastically, he will say, 'I have some movies to show,' " a guest recalled. Everyone moves into the library, where the Mayor treats the guests to two films—of himself. One offering is an Academy Award-winning animated cartoon featuring a clay likeness of Koch having some odd experiences, such as being tossed into the back of a garbage truck, to the tune of "New York, New York." The Mayor then moves from this opening short to the main feature, "Doin' My Job," a ten-minute propaganda film that shows Koch traveling around the city, giving speeches, shaking hands, and just plain meeting the folks. The film is replete with upbeat tunes with lyrics such as "What a mind, what a mouth." The film was made possible by the generosity of Merrill Lynch, the brokerage house.

Koch, who says he never gets tired of seeing the films, maintains that he uses them as a quick, painless way to end the evening. "After the films are over," the Mayor explained, without apparent irony, "everybody looks at their watch, and says, 'Oh gee, it's 10:30,' and everybody gets up and leaves."

The films are but a small part of the Mayor's video tribute to himself. Koch has amassed a library of more than 400 videotapes of himself covering some 200 hours of his interviews and appearances. The security-conscious Mayor has placed the library under lock and key at the Department of Investigation. In addition to more than 300 television appearances a year on various news programs, Koch has been on so many entertainment programs that he was asked in 1984 to join a union—the American Federation of Television and Radio Artists. He has appeared three times on "Saturday Night Live," and has also shown up on "Romper Room," "Gimme a Break," the Johnny Carson show, MTV, quiz shows, television movies, and "All My Children." His debut on the silver screen came in 1984 with the release of *The Muppets Take Manhattan*. Talk of turning his book into a movie fell through, but he sold the rights to make it a Broadway musical.

The evening isn't over soon enough for some guests, especially those who have seen the films enough times to memorize them. A Koch aide once suggested that a good game to play would be to do imitations of Ed Koch watching himself on television. He immediately dropped his jaw and lapsed into a beatific smile. Former Police Commissioner Bob McGuire said, when he resigned, "Now I won't have to watch those damn movies anymore." He insists he was joking, saying he hadn't seen the films "that" many times.

When the guests are gone and the mansion grows quiet, Koch

goes through his solitary nightly routine of reading the next day's papers and watching the late news. He is particularly curious about what is going on these days because it's an election year and he's worried about his opposition. He's rated the overwhelming favorite, but he's not entirely sanguine, in part because that's the position he was in against Cuomo in 1982. He survived that defeat, but now he's got so much more to lose. He's grown rich in office, particularly from the sales of his book, but being defeated again would mean giving up everything—the title, City Hall, the mansion, press attention, chauffeurs—it would all be gone in a minute. Ed Koch would go back to being just Ed Koch. And so he reads and watches and worries before he goes to bed, alone.

His family and friends worry too, because they also know how much of his life and identity are wrapped up in being Mayor.

"My greatest concern for my brother is what happens to him when this is all over, when he's no longer in the center of the storm," says Harold Koch. "Whether it's this year, four years from now, or whenever, that's going to be the most difficult period of his life."

INDEX